P9-CQB-675

ARE YOU Politically Correct?

Contemporary Issues

Series Editors: Robert M. Baird
Stuart E. Rosenbaum

Other titles in this series:

ARE YOU Politically Correct?

Debating America's Cultural Standards

Edited by
Francis J. Beckwith & Michael E. Bauman

Prometheus Books • Buffalo, New York

Published 1993 by Prometheus Books

Are You Politically Correct?: Debating America's Cultural Standards. Copyright
© 1993 by Francis J. Beckwith and Michael E. Bauman. All rights reserved.

97 96 95 94 93   5 4 3 2 1

Library of Congress Cataloging-in-Publication Data

Are you politically correct? : debating America's cultural standards /
    edited by Francis J. Beckwith and Michael E. Bauman.
        p.   cm. — (Contemporary issues)
    Includes bibliographical references.
    ISBN 0-87975-769-8
    1. Education, Higher—Political aspects—United States.
2. Political correctness—United States. I. Bauman, Michael.
II. Beckwith, Francis. III. Series: Contemporary issues (Buffalo, N.Y.)
LC89.A82   1992
378.73—dc20   92-33259
                                                                    CIP

Printed in the United States of America on acid-free paper.

Contents

5

132863

Acknowledgments

We would like to thank several people who were instrumental in providing us with either important suggestions or research help for this work: Bruce Pencek (University of Nevada, Las Vegas), Louis Pojman (University of Mississippi), Christina Hoff Sommers (Clark University), Frederick R. Lynch (Claremont-McKenna College), Jan H. Blits (University of Delaware), Steven L. Mitchell (Prometheus Books), Orem Ryssman, Daniel Pressler (Hillsdale College), Michelle McCoullough (Hillsdale College), and Lissa Roche (Center for Constructive Alternatives, Hillsdale College).

Introduction

In his 1991 article in *New York* magazine, journalist John Taylor asked the question, "Are You Politically Correct?" Followed by articles in *Newsweek, Time, Atlantic Monthly,* and other publications, the American public was confronted with an issue that has brought the most controversy to the American college campus and public education since the turbulent 1960s. But exactly what is Mr. Taylor asking?

He refers to a web of interconnected, though not mutually dependent, ideological beliefs that have challenged the traditional nature of the university as well as traditional curriculum, standards of excellence, and views about truth, justice, and the objectivity of knowledge, while accentuating our cultural, gender, class, and racial differences in the name of campus diversity. Typically, the politically correct (PC) movement is politically leftist, although, as will be evident in the readings, some of its harshest critics are on the political left, just as forty years ago many critics of McCarthyism were on the political right.

To explain by way of example, the PC person sees the exclusion of black female lesbian authors from the "Great Books of the Western World" as a purely political phenomenon. The traditional response that black female lesbian authors are excluded because canon inclusion is based on objective standards of excellence and that none have met these standards is, according to the PCer, evidence that these "objective standards" are racist, sexist, and homophobic.[1] The traditionalist, although decrying oppression, argues that the historical absence of such authors has to do with the fact that they wrote and studied very little *precisely because* they were oppressed. The standards of excellence are just fine. To use an analogy,

9

the absence of blacks from major league baseball, prior to the arrival of Jackie Robinson in 1947, had nothing to do with the rules of baseball or the game's standards of excellence, but everything to do with bigotry, prejudice, and racism.

Other issues central to the debate over political correctness include speech codes and multiculturalism. Concerning the former, many college campuses have instituted rules forbidding "racist," "sexist," or "homophobic" speech. For those opposed to these codes the question is not whether colleges should forbid verbal harassment, but rather who is to define what is racist, sexist, or homophobic. Civil libertarians view these speech codes as an attempt to silence unpopular ideas in the name of limiting "harassment." Those who defend the codes argue that students and faculty have a right not to be subject to offensive speech. At some schools, instructors have gone so far as to provide students with a list of politically incorrect "isms." Consider the following, excerpted from a handout at Smith College, "Specific Manifestations of Oppression":

[P]eople can be oppressed in many ways and for many reasons because they are perceived to be different. As groups begin the process of realizing that they are oppressed and why, new words tend to be created to express the concepts that the existing language cannot. Thus, some of the words below may be familiar to you while others may be new.

ABELISM: oppression of the differently abled, by the temporarily able.

* * *

ETHNOCENTRISM: oppression of cultures other than the dominant one in the belief that the dominant way of doing things is the superior way.

HETEROSEXISM: oppression of those of sexual orientations other than heterosexual, such as gays, lesbians, and bisexuals; this can take place by not acknowledging their existence. Homophobia is the fear of lesbians, gays, or bisexuals.

LOOKISM: the belief that appearance is an indicator of a person's value; the construction of a standard for beauty/attractiveness; and oppression through stereotypes and generalizations of both those who do not fit that standard and those who do.

RACISM: the belief that one group of people [is] superior to another and therefore [has] the right to dominate, and the power to institute and enforce [its] prejudices and discriminations.[2]

Multiculturalism, as popularly defined, is a philosophy of education that stresses the unique contributions of different cultures to the history of the world. According to this view, to emphasize "Western thought" at the expense of other types of thought is "Eurocentric." Multiculturalists argue that an African-American student who studies only Dead White European Males (DWEMs), such as Plato, Aristotle, and Galileo, will not do as well as he would if that student were studying the greats of "African" culture. This widespread notion has reshaped curricula not only on the university level, but also in elementary and secondary public schools, and its effect is filtering through to corporate America, influencing hiring practices.

The radical forms of multiculturalism makes at least three controversial assumptions: (1) all cultures have contributed equally to the history of the human race; (2) the ideas of those produced by members of one's own ethnic or racial group are easier for one to understand and comprehend; and (3) every judgment can be reduced to a "cultural perspective." Concerning the first assumption, we are reminded of the multiculturalist professor who told his students that we in the West have ignored for too long the valuable and revolutionary "scientific" and "magical" insights of the hut people of South America, to which a student replied, "If these insights are so valuable, why are they still hut people?" The second assumption is self-refuting if it is proposed by an African American to a white audience, since the white audience would, according to this proposition, have grave difficulty comprehending it. If certain values are not transpersonal and transcultural, then racism cannot be morally judged as objectively evil, which is absurd. The third assumption is self-refuting as well, for it is a judgment, and hence (on its own terms) merely a cultural perspective, something that cannot be objectively and universally true. But if it is objectively and universally true, then this statement is false, because it asserts that "every judgment can be reduced to a 'cultural perspective.' "

Other key issues in the political correctness debate include the objectivity of human knowledge, cultural diversity and student enrollment, and affirmative action and regional accreditation. Many PCers deny that any transcultural values and norms of excellence even exist. They believe that accepting students to their universities should be based on race and gender quotas, not upon academic performance alone. Some accrediting agencies—recognized for assessing the extent to which institutions of higher education meet basic standards of faculty, staffing, and curriculum—believe that schools that do not have the "correct" number of minority and female faculty members as well as multicultural representation in the student body should not be fully accredited.

All these issues are addressed in this anthology. We have tried to provide the reader representative arguments from all sides of the debate as well as from differing political perspectives. We could not, of course, be exhaustive. The limitations of space and time preclude it. But we have tried to be fair. Consequently, this is not a simple pro/con anthology with half of the authors pro-PC and the other half anti-PC. The debate, of course, is not that simple. For this reason, this text contains defenses of PC, moderate views, and critiques of the PC movement from right-wing, left-wing, and libertarian perspectives as well as from some which are difficult to label precisely.

If, as editors, we might be permitted briefly to editorialize, perhaps it is time to return to those enduring and resilient ideals upon which our educational foundation has rested for nearly two millennia: "The unexamined life is not worth living" and "You shall know the truth and the truth shall set you free." If this volume serves to foster these ideals, we shall be both pleased and grateful.

Francis J. Beckwith, Ph.D.
University of Nevada, Las Vegas

Michael E. Bauman, Ph.D.
Hillsdale College, Hillsdale, Michigan

NOTES

1. To call someone "homophobic" is logically as well as psychologically futile. First, it is logically fallacious when used against someone who is arguing that homosexuality is immoral, because whether or not one fears homosexuals is irrelevant to the question of whether homosexual practice is moral. No one would say that the arguments of an anti-war protestor should not be taken seriously on the grounds that he is "hemophobic," that is, fearful of bloodshed. To do so would be to commit the ad hominem fallacy in logic. Second, if one is homophobic, that is, suffering from a phobia as one would suffer from claustrophobia, then the homophobe cannot help himself and is therefore suf-fering from a mental disorder. Consequently, calling someone homophobic is tantamount to making fun of the handicapped, unless of course the accuser is himself homophobephobic.

2. John Taylor, "Are You Politically Correct?" *New York* magazine, January 21, 1991, p. 34.

3. Although some of these "isms" truly hurt people, others border on the humorous. For example, one school requires that short people be called the "vertically challenged." What shall we call the impotent, "The horizontally challenged"?

Part One

The Media
and
Political Correctness

1

Are You Politically Correct?

John Taylor

"Racist."

"Racist."

"The man is a racist!"

"A *racist!*"

Such denunciations, hissed in tones of self-righteousness and contempt, vicious and vengeful, furious, smoking with hatred—such denunciations haunted Stephan Thernstrom for weeks. Whenever he walked through the campus that spring, down Harvard's brick paths, under the arched gates, past the fluttering elms, he found it hard not to imagine the pointing fingers, the whispers. Racist. There goes *the racist.* It was hellish, this persecution. Thernstrom couldn't sleep. His nerves were frayed, his temper raw. He was making his family miserable. And the worst thing was that he didn't know who was calling him a racist, or why.

Thernstrom, fifty-six, a professor at Harvard University for twenty-five years, is considered one of the preeminent scholars of the history of race relations in America. He has tenure. He has won prizes and published numerous articles and four books and edited the *Harvard Encyclopedia of American Ethnic Groups.* For several years, Thernstrom and another professor, Bernard Bailyn, taught an undergraduate lecture course on the history of race relations in the United States called "Peopling of

America." Bailyn covered the colonial era. Thernstrom took the class up to the present.

Both professors are regarded as very much in the academic mainstream, their views grounded in extensive research on their subject, and both have solid liberal democratic credentials. But all of a sudden, in the fall of 1987, articles began to appear in the *Harvard Crimson* accusing Thernstrom and Bailyn of "racial insensitivity" in "Peopling of America." The sources for the articles were anonymous, the charges vague, but they continued to be repeated, these ringing indictments.

Finally, through the intervention of another professor, two students from the lecture course came forward and identified themselves as the sources for the articles. When asked to explain their grievances, they presented the professors with a six-page letter. Bailyn's crime had been to read from the diary of a southern planter without giving equal time to the recollections of a slave. This, to the students, amounted to a covert defense of slavery. Bailyn, who has won two Pulitzer Prizes, had pointed out during the lecture that no journals, diaries, or letters written by slaves had ever been found. He had explained to the class that all they could do was read the planter's diary and use it to speculate about the experience of slaves. But that failed to satisfy the complaining students. Since it was impossible to give equal representation to the slaves, Bailyn ought to have dispensed with the planter's diary altogether.

Thernstrom's failures, according to the students, were almost systematic. He had, to begin with, used the word *Indians* instead of *Native Americans*. Thernstrom tried to point out that he had said very clearly in class that *Indian* was the word most Indians themselves use, but that was irrelevant to the students. They considered the word racist. Thernstrom was also accused of referring to an "Oriental religion." The word *Oriental,* with its imperialist overtones, was unacceptable. Thernstrom explained that he had used the word as an adjective, not as a noun, but the students weren't buying any wriggling, sophistic evasions like that.

Even worse, they continued, Thernstrom had assigned a book to the class that mentioned that some people regarded affirmative action as preferential treatment. That was a racist opinion. But most egregiously, Thernstrom had endorsed, in class, Patrick Moynihan's emphasis on the breakup of the black family as a cause of persistent black poverty. That was a racist idea.

All of these words and opinions and ideas and historical approaches were racist. *Racist!* They would not be tolerated.

The semester was pretty much over by then. But during the spring, when Thernstrom sat down to plan the course for the following year, he had to think about how he would combat charges of racism should they crop up again. And they assuredly would. All it took was one militant student, one word like *Oriental* taken out of context, one objection that a professor's account of slavery was insufficiently critical or that, in discussing black poverty, he had raised the "racist" issue of welfare dependency. And a charge of racism, however unsubstantiated, leaves a lasting impression. "It's like being called a Commie in the fifties," Thernstrom says. "Whatever explanation you offer, once accused, you're always suspect."

He decided that to protect himself in case he was misquoted or had comments taken out of context, he would need to tape all his lectures. Then he decided he would have to tape his talks with students in his office. He would, in fact, have to tape everything he said on the subject of race. It would require a tape-recording system worthy of the Nixon White House. Microphones everywhere, the reels turning constantly. That was plainly ridiculous. Thernstrom instead decided it would be easier just to drop the course altogether. "Peopling of America" is no longer offered at Harvard.

THE NEW FUNDAMENTALISM

When the Christian-fundamentalist uprising began in the late seventies, Americans on the left sneered at the Bible thumpers who tried to ban the teaching of evolution in public schools, at the troglodytes who wanted to remove *Catcher in the Rye* from public libraries. They heaped scorn on the evangelists who railed against secular humanism and the pious hypocrites who tried to legislate patriotism and Christianity through school prayer and the Pledge of Allegiance. This last effort was considered particularly heinous. Those right-wing demagogues were interfering with individual liberties! They were trying to indoctrinate the children! It was scandalous and outrageous, and unconstitutional too.

But curiously enough, in the past few years, a new sort of fundamentalism has arisen precisely among those people who were the most appalled by Christian fundamentalism. And it is just as demagogic and fanatical. The new fundamentalists are an eclectic group; they include multiculturalists, feminists, radical homosexuals, Marxists, New Historicists. What unites them—as firmly as the Christian fundamentalists are united in the belief that the Bible is the revealed word of God—is their conviction that Western culture and American society are thoroughly and hopelessly racist, sexist, oppressive. "Racism and sexism are pervasive in America and fundamentally present in all American institutions," declares a draft report on "race and gender enrichment" at Tulane University. A 1989 report by a New York State Board of Education task force was even more sweeping: "Intellectual and educational oppression . . . has characterized the culture and institutions of the United States and the European American world for centuries."

The heart of the new fundamentalists' argument is not just that, as most everyone would agree, racism and sexism historically have existed within political systems designed to promote individual liberties. They believe that the doctrine of individual liberties *itself* is inherently oppressive. At the University of Pennsylvania, an undergraduate on the "diversity education committee" wrote a memo to committee members describing her "deep regard for the individual and my desire to protect the freedoms of all members of society." The tone was earnest and sincere. The young woman clearly considered herself an idealist of the Jeffersonian persuasion. Individual freedom, she seemed to indicate, was a concept to be cherished above all else.

But in the prevailing climate, Thomas Jefferson and all the Founding Fathers are in disrepute. (The Constitution, according to the 1989 New York State report, is "the embodiment of the White Male with Property Model.") One college administrator had no patience with the young woman's naive and bourgeois sentiments. He returned her memo with the word *individual* underlined. "This is a 'RED FLAG' phrase today, which many consider RACIST," the administrator wrote. "Arguments that champion the individual over the group ultimately privilege the 'INDIVIDUALS' belonging to the largest or dominant group."

Defenders of Western culture try to point out that other civilizations— from the Islamic and the Hindu to the Confucian and the Buddhist— are rife with racism and sexism. They find it odd that while Eastern Europeans are rushing to embrace Western democracy, while the pro-democracy movement in China actually erected a replica of the Statue of Liberty in Tiananmen Square, this peculiar intellectual cult back in the States continues to insist that Western values are the source of much of the world's evil.

But one of the marvels of the new fundamentalism is the rationale it has concocted for dismissing all dissent. Just as Christian fundamentalists attack nonbelievers as agents of Satan, so the politically correct dismiss their critics as victims of, to use the famous Marxist phrase, "false consciousness." Anyone who disagrees is simply too soaked in the oppressors' propaganda to see the truth. "Racism and sexism are subtle and, for the most part, subconscious or at least subsurface," the Tulane report continues. "It is difficult for us to see and overcome racism and sexism because we are all a product of the problem, i.e., we are all the progeny of a racist and sexist society."

This circular reasoning enables the new fundamentalists to attack not just the opinions of their critics but the right of their critics to disagree. Alternate viewpoints are simply not allowed. Though there was little visible protest when Louis Farrakhan was invited to speak at the University of Wisconsin, students at the University of Northern Colorado practically rioted when Linda Chavez, a Hispanic member of the Reagan administration who opposes affirmative action and believes immigrants should be encouraged to learn English, was asked to talk. The invitation was withdrawn. Last February, Patrick Moynihan declared during a lecture at Vassar that America was "a model of a reasonably successful multiethnic society." Afterward, he got into an argument with a black woman who disagreed with him, and when she claimed the senator had insulted her, militant students occupied a school building until Moynihan returned his lecture fee. "The disturbing factor in the success of totalitarianism is . . . the true selflessness of its adherents," Hannah Arendt wrote in *The Origins of Totalitarianism*. "The fanaticized members can be reached by neither experience nor argument."

It is this sort of demand for intellectual conformity, enforced with harassment and intimidation, that has led some people to compare the atmosphere in universities today to that of Germany in the thirties. "It's fascism of the left," says Camille Paglia, a professor at the University of the Arts in Philadelphia and the author of *Sexual Personae*. "These people behave like the Hitler Youth."

It reminds others of America in the fifties. "This sort of atmosphere, where a few highly mobilized radical students can intimidate everyone else, is quite new," Thernstrom says. "This is a new McCarthyism. It's more frightening than the old McCarthyism, which had no support in the academy. Now the enemy is within. There are students and faculty who have no belief in freedom of speech."

And it reminds still others of China during the Cultural Revolution of the sixties, when thought criminals were paraded through towns in dunce caps. "In certain respects, the University of Pennsylvania has become like the University of Peking," says Alan Kors, a professor of history.

Indeed, schools like Berkeley and Carleton require courses in race relations, sometimes called "oppression studies." A proposed course book for a required writing seminar at the University of Texas contains, instead of models of clarity like E. B. White, essays such as "is not so gd [*sic*] to be born a girl," by Ntozake Shange. Many schools—including Stanford, Pennsylvania, and the University of Wisconsin—have adopted codes of conduct that require students who deviate from politically correct thinking to undergo thought reform. When a student at the University of Michigan read a limerick that speculated jokingly about the homosexuality of a famous athlete, he was required to attend gay-sensitivity sessions and publish a piece of self-criticism in the student newspaper called "Learned My Lesson."

But is any of this so awful? In the minds of its advocates, thought reform is merely a well-intentioned effort to help stop the spread of the racial tensions that have proliferated in universities in recent years. "I don't know of any institution that is saying you have to adore everyone else," says Catharine Stimpson, dean of the graduate school at Rutgers. "They are saying you have to learn to live with everyone. They are taking insulting language seriously. That's a good thing. They're not laughing off anti-Semitic and homophobic graffiti."

After all, it is said, political indoctrination of one sort or another has always taken place at universities. Now that process is simply being made overt. And anyway, all these people complaining about the loss of academic freedom and the decline in standards are only trying to disguise their own efforts to retain power. "The attack on diversity is a rhetorical strategy by neo-conservatives who have their own political agenda," says Stimpson. "Under the guise of defending objectivity and intellectual rigor, which is a lot of mishmash, they are trying to preserve the cultural and political supremacy of white heterosexual males."

EVERYTHING IS POLITICAL

If the debate over what students should be taught has become an openly political power struggle, that is only because, to be politically correct, *everything* is political. And nothing is more political, in their view, than the humanities, where much of the recent controversy has been centered.

For most of the twentieth century, professors in the humanities modeled themselves on their counterparts in the natural sciences. They thought of themselves as specialists in the disinterested pursuit of the truth. Their job, in the words of T. S. Eliot, was "the elucidation of art and the correction of taste," and to do so they concentrated on what Matthew Arnold called "the best that has been thought and written."

That common sense of purpose began to fracture in the sixties. The generation of professors now acquiring prominence and power at universities—Elaine Showalter, the head of the English department at Princeton; Donna Shalala, chancellor of the University of Wisconsin; James Freedman, the president of Dartmouth—came of age during that period. They witnessed its upheavals and absorbed its political commitments.

And by and large, they have retained them. Which means that, though much of the country subsequently rejected the political vision of the sixties, it has triumphed at the universities. "If the undergraduate population has moved quietly to the right in recent years, the men and women who are paid to introduce students to the great works and ideas of our civilization have by and large remained true to the emancipationist ideology of the sixties," writes Roger Kimbal in his book *Tenured Radicals*. The professors themselves eagerly admit this. "I see my scholarship as an extension of my political activism," said Annette Kolodny, a former Berkeley radical and now the dean of the humanities faculty at the University of Arizona.

In the view of such activists, the universities were hardly the havens of academic independence they pretended to be. They had hopelessly compromised their integrity by accepting contracts from the Pentagon, but those alliances with the reviled "military-industrial Establishment" were seen as merely one symptom of a larger conspiracy by white males. Less obviously, but more insidiously, they had appointed themselves guardians of the culture and compiled the list of so-called Great Books as a propaganda exercise to reinforce the notion of white-male superiority. "The canon of great literature was created by high-Anglican ass----s to underwrite their social class," Stanley Hauerwas, a professor at Duke's Divinity School, put it recently.

Several schools of French critical theory that became fashionable during the seventies provided the jargon for this critique. Semiotics and Lacanian psychoanalysis argued that language and art conveyed subliminal cultural prejudices, power configurations, metaphoric representations of gender. Deconstruction declared that texts, to use the preferred word, had no meaning outside themselves. "There is no such thing as literal meaning . . . there is no such thing as intrinsic merit," wrote Stanley Fish, the head of Duke's English department.

That being the case, any attempt to assign meaning to art, literature, or thought, to interpret it and evaluate it, was nothing more than an exercise in political power by the individual with the authority to impose his or her view. It then followed that the only reason to require students to read certain books is not to "correct taste" or because the books were "the best that has been thought or written" but because they promoted politically correct viewpoints. That ideological emphasis also applied to scholarship generally. "If the work doesn't have a strong political thrust, I don't see how it matters," said Eve Sedgwick, a professor of English at Duke and the author of such papers as "Jane Austen and the Masturbating Girl."

This agenda can produce a rather remarkable, not to say outré, reading list. Catharine Stimpson has declared that her ideal curriculum would contain the little-known book *Stars in My Pocket Like Grains of Sand.* "Like many contemporary speculative fictions," Stimpson wrote, "*Stars in My Pocket* finds conventional heterosexuality absurd. The central characters are two men, Rat Korga and Marq Dyeth, who have a complex but ecstatic affair. Marq is also the product of a rich 'nurture stream.' His ancestry includes both humans and aliens. His genetic heritage blends differences. In a sweet scene, he sees three of his mothers.*"

ETHNIC AND IDEOLOGICAL PURITY

The multicultural and ethnic-studies programs now in place at most universities tend to divide humanity into five groups—whites, blacks, Native Americans, Hispanics, and Asians. (Homosexuals and feminists are usually included on the grounds that, though they are not a distinct ethnic group, they, too, have been oppressed by the "whitemale," to use the neologism of black literature professor Houston Baker, and prevented from expressing their "otherness.") These are somewhat arbitrary categories, and, in fact, the new fundamentalists have two contradictory views about just what constitutes an ethnic group and who can belong.

On the one hand, there is a reluctance to confer ethnic status on certain groups. At the University of Washington, a student-faculty Task Force on Ethnicity denied Jews, Italians, and Irish-Americans certification as ethnic groups. Status as an oppressed ethnic group is guarded even more jealously. The Washington task force also decided that a required ethnic-studies program exploring the pervasiveness of racism in America would not take up the subject of anti-Semitism. The reason, *Commentary* quoted professor Johnnella Butler as having said, was that "anti-Semitism is not institutionalized in this country."

At the same time, the racial credentials of people aspiring to membership in the officially sanctioned ethnic categories are examined with an attention to detail associated with apartheid. Recently, a Hispanic who had been turned down for an affirmative-action promotion in the San Francisco fire department filed a complaint because the person who got the job instead was from Spain rather than Latin America. Colleges are becoming equally obsessed with such distinctions. Three years ago, the faculty at Hampshire College in Amherst began interviewing candidates for a professorship in Latin American literature. The professor, of course, needed to be Latin. *Pure* Latin. One woman who applied for the job was turned down because, though she was Argentine, she had, like many Argentines, Jewish and Italian blood, and thus her Third World ethnicity was considered insufficiently pure. Her heritage made her, in the words of one faculty member, "Eurocentric."

But even as these standards become increasingly exacting, more and more groups are clamoring for oppressed status. While supporters of American involvement in the Vietnam War were denounced as "war criminals" at the University of Michigan in the sixties, the school now counts Vietnam veterans as an oppressed group. In fact, the politically correct have concluded that virtually *any* one with *any* sort of trait, anxiety, flaw, impediment, or unusual sexual preference qualifies for membership in an oppressed group. This past fall, a handout from the Office of Student Affairs at Smith College explained that many people are *unaware* they are oppressed, though with help they are finding out: "As groups of people begin the process of realizing that they are oppressed, and why, new words tend to be created to express the concepts that the existing language cannot."

This obsessive tendency to see oppression everywhere is creating a sort of New Age caste system. The Smith handout listed various categories of oppression that ranged from "classism" and "ageism" to "ableism" (identified as "oppression of the differently abled by the temporarily able") and "lookism," which was revealed to be "the construction of a standard for beauty/attractiveness; and oppression through stereotypes and generalizations of both those who do not fit that standard and those who do." Heightism may be next. In a joke now making the rounds, short people are demanding to be known as "the vertically challenged."

But joking isn't allowed! Even the most harmless, lighthearted remarks can lead to virulent denunciations. In October, Roderick Nash, a professor at the University of California at Santa Barbara, pointed out during a lecture on environmental ethnics that there is a movement to start referring to pets as animal companions. (Apparently, domesticated animals are offended by the word *pet.*) Nash then made some sort of off-the-cuff observation about how women who pose for *Penthouse* are still called Pets (and not *Penthouse* Animal Companions). Inevitably, several female students filed a formal sexual-harrassment complaint against him. Susan Rode, one of the signers, said, "Maybe this will make more people aware in other classes and make other faculty watch what they say."

Indeed, making people *watch what they say* is the central preoccupation of politically correct students. Stephan Thernstrom is not the only professor who has been forced to give up a course on race relations. Reynolds Farley, one of the leading scholars on race relations, dropped a course he had taught for nearly ten years at the University of Michigan after he was accused of racial insenstivity for reading Malcolm X's description of himself as a pimp and a thief and for discussing the southern defense of slavery. "Given the climate at Michigan," Farley said, "I could be hassled for anything I do or don't say in that class."

Watch what you say: And it's not enough just to avoid racism. One must display absolute ideological purity. The search committee at Hampshire College also considered a highly qualified Chicano candidate for the Latin American literature post. Unfortunately for him, in his dissertation on Chicano literature he drew parallels between Shakespeare and Mexican writers. This demonstrated dangerous "Eurocentric" tendencies. Certain faculty members, doubting the candidate's ethnic purity as well, wondered whether someone of Mexican heritage was *really* Latin American. They thought a Puerto Rican might be better. He didn't get the job.

It was finally offered to Norman Holland, who seemed both ethnically and ideologically pure. But this past summer, Holland's contract was not renewed, and Holland claims it is because he also was branded "Eurocentric." Though the school's official position is that Holland was an ineffective teacher, two of the professors who reviewed his work insinuated that he had a European bias. Holland, one professor declared, had "focused mainly on Western Europe to the exclusion of cultural issues Third World students perceive as uniquely relevant." "I suppose I committed certain kinds of sins," says Holland. "When I was teaching *One Hundred Years of Solitude,* I would talk about colonial rape, but I would also talk about how the novel originated in Europe and how García Márquez was working in that tradition and addressing ideas in Proust and Joyce. I didn't limit myself to considering it as a sociological document."

THE GENDER FEMINISTS AND DATE RAPE

"Misogynistic!"
   "Patriarchal!"
   "Gynophobic!"
   "Phallocentric!"
   Last fall, Camille Paglia attended a lecture by a "feminist theorist" from a large Ivy League university who had set out to "decode" the subliminal sexual oppressiveness in fashion photography. The feminist theorist stood at the front of the room showing slides of fashion photography and cosmetics ads and exposing, in the style of Lacanian psychoanalysis, their violent sexism. She had selected a Revlon ad of a woman

with a heavily made-up face who was standing up to her chin in a pool of water. When it came up on the screen, she exclaimed, "Decapitation!"

She showed a picture of a black woman who was wearing aviator goggles and had the collar of her turtleneck sweater pulled up. "Strangulation!" she shouted. "Bondage!"

It went on like this for the entire lecture. When it was over, Paglia, who considers herself a feminist, stood up and made an impassioned speech. She declared that the fashion photography of the past forty years is great art, that instead of decapitation she saw the birth of Venus, instead of strangulation she saw references to King Tut. But political correctness has achieved a kind of exquisitely perfect rigidity among the group known as the gender feminists, and she was greeted, she says, "with gasps of horror and angry murmuring. It's a form of psychosis, this slogan-filled machinery. The radical feminists have contempt for values other than their own, and they're inspiring in students a resentful attitude toward the world."

Indeed, the central tenet of gender feminism is that Western society is organized around a "sex/gender system." What defines the system, according to Sandra Harding, a professor of philosophy at the University of Delaware and one of its exponents, is "male dominance made possible by men's control of women's productive and reproductive labor."

The primary arena for this dominance is, of course, the family, which Alison Jaggar, a professor at the University of Cincinnati and the head of the American Philosophical Association's Committee on the Status of Women in Philosophy, sees as "a cornerstone of women's oppression." The family, in Jaggar's view, "enforces heterosexuality" and "imposes the prevailing masculine and feminine character structures on the next generation."

This position makes gender feminists, as Christina Sommers has written in an article in *Public Affairs Quarterly,* from which some of these quotes were taken, "oddly unsympathetic to the women whom they claim to represent." But that poses no problem. Women who have decided to get married and raise families, women who want to become mothers, are, naturally, victims of false consciousness. The radical feminists are fond of quoting Simone de Beauvoir, who said, "No woman should be authorized to stay at home and raise children . . . precisely because if there is such a choice, too many women will make that one."

Jaggar, for one, would like to abolish the family altogether and create a society where, with the aid of technology, "one woman could inseminate another . . . men . . . could lactate . . . and fertilized ova could be transferred into women's or even men's bodies." All that is preventing this, according to the gender feminists, is "phallocentricity" and "androcentricity," the view that society is organized around the male and his sexual organs. The feminists, ablaze with revolutionary rhetoric, have set out to overthrow this system. "What we feminists are doing," the philosopher Barbar Minnich has said, "is comparable to Copernicus shattering our geocentricity, Darwin shattering our species-centricity. We are shattering androcentricity, and the change is as fundamental, as dangerous, as exciting."

But unlike the pre-Copernican view that the Earth was at the center of the universe, androcentricity is not, in the view of the gender feminists, merely a flawed theory. It is a moral evil, dedicated to the enslavement of women. And since most of Western culture, according to this view, has been a testament to "male power and transcendence," it is similarly evil and must be discarded. This includes not only patriarchal books like the Bible and sexist subjects like traditional history, with its emphasis on great men and great deeds, but also the natural sciences and even the very process of analytical thinking itself. "To know is to f---" has become a radical-feminist rallying cry. Indeed, scientific inquiry itself is seen as "the rape of nature." A project sponsored by the state of New Jersey to integrate these views into college campuses has issued a set of "feminist scholarship guidelines" that declares "mind was male. Nature was female, and knowledge was created as an act of aggression—a passive nature had to be interrogated, unclothed, penetrated, and compelled by man to reveal her secrets."

To certain women, however, this is just a veiled restatement of the old idea that women don't make good scientists. "As a liberal feminist, I encourage women to study science," says Christina Sommers. "I'm not impugning science itself as hostile to the female sensibility."

But it is not just the coldly analytical and dualistic structures of male thinking that the gender feminists find so contemptible. It is males themselves, or at least heterosexual males. After all, heterosexuality is responsible for the subjugation of women, and so, in the oppressive culture of the West, any woman who goes on a date with a man is a prostitute. "Both man and woman might be outraged at the description of their candlelight dinner as prostitution," Jaggar has written. "But the radical feminist argues this outrage is simply due to the participants' failure or refusal to perceive the social context in which the dinner occurs." In other words, they are victims of—what else?—false consciousness.

This eagerness to see all women as victims, to describe all male behavior with images of rape and violation, may shed some light on the phenomenon of date rape, a legitimate issue that has been exaggerated and distorted by a small group with a specific political agenda. As with the hysteria a few years ago over the sexual abuse of children, endless talk shows, television news stories, and magazine articles have been devoted to date rape, often describing it as "an epidemic" that, as the Chicago *Tribune* put it, "makes women campus prisoners" and forces them, as at Brown, to list supposed rapists on bathroom walls.

Much of this discussion starts off with the claim that one in four female students is raped by a date. The figure seems staggeringly high, and debate tends to focus on whether actual rape or merely the reporting of rape is on the rise. But the journalist Stephanie Gutmann has pointed out in *Reason* magazine the gross statistical flaws in the survey of date rape that produced this figure. According to Gutmann, "The real story about campus date rape is not that there's been any significant increase of rape on college campuses, at least of the acquaintance type, but that the word *rape* is being stretched to encompass any type of sexual interaction."

In fact, rape under the new definition does not have to involve physical assault at all. Andrea Parrot, a professor at Cornell who has promoted the idea of the date-rape epidemic, has declared that "any sexual intercourse without mutual desire is a form of rape." In other words, a woman is being raped if she has sex when not in the mood, even if she fails to inform her partner of that fact. As a former director of Columbia's date-rape-education program told Gutmann, "Every time you have an act of intercourse, there must be explicit consent, and if there's no explicit consent, then it's rape. . . . Stone silence throughout an entire physical encounter with someone is not explicit consent." And rape is no longer limited to actual intercourse. A training manual at Swarthmore College states that "Acquaintance rape . . . spans a spectrum of incidents and behaviors ranging from crimes legally defined as rape to verbal harassment and inappropriate innuendo."

It is no surprise then that Catherine Nye, a University of Chicago psychologist interviewed by Gutmann, found that 43 percent of the women in a widely cited rape study "had not realized they had been raped." In other words, they were victims of, yes, false consciousness. But by the definition of the radical feminists, all sexual encounters that involve any confusion or ambivalence constitute rape. "Ordinary bungled sex—the kind you regret in the morning or even during—is being classified as rape," Gutmann says. "Bad or confused feelings after sex becomes someone else's fault." Which is fine with the feminists. "In terms of making men nervous or worried about overstepping their bounds, I don't think that's a bad thing," Parrot said. Indeed, since it encourages a general suspicion of all men, it's a good thing. As Parrot has put it, "Since you can't tell who has the potential for rape simply by looking, be on your guard with every man."

AFROCENTRISM

For all their fury, the gender feminists are surpassed in ideological rage by an even more extreme wing of the politically correct: the Afrocentrists. Afrocentrists argue that not only is Western culture oppressive, it isn't even really *Western.* Key accomplishments, from mathematics and biology to architecture and medicine, were in fact the work of Africans. "Very few doctors, African-American or otherwise in America, are aware of the fact that when they take their medical oath, the hypocratic [*sic*] oath, they actually swear to Imhotep, the African God of Medicine," Asa Hilliard, a professor of Afro-American history at Georgia State, has written.

The theory that Africa was the true source of Western civilization hinges on the claim that the ancient Egyptians were black. "The first 12 dynasties plus dynasties 18 and 25 were native-black-African dynasties," Hilliard has asserted. Traditional Egyptologists generally believe that while blacks, from Nubia to the south, were active in Egyptian society, ancient Egyptians, like their contemporary counterparts, tended to be of Semitic stock. But to the Afrocentrists, that explantion is merely part of the long-running conspiracy by Western whites to deny the African contribution to civilization.

The conspiracy began, in the Afrocentric view, when the ancient Greeks "stole" African philosophy and science from the Egyptians. To claim European credit for these discoveries, Romans and, later, Christians burned the library of Alexandria in Egypt. The conspiracy has continued ever since. Napoleon's soldiers shot off the nose and lips of the Sphinx to obliterate its Negroid features. Beethoven and Robert Browning were actually blacks whose ethnicity has been hidden. "African history has been lost, stolen, destroyed, and suppressed," Hilliard maintains.

Leonard Jeffries, chairman of the black-studies department at City College and one of the most extreme exponents of Afrocentrism, has worked up a sort of anthropological model to explain why Europeans have oppressed Africans. The human race, according to Jeffries, is divided into the "ice people" and the "sun people." The ethnic groups descended from the ice people are materialistic, selfish, and violent, while those descended from the sun people are nonviolent, cooperative, and spiritual. In addition, blacks are biologically superior to whites, Jeffries maintains, because they have more melanin, and melanin regulates intellect and health.

Despite the spiritual benevolence one might expect from a "sun person," Jeffries is known for making the sort of hostile denunciations that, if he were at the other end of the political spectrum, would no doubt provoke howls of indignation. According to Fred Rueckher, a white student who took his course, Jeffries attacked black males for succumbing to the "white pussy syndrome," that is, pursuing white women. He called Diana Ross an "international whore" for her involvement with white men. And he applauded the destruction of the Challenger space shuttle because it would deter white people from "spreading their filth throughout the universe."

Jeffries's wild remarks are excused by the politically correct on the grounds that to be a racist, you have to have "institutional power," and since blacks do not have "institutional power," they cannot be considered racist. The somewhat flimsy propositions of Afrocentrism are excused with equal finesse. First of all, since everything is political, there has never been disinterested scholarship, only power plays by various groups to justify their own claims. And even if there are some holes in Afrocentrism, the approach is useful because it raises the "self-esteem" of black students.

Such was the reasoning of the New York Board of Education's Task Force on Minorities, to which Leonard Jeffries was a consultant. Its report suggested that "All curricular materials [including math and science] be prepared on the basis of multicultural contributions." As a result, the report said, children from minority cultures "will have higher self-esteem and self-respect, while children from European cultures will have a less arrogant perspective." The notion has already been put into effect in public schools in Portland, Indianapolis, and Washington, D.C., where students are taught subjects like Yoruba mathematics and ancient Egyptian astronomy.

The idea that the "self-esteem" of students—rather than historical relevance—should be the basis for including material in textbooks does have its critics. Among the most prominent is Diane Ravitch, who has said the idea "that children can learn only from the experiences of people from the same race" represents a sort of "racial fundamentalism." The success of Chinese students in math is due not to a "Sinocentric" approach to numbers but to hard work. If the "self-esteem" model had any validity, Italian American students—the descendants of Caesar and Michelangelo—would excel in school, but in fact they have the highest dropout rate of any white group in New York City schools. By promoting a brand of history "in which everyone is either a descendant of victims or oppressors," Ravitch has declared, "ancient hatreds are fanned and re-created in each new generation."

Ravitch naturally was branded a racist for this position. Participants at a recent Afrocentrism conference in Atlanta derided her as "Miss Daisy." She has been attacked in the *City Sun* and on black television and radio programs. As a result, she has received so many threats that when we first agreed to meet, she was afraid to tell me where she lived. "They've written saying things like 'We're going to get you, bitch. We're going to beat your white ass.' "

MOONIES IN THE CLASSROOM

The supreme irony of the new fundamentalism is that the generation that produced the free-speech movement in Berkeley and rebelled against the idea of *in loco parentis*—that university administrators should act as surrogate parents—is now trying to restrict speech and control the behavior of a new generation of students. The enterprise is undertaken to combat racism, of course, and it is an article of faith among the politically correct that the current climate of racial hostility can be traced to the Reagan and Bush presidencies, to conservative-Republican efforts to gut civil-rights legislation and affirmative-action programs. However true that may be, scholars like Shelby Steele, a black essayist and English professor, have also argued that the separatist movements at universities—black dorms, Native American student centers, gay-studies programs, the relentless harping on "otherness"—have heightened tensions and contributed to the culture of victimization. "If you sensitize people from day one to look at everything in terms of race and sex, eventually they will see racism and sexism at the root of everything," says Alan Kors. "But not all the problems and frustrations in life are due to race and gender."

Furthermore, they say, instead of increasing self-esteem, schools that offer an Afrocentric education will only turn out students who are more resentful, and incompetent, than ever. Indeed, while the more rabid Afrocentrics have claimed that crack and AIDS are conspiracies by whites to eliminate blacks, it could just as easily be argued that white indulgence of Afrocentric education represents a conspiracy to provide blacks with a useless education that will keep them out of the job market.

Of course, to make such a statement is invariably to provoke a charge of racism. But part of the problem with this reaction is that it trivializes the debate. In fact, it makes debate impossible. But that is just as well, according to the new fundamentalists. Debate, and the analytic thinking it requires, is oppressive. It's logocentric. It favors the articulate at the expense of the inarticulate. It forces people to make distinctions, and since racism is the result of distinctions, they should be discouraged. "I have students tell me they don't need to study philosophy because it's patriarchal and logocentric," says Christina Sommers. "They're unteachable and scary. It's like having a Moonie in the classroom."

Resistance to this sort of robotic sloganeering is beginning. "Today, routinized righteous indignation has been substituted for rigorous criticism," Henry Louis Gates, a black English professor at Duke, recently declared. Some professors are actually arguing that colleges should begin to emphasize what whites, homosexuals, minorities, and women have in common rather than dwelling constantly on "difference." In November, writing in the *Stanford Daily* about a proposal to require Stanford students to take a course in diversity, David Kennedy, chairman of American studies at Stanford and previously a champion of multiculturalism, said, "I worry that the proposal will add to the already considerable weight that Stanford culture places on racial and ethnic divisiveness, rather than shared participation. I question whether this is socially wise and, further, whether it is intellectually true to the lived experience of members of this society."

A few emboldened administrators are actually suggesting that it is not unreasonable for Western culture to enjoy a certain prominence at American colleges. In an address to incoming Yale students in September, Donald Kagan, dean of the college, encouraged them to center their undergraduate studies around Western culture. He argued that the West "has asserted the claims of the individual against those of the state, limiting its power and creating a realm of privacy into which it cannot penetrate." The West's tradition of civil liberties has produced "a tolerance and respect for diversity unknown in most cultures."

But many of the Yale freshmen—or "freshpeople," as the *Yale Daily News* puts it—considered the dean's statements "quite disturbing." And the dean was denounced with the obligatory mind-numbing litany.

"Paternalistic!"

"Racist!"

"Fascist!"

2

What Campus Radicals?

The P.C. Undergrad Is a Useful Specter

Rosa Ehrenreich

A national survey of college administrators released last summer found that "political correctness" is not the campus issue it has been portrayed to be by pundits and politicians of the political right. During the 1990–91 academic year, according to the survey's findings, faculty members complained of pressure from students and fellow professors to alter the political and cultural content of their courses at only *5 percent* of all colleges. So much for the influence of the radicals, tenured or otherwise.

The survey's findings came as no real surprise to me. The hegemony of the "politically correct" is not a problem at Harvard, where I've just completed my undergraduate education, or at any other campus I visited during my student years. But then none among those who have escalated the P.C. debate in the past year—Dinesh D'Souza and Roger Kimball, George Will and George Bush, *Time* and *New York* magazines—is actually interested in what is happening on the campuses. In all the articles and op-ed pieces published on P.C., multiculturalism, etc., very few student voices have been heard. To be a liberal arts student with progressive politics today is at once to be at the center of a raging national debate and to be completely on the sidelines, watching others far from campus describe you and use you for their own ends.

For instance: During the spring semester of my freshman year at Harvard, Stephan Thernstrom, an American history professor, was criticized by several black students for making "racially insensitive" comments during lectures. The incident made the *Harvard Crimson* for a few days, then blew over after a week or so and was quickly forgotten by most students. It continued a kind of mythic afterlife, however, in the P.C. debate. Here is how it was described last January in a *New York* magazine cover story by John Taylor on, in the author's words, the "moonies in the classroom" propagating the "new fundamentalism":

> "Racist." "Racist!" "The man is a racist!" "A *racist!*"
> Such denunciations, hissed in tones of self-righteousness and contempt, vicious and vengeful, furious, smoking with hatred—such denunciations haunted Stephan Thernstrom for weeks. Whenever he walked through the campus that spring, down Harvard's brick paths, under the arched gates, past the fluttering elms, he found it hard not to imagine the pointing fingers, the whispers.

The operative word here is "imagine." Taylor seriously distorted what actually happened. In February of 1988, several black female students told classmates that they had been disturbed by some "racially insensitive" comments made by Professor Thernstrom. Thernstrom, they said, had spoken approvingly of Jim Crow laws, and had said that black men, harboring feelings of inadequacy, beat their female partners. The *students,* fearing for their grades should they anger Professor Thernstrom by confronting him with their criticisms—this is not an unusual way for college students to think things through, as anyone who's been an undergraduate well knows—never discussed the matter with him. They told friends, who told friends, and the *Crimson* soon picked up word of the incident and ran an article.

Professor Thernstrom, understandably disturbed to learn of the matter in the *Crimson,* wrote a letter protesting that no students had ever approached him directly with such criticisms. He also complained that the students' vague criticisms about "racial insensitivity" had "launched a witch-hunt" that would have "chilling effect upon freedom of expression." Suddenly, Professor Thernstrom was to be understood as a victim, falsely smeared with the charge of racism. But no one had ever accused him of any such thing. "I do not charge that [Thernstrom] is a racist," Wendi Grantham, one of the students who criticized Thernstrom, wrote in the *Crimson* in response to his letter. Grantham believed the professor gave "an incomplete and over-simplistic presentation of the information. . . . I am simply asking questions about his presentation of the material. . . ." As for the professor's comment that the criticisms were like a "witch-hunt," Grantham protested that Thernstrom had "turned the whole situation full circle, proclaimed himself victim, and resorted to childish name-calling and irrational comparisons . . . 'witch-hunt'[is] more than a little extreme. . . ." But vehement, even hysterical language is more and more used to demonize students who question and comment. Terms like "authoritarian" and "Hitler youth" have been hurled at students who, like Grantham, dare to express any sort of criticism of the classroom status quo.

In my four years as a student at Harvard, I found few signs of a new fascism of the left. For that matter, there are few signs of the left at all. The Harvard-Radcliffe Democratic Socialists Club collapsed due to lack of members, as did the left-wing newspaper, the *Subterranean Review*. As to the neoconservative charge that the traditional political left has been supplanted by a feminist-gay-multicultural left: In my senior year the African-American Studies department and the Women's Studies committee each had so few faculty that the same woman served as chair of both. I got through thirty-two courses at Harvard, majoring in the history and literature of England and America, without ever being required to read a work by a black woman writer, and of my thirty-two professors only two were women. I never even *saw* a black or Hispanic professor. (Fewer than 10 percent of tenured professors at Harvard are women, and fewer than 7 percent are members of minorities.)

Perhaps, as some conservatives have maintained, even a few radical professors can reach hundreds of students, bending their minds and sending them, angry and politicized, out into society upon graduation. To cure such fears, drop by Harvard's Office of Career Services. Most staffers there spend their days advising those who would be corporate execs, financial consultants, and investment bankers. Nearly 20 percent of the class of 1990 planned to go to law school. This compares with 10 percent who claimed that they would eventually go into government or one of what Career Services calls the "helping professions."

President Bush, speaking at the University of Michigan's commencement exercises last spring, went on about radical extremists on campus. It would be interesting to know how he calculated this rise in radicalism. Two thirds of Harvard students wholeheartedly supported the Gulf War, according to one *Crimson* poll. That's more support for the war than was found in the country at large. And during my years at Harvard I found that most women on campus, including those who consider themselves politically liberal, would not willingly identify themselves as feminists.

The very notion of "politicization" makes most Harvard students nervous. I discovered this in the fall of 1989, when I was elected president of Harvard's community service organization, Phillips Brooks House Association. I had been reckless enough to suggest that volunteers would benefit from having some awareness of the social and political issues that affected the communities in which they did their volunteer work. I was promptly attacked in the *Crimson* for trying to inappropriately "politicize" public service. The paper also suggested that under my leadership volunteer training might mimic a "party line," with Brooks House as a "central planning office." This used to be called red-baiting. (So much for the liberal campus media.)

Meanwhile—and unremarked upon by D'Souza, et al.—the campus right thrives nationally. Two new right-wing vehicles have popped up on Harvard's campus in recent years. The Association Against Learning in the Absence of Religion and Morality (AALARM) initially made a splash with its uninhibited gay-bashing. The magazine *Peninsula,* closely tied to AALARM, bears an uncanny editorial resemblance to the notorious *Dartmouth Review,* claims to uphold Truth, and has a bizarre propensity for centerfold spreads of mangled fetuses. And older, more traditional conservative groups have grown stronger and more ideological. The Harvard Republican Club, once a stodgy and relatively inactive group, suffered a rash of purges and resignations as more moderate members were driven out by the far right. It is inactive no more.

There *are* those on the left who are intolerant and who could stand to lighten up a bit—these are the activists whom *progressive* and *liberal* students mockingly called "politically correct" years before the right appropriated the term, with a typical lack of irony. But on the whole, intolerance at Harvard—and, I suspect, elsewhere—is the province mostly of extreme conservatism. Posters put up at Harvard by the Bisexual, Gay and Lesbian Students Association are routinely torn down. I don't recall any Republican Club posters being ripped up or removed.

The day after the bombing started in Iraq, I went to an event advertised as "a nonpartisan rally to support our troops," sponsored by the Republican Club. After the scheduled speakers—and several other non-scheduled speakers—had finished, I tried to speak. The rally organizers promptly turned off the microphone. I kept speaking, saying that I supported the troops but not the war. I added that I had been disturbed to hear it said by rally organizers—and applauded by the audience—that the time for debate was over. In a democracy, I said, the time for debate is never over.

I would have gone on, but at this point a group of men in the audience felt the need to demonstrate their conviction that there should be no debate. They began to loudly chant "victory" over and over, quite effectively drowning me out. By way of contrast, supporters of the war were listened to in polite silence by the crowd at an anti-war rally the next day.

In the classroom, too, right-wing political views are heard without disruption. One of Harvard's largest core courses, taken by nearly half of all undergraduates while I was there, is Social Analysis 10, Principles of Economics. It was taught during my undergrad years by two of President Reagan's top economic advisers, Martin Feldstein and Larry Lindsay. Students did not rise up *en masse* to protest the course's right-wing political bias; instead, they sat scribbling feverishly in their notebooks: Ec-10 had a notoriously steep grading curve. (No one seemed worried that each year some 750 innocent Harvard students were being lectured to by the engineers of what George Bush, in one of his more forthright moments, once referred to as "voodoo economics.")

There are many other politically conservative professors at Harvard whose courses are quite popular—Richard Pipes on Russian history and Samuel P. Huntington on modern democracy, to name two of the most prominent—and in their classrooms, as in all undergrad classrooms I was in, free and open discussion did quite well. I took many classes in which fearless conservatives rushed to take part in entirely civil discussions about the efficacy and justice of affirmative action, about whether books like *Uncle Tom's Cabin* and Frederick Douglass's autobiography are "really *literature*," as opposed to just interesting historical documents, and about whether it's at all fair or even interesting to condemn Jefferson for owning slaves even as he decried slavery. These are all valid questions, and all sides deserve a hearing—which, in my experience, is exactly what they always got.

And my experience was not unique. Most other Harvard students seemed to agree that there's no such thing as a cadre of P.C. thought police. Last winter the Republican Club laid huge sheets of poster board across several dining-hall tables and put up a sign asking students to scribble down their responses to the question "Is there free speech at Harvard?" The vast majority of students wrote things like "What's the big deal? Of course there's free speech here." And the lively, cheerful discussion going on among the students gathered around the tables attested to that fact.

Conservatives like D'Souza and Kimball charge that traditional Western culture courses barely exist anymore at schools like Harvard, because of some mysterious combination of student pressure and the multiculturalist, post-structuralist tendencies of radical professors. Writing in the *Atlantic Monthly* last year, Caleb Nelson, a former editor of the conservative *Harvard Salient,* complained that in the 1989–90 Harvard course catalogue:

No core Literature and Arts course lists any of the great nineteenth-century British novelists among the authors studied, nor does any list such writers as Virgil, Milton, and Dostoevsky. In the core's history areas even students who . . . took every single course would not focus on any Western history before the Middle Ages, nor would they study the history of the Enlightenment, the Renaissance, the American Civil War, or a host of other topics that one might expect a core to cover.

Nelson's major complaint is that Harvard is not properly educating all of its students. I agree with him here; in Caleb Nelson, Harvard has let us all down by producing a student so poorly educated that he's unable even to read the course catalogue.

I have the 1989–90 catalogue in front of me as I write, and a quick sampling of some of the entries gives us, from the Literature and Arts and the Historical Study sections of the core curriculum, the following courses: Chaucer, Shakespeare, The Bible and Its Interpreters, Classical Greek Literature and 5th-Century Athens, The Rome of Augustus, The British Empire, The Crusades, The Protestant Reformation. Perhaps Chaucer and Shakespeare are somehow, to Caleb Nelson, not "such writers" as Milton and Dostoevsky and the Protestant Reformation is a historically trivial topic.

Nelson also worries that students will have "no broad look on . . . philosophy"—by which he really means Western philosophy. Yet in the Moral Reasoning section of the core, seven of the ten courses listed have at least four of the following authors on their primary reading lists: Plato, Aristotle, Thucydides, Machiavelli, Locke, Kant, Rousseau, Hume, Mill, Nietzsche, Marx, and Weber. There is one course devoted to a non-Western philosopher: Confucius. The remaining two Moral Reasoning courses focus, respectively, on the writings of "Aristotle . . . [and] Maimonides," and of "Jesus as presented in the Gospels."

These courses are far more representative of those taken by most Harvard undergraduates than the titillating and much denounced 1991 English course on Cross-Dressing and Cultural Anxiety—a graduate seminar listed in the course catalogue but ultimately never held. But then, if you are a right-winger looking for something to replace the commies on campus—remember them?—you aren't going to sell books or raise funds or win votes complaining about undergrads studying Confucian Humanism and Moral Community.

Many of the loudest complainers about P.C. thought police are those who are doing their best to curb free expression in other areas. It doesn't appear to bother Dinesh D'Souza that the word "abortion" cannot be uttered at a federally funded family clinic. More broadly, the brouhaha about political conformity on campus serves as a perfect smoke screen, masking from Americans—from ourselves—the rigid political conformity *off* campus: the blandness of our political discourse, the chronic silence in Washington on domestic matters, the same faces returned to office each year, the bipartisanship that keeps problems from becoming issues. During the Gulf War, the number of huge yellow bouquets in public places rivaled the number of larger-than-life photos of Saddam Hussein displayed on Iraqi billboards. Patriotically correct.

The campuses are no more under siege by radicals than is the society at large. It has been clever of the Kimballs and D'Souzas to write as if it were so. It is always clever of those in ascendance to masquerade as victims. Rebecca Walkowitz, the newly elected president of the *Harvard Crimson,* understands perfectly how this dynamic works. Referring to the 1988 incident involving Professor Thernstrom and several of his black students, Walkowitz has said: "People call the *Crimson* and ask me what we 'did to that man.' It's important to remember who has the power here, because it's not students. Who would dare criticize a professor for political reasons now? In addition to fearing for your grade, you'd fear being pilloried in the national press."

Part Two

Freedom of Expression
on Campus

3

There's No Such Thing as Free Speech and It's a Good Thing, Too

Stanley Fish

"Nowadays the First Amendment is the first refuge of scoundrels."
—Samuel Johnson and Stanley Fish

Lately many on the liberal and progressive left have been disconcerted to find that words, phrases, and concepts thought to be their property and generative of their politics have been appropriated by the forces of neoconservatism. This is particularly true of the concept of free speech, for in recent years First Amendment rhetoric has been used to justify policies and actions the left finds problematical if not abhorrent: pornography, sexist language, campus hate-speech. How has this happened? The answer I shall give in this essay is that abstract concepts like free speech do not have any "natural" content but are filled with whatever content and direction one can manage to give them. Free speech, in short, is not an independent value but a political prize, and if that prize has been captured by a politics opposed to yours, it can no longer be invoked in ways that further your purposes for it is now an obstacle to those purposes. This is something that the liberal left has yet to understand

From *Boston Review* (February 1992). Copyright © 1992 by Stanley Fish. Reprinted by permission.

and what follows is an attempt to pry its members loose from a vocabulary that may now be a disservice to them.

Not far from the end of his *Areopagitica,* and after having celebrated the virtues of toleration and unregulated publication in passages that find their way into every discussion of free speech and the First Amendment, John Milton catches himself up short and says, of course I didn't mean Catholics, *them* we exterminate:

> I mean not tolerated popery, and open superstition, which as it extirpates all religious and civil supremacies, so itself should be extirpated . . . that also which is impious or evil absolutely against faith or manners no law can possibly permit that intends not to unlaw itself.

Notice that Milton is not simply stipulating a single exception to a rule generally in place; the kinds of utterance that might be regulated and even prohibited on pain of trial and punishment comprise an open set; popery is named only as a particularly perspicuous instance of the advocacy that cannot be tolerated. No doubt there are other forms of speech and action that might be categorized as "open superstitions" or as subversive of piety, faith, and manners, and presumably these too would be candidates for "extirpation." Nor would Milton think himself culpable for having failed to provide a list of unprotected utterances. The list will fill itself out as utterances are put to the test implied by his formulation: Would this form of speech or advocacy, if permitted to flourish, tend to undermine the very purposes for which our society is constituted? One cannot answer this question with respect to a particular utterance in advance of its emergence on the world's stage; rather, one must wait and ask the question in the full context of its production and (possible) dissemination. It might appear that the result would be ad hoc and unprincipled, but for Milton the principle inheres in the core values in whose name men of like mind come together in the first place. Those values, which include the search for truth and the promotion of virtue, are capacious enough to accommodate a diversity of views. But at some point—again impossible of advance specification—capaciousness will threaten to become shapelessness, and at that point fidelity to the original values will demand acts of extirpation.

I want to say that all affirmations of freedom of expression are like Milton's, dependent for their force on an exception that literally carves out the space in which expression can then emerge. I do not mean that expression (saying something) is a realm whose integrity is sometimes compromised by certain restrictions but that restriction, in the form of an underlying articulation of the world that necessarily (if silently) negates alternatively possible articulations, is constitutive of expression. Without restriction, without an in-built sense of what it would be meaningless to say or wrong to say, there could be no assertion and no reason for asserting it. The exception to unregulated expression is not a negative restriction, but a positive hollowing out of value—we are for *this,* which means we are against *that*—in relation to which meaning assertion can then occur. It is in reference to that value—constituted as all values are by an act of exclusion—that some forms of speech will be heard as (quite literally) intolerable. Speech, in short, is never a value, but is always in and of itself produced within the precincts of some assumed conception of the good to which it must yield in the event of conflict. When the pinch comes (and sooner or later it will always come) and the institution (be it church, state, or university) is confronted by behavior subversive of its core rationale, it will respond by declaring "of course we mean not tolerated ———, that we extirpate"; not because an exception to a general freedom has suddenly and contradictorily been announced but because the freedom has never been general and has always been understood against the background of an originary exclusion that gives it meaning.

This is a large thesis, but before tackling it directly I want to buttress my case with another example, taken not from the seventeenth century but from the Charter and case law of Canada. Canadian thinking about freedom of expression departs from the line usually taken in the United States in ways that bring that country very close to the *Areopagitica* as I have expounded it. The differences are fully on display in a recent landmark case, *R.* v. *Keegstra.* James Keegstra was a high school teacher in Alberta who, it was established by evidence, "systematically denigrated Jews and Judaism in his classes." He described Jews as treacherous, subversive, sadistic, money-loving, power-hungry, and child-killers. He declared them "responsible for depressions, anarchy, chaos, wars, and revolution," and required his students "to regurgitate these notions in essays and examinations." Keegstra was indicted under section 319(2) of the Criminal Code and convicted. The Court of Appeal reversed, and the Crown appealed to the Supreme Court, which reinstated the lower court's verdict.

Section 319(2) reads in part, "Everyone who, by communicating statements other than in private conversation, willfully promotes hatred against any identifiable group is guilty of . . . an indictable offense and is liable to imprisonment for a term not exceeding two years." In the United States, this provision of the code would almost certainly be struck down because, under the First Amendment, restrictions on speech are apparently prohibited without qualification. To be sure, the Canadian

Charter has its own version of the First Amendment, in section 2(b): "Everyone has the following fundamental freedoms . . . (b) freedom of thought, belief, opinion, and expression, including freedom of the press and other media of communication." But section 2(b), like every other section of the Charter, is qualified by section 1: "The Canadian Charter of Rights and Freedoms guarantees the rights and freedoms set out in it subject only to such reasonable limits prescribed by law as can be demonstrably justified in a free and democratic society." Or in other words, every right and freedom herein granted can be trumped if its exercise is found to be in conflict with the principles that underwrite the society.

This is what happens in *Keegstra,* as the majority finds that section 319(2) of the Criminal Code does in fact violate the right of freedom of expression guaranteed by the Charter but is nevertheless a *permissible* restriction because it accords with the principles proclaimed in section 1. There is, of course, a dissent which reaches the conclusion that would have been reached by most, if not all, U.S. courts; but even in dissent the minority is faithful to Canadian ways of reasoning. "The question," it declares, "is always one of tolerance," and thus even when a particular infringement of Charter section 2(b) has been declared unconstitutional, as it would have been by the minority, the question remains open with respect to the next case. In the United States the question is presumed closed and can be pried open only by special tools. In our legal culture as it is presently constituted, if one yells "free speech" in a crowded courtroom and makes it stick, the case is over.

Of course, it is not that simple. Despite the apparent absoluteness of the First Amendment, there are any number of ways to getting around it, ways that are known to every student of the law. In general, the preferred strategy is to manipulate the distinction, essential to First Amendment jurisprudence, between speech and action. The distinction is essential because no one would think to frame a First Amendment that began "Congress shall make no law abridging freedom of action," for that would amount to saying "Congress shall make no law," which would amount to saying "There shall be no law," only actions uninhibited and unregulated. If the First Amendment is to make any sense, have any bite, speech must be declared not to be a species of action, or to be a special form of action lacking the aspects of action that cause it to be the object of regulation. The latter strategy is the favored one and usually involves the separation of speech from consequences. This is what Archibald Cox does when he assigns to the First Amendment the job of protecting "expressions separable from conduct harmful to other individuals and the community." The difficulty of managing this segregation is well known: Speech always seems to be crossing the line into action where it becomes, at least potentially, consequential. In the face of this categorical instability, First Amendment theorists and jurists fashion a distinction within the distinction: Some forms of speech are not really speech because they have a tendency to incite violence; they are, as the court declares in *Chaplinsky* v. *New Hampshire* (1942), "fighting words," words "likely to provoke the average person to retaliation, and thereby cause a breach of the peace."

The trouble with this definition is that it distinguishes not between fighting words and words that remain safely and merely expressive, but between words that are provocative to one group (the group that falls under the rubric "average person") and words that might be provocative to other groups, groups of persons not now considered average. And if you ask what words are likely to be provocative to those nonaverage groups, what are likely to be *their* fighting words, the answer is anything and everything, for as Justice Holmes said long ago (in *Gitlow* v. *New York*), every idea is an incitement to somebody, and since ideas come packaged in sentences, in words, every sentence is potentially, in some situation that might occur tomorrow, a fighting word and therefore a candidate for regulation. That may be why the doctrine of "fighting words" has been more invoked than honored since 1942. If the category is not a formal one, but one that varies with the varying sensitivies of different groups, there is no utterance that it does not include, and we are led to the conclusion that there is nothing for the First Amendment to protect, no such thing as "speech alone" or speech separable from harmful conduct, no such thing as "mere speech" or the simple nonconsequential expression of ideas. It would follow from this conclusion that when a court rules in the name of these nonexistent things, it is really doing something else; it is deciding to permit certain harms done by words because it believes that by permitting them it upholds a value greater than the value of preventing them. That value will not, however, be the value of speech, per se, but of whatever set of concerns is judged by the court to override the concerns of those who find a form of speech harmful.

At this point a First Amendment purist might ask, "Why couldn't that overriding concern be the protection of speech? Why couldn't freedom of speech be the greater value to which other values must yield in the event of a clash?" The answer is that freedom of expression would be a primary value only if it didn't matter what was said; didn't matter in the sense that no one gave a damn, but just liked to hear talk. There are contexts like that, a Hyde Park corner or a radio talk show where people get to sound off for the sheer fun of it. These, however, are special contexts, artificially bounded spaces designed to assure that talking is not taken seriously. In ordinary contexts, talk is produced with the goal of trying to move the world in one direction rather than another. In these contexts—the contexts of everyday life—you go to the trouble of asserting that x is y only because you suspect that some people are asserting that x is z or that x doesn't exist. You assert, in short, because you give a damn, not about assertion—as if it were a value in and of itself—but about what your assertion is about. It may seem paradoxical, but free expression could only be a primary value if what you are valuing is the right to make noise; but if you are engaged in some purposive activity in the course of which speech happens to be produced, sooner or later you will come to a point when you decide that some forms of speech do not further but endanger that purpose.

Take the case of universities and colleges. Could it be the purpose of such places to encourage free expression? If the answer were "yes," it would be hard to say why there would be any need for classes, or examinations, or departments, or disciplines, or libraries, since freedom of expression requires nothing but a soapbox or an open telephone line. The very fact of the university's machinery—of the events, rituals and procedures that fill its calendar—argues for some other, more substantive, purpose. In relation to that purpose (which will be realized differently in different kinds of institutions), the flourishing of free expression will in almost all circumstances be an obvious good; but in some circumstances, freedom of expression may pose a threat to that purpose, and at that point, it may be necessary to discipline or regulate speech, lest, to paraphrase Milton, the institution were to sacrifice itself to one of its accidental features.

Interestingly enough, the same conclusion is reached (inadvertently) by Congressman Henry Hyde, who is addressing these very issues in a recently offered amendment to Title VI of the Civil Rights Act. The first section of the amendment states its purpose, to protect "the free speech rights of college students" by prohibiting private as well as public educational institutions from "subjecting any student to disciplinary sanctions solely on the basis of conduct that is speech." The second section enumerates the remedies available to students whose speech rights may have been abridged; and the third, which is to my mind the nub of the matter, declares as an exception to the amendment's jurisdiction any "educational institution that is controlled by a religious organization," on the reasoning that the application of the amendment to such institutions "would not be consistent with the religious tenets of such organizations." In effect, what Congressman Hyde is saying is that at the heart of these colleges and universities is a set of beliefs, and it would be wrong to require them to tolerate behavior, including speech behavior, inimical to those beliefs. But insofar as this logic is persuasive, it applies across the board; for all educational institutions rest on some set of beliefs—no institution is "just there" independent of any purpose—and it is hard to see why the rights of an institution to protect and preserve its basic "tenets" should be restricted only to those that are religiously controlled. Read strongly, the third section of the amendment undoes sections one and two—the exception becomes, as it always was, the rule—and points us to a balancing test very much like that employed in Canadian law: Given that any college or university is informed by a core rationale, an administrator faced with complaints about offensive speech should ask whether damage to the core would be greater if the speech were tolerated or regulated.

The objection to this line of reasoning is well known and has recently been reformulated by Benno Schmidt, president of Yale University. According to Schmidt, speech-codes on campuses constitute "well-intentioned but misguided efforts to give values of community and harmony a higher place than freedom" (*Wall Street Journal,* May 6, 1991). "When the goals of harmony collide with freedom of expression," he continues, "freedom must be the paramount obligation of an academic community." The flaw in this logic is on display in the phrase "academic community"; for the phrase recognizes what Schmidt would deny, that expression occurs only in communities, if not in an academic community, then in a shopping-mall community or a dinner-party community or an airplane-ride community or an office community. Arguments like Schmidt's get their purchase by imagining expression occurring in *no* community, in an environment without the pervasive pressures and pressurings that come along with any socially organizing activity. The same (impossibly) quarantined and pristine space is the location of his preferred value, freedom, which in his conception is not freedom *for* anything but just "freedom," an urge without direction, as expression is for him an emission without assertive content. Of course the speech to which campus codes are a response is full of content and productive of injury; but Schmidt is able to skirt this difficulty by reducing the content to a matter of style and the injury to an offense against sensibility. This is the work done by the word "obnoxious" when Schmidt urges us to protect speech "no matter how obnoxious in content." In this formulation, obnoxiousness becomes the content of the speech and the deeper affront that might provoke efforts to curtail it is pushed into the background. "Obnoxious" suggests that the injury or offense is a surface one that a large-minded ("liberated and humane") person should be able to tolerate if not embrace. The idea that the effects of speech can penetrate to the core—either for good or for ill—is never entertained; everything is kept on the level of weightless verbal exchange;

there is no sense of the lacerating harms that speech of certain kinds can inflict.

To this Schmidt would no doubt reply, as he does in his essay, that harmful speech should be answered not by regulation but by more speech; but that would make sense only if the effects of speech could be canceled out by additional speech, only if the pain and humiliation caused by racial or religious epithets could be ameliorated by saying something like, "So's your old man." What Schmidt fails to realize at every level of his argument is that expression is more than a matter or proffering and receiving propositions, that words do work in the world of a kind that cannot be confined to a purely cognitive realm of "mere" ideas.

It could be said, however, that I myself mistake the nature of the work done by freely tolerated speech because I am too focused on short-run outcomes and fail to understand that the good effects of speech will be realized not in the present, but in a future whose emergence regulation could only inhibit. This line of reasoning would also have the advantage of blunting one of my key points, that speech in and of itself cannot be a value and is only worth worrying about if it is in the service of something with which it cannot be identical. My mistake, it could be said, is to equate the something in whose service speech is with some locally espoused value (e.g., the end of racism, the empowerment of disadvantaged minorities), whereas in fact we should think of that "something" as a now inchoate shape that will be given firm lines only by time's pencil. That is why the shape now receives such indeterminate characterizations (e.g., true self-fulfillment, a more perfect polity, a more capable citizenry, a less partial truth); we cannot now know it, and therefore we must not prematurely fix it in ways that will bind successive generations to error.

This forward-looking view of what the First Amendment protects has a great appeal, in part because it continues in a secular form the Puritan celebration of millenarian hopes, but it imposes a requirement so severe that one would expect more justification than is usually provided. The requirement is that we endure whatever pain racist and hate speech inflicts for the sake of a future whose emergence we can only take on faith. In a specifically religious vision like Milton's, this makes perfect sense (it is indeed the whole of Christianity), but in the context of a politics that puts its trust in the world and not in the Holy Spirit, it raises more questions than it answers and could be seen as the other prong of a strategy designed to delegitimize the complaints of victimized groups. The first strategy, as I have noted, is to define speech in such a way as to render it inconsequential (on the model of "sticks and stones will break my bones, but . . ."); the second strategy is to acknowledge the (often grievous) consequences but declare that we must suffer them in the name of something that cannot be named. The two strategies are denials from slightly different directions of the *present* effects of racist speech: one confines those effects to a closed and safe realm of pure mental activity; the other imagines the effects of speech spilling over into the world, but only in an ever-receding future for whose sake we must forever defer taking action.

I find both strategies unpersuasive, but my own skepticism concerning them is less important than the fact that in general they seem to have worked; in the parlance of the marketplace (a parlance First Amendment commentators love), many in the society seemed to have bought them. Why? The answer, I think, is that people cling to First Amendment pieties because they do not wish to face what they correctly take to be the alternative. That alternative is *politics,* the realization (at which I have already hinted) that decisions about what is and is not protected in the realm of expression will rest not on principle or firm doctrine, but on the ability of some persons, to interpret—recharacterize or rewrite—principle and doctrine in ways that lead to the protection of speech they want heard and the regulation of speech they want silenced. (That is how George Bush can argue *for* flag-burning statutes and *against* campus hate-speech codes.) When the First Amendment is successfully invoked the result is not a victory for free speech in the face of a challenge from politics, but a *political victory* won by the party that has managed to wrap its agenda in the mantle of free speech. It is from just such a conclusion—a conclusion that would put politics *inside* the First Amendment—that commentators recoil, saying things like "this could render the First Amendment a dead letter," or "this would leave us with no normative guidance in determining when and what speech to protect," or "this effaces the distinction between speech and action," or "this is incompatible with any viable notion of freedom of expression." To these statements (culled more or less at random from recent law review pieces) I would reply that the First Amendment has always been a dead letter if one understood its "liveness" to depend on the identification and protection of a realm of "mere" expression or discussion distinct from the realm of regulatable conduct; the distinction between speech and action has always been effaced in principle, although in practice it can take whatever form the prevailing political conditions mandate; we have never had any normative guidance for marking off protected from unprotected speech; rather, the guidance we have has been fashioned (and refashioned) in the very political struggles over which it then (for a time) presides. In short, the name of the game has always been politics, even when (indeed, especially when) it is played by stigmatizing politics as the area to be avoided.

It is important to be clear as to what this means. It does *not* mean that in the absence of normative guidelines we should throw up our hands and either regulate everything or allow everything. Rather, it means that the question of whether or not to regulate will always be a local one and that we cannot rely on abstractions that are either empty of content or filled with the content of some partisan agenda to generate a "principled" answer. Instead we must consider in every case what is at stake and what are the risks and gains of alternative courses of action. In the course of this consideration many things will be of help, but among them will not be phrases like "freedom of speech" or "the right of individual expression," which, at least as they are used now, these phrases tend to obscure rather than clarify our dilemmas. Once they are deprived of their talismanic force, once it is no longer strategically effective simply to invoke them in the act of walking away from a problem, the conversation could continue in directions that are now blocked by a First Amendment absolutism that has only been honored in the breach anyway. To the student reporter who complains that in the wake of the promulgation of a speech code at the University of Wisconsin there is now something in the back of his mind as he writes, one could reply, "There was always something in the back of your mind and perhaps it might be better to have this code in the back of your mind than whatever was in there before." And when someone warns about the slippery slope and predicts mournfully that if you restrict one form of speech, you never know what will be restricted next, one could reply, "Some form of speech is always being restricted; else there could be no meaningful assertion; we have always and already slid down the slippery slope; someone is always going to be restricted next, and it is your job to make sure that the someone is not you." And when someone observes, as someone surely will, that anti-harassment codes chill speech, one could reply that since speech becomes intelligible only against the background of what isn't being said, the background of what has already been silenced, the only question is the political one of which speech is going to be chilled, and, all things considered, it seems a good thing to chill speech like "nigger," "cunt," "kike," and "faggot." And if someone then says, "But what happened to free-speech principles?" one could say what I have now said a dozen times—free speech principles don't exist except as a component in a bad argument in which such principles are invoked to mask motives that would not withstand close scrutiny.

An example of a wolf wrapped in First Amendment clothing is an advertisement that ran recently in the Duke University student newspaper, *The Chronicle*. Signed by Bradley R. Smith, well-known as a purveyor of anti-Semitic neo-Nazi propaganda, the ad is packaged as a scholarly treatise: four densely packed columns complete with "learned" references, undocumented statistics, and an array of so-called authorities. The message of the ad is that the Holocaust never occurred and that the German state never "had a policy to exterminate the Jewish people (or anyone else) by putting them to death in gas chambers." In a spectacular instance of the increasingly popular "blame the victim" strategy, the Holocaust "story" or "myth" is said to have been fabricated in order "to drum up world sympathy for Jewish causes." The "evidence" supporting these assertions is a slick blend of supposedly probative facts—"not a single autopsied body has been shown to be gassed"—and sly insinuations of a kind familiar to readers of *Mein Kampf* and *The Protocols of the Elders of Zion*.

The slickest thing of all, however, is the presentation of the argument as an exercise in free speech—the ad is subtitled *The Case for Open Debate*—that could be objected to only by "thought police" and censors. This strategy bore immediate fruit in the decision of the newspaper staff to accept the ad despite a longstanding (and historically honored) policy of refusing materials that contain ethnic and racial slurs or are otherwise offensive. The reasoning of the staff (explained by the editor in a special column) was that, under the First Amendment, advertisers have the "right" to be published. "American newspapers are built on the principles of free speech and free press, so how can a newspaper deny these rights to anyone?" The answer to this question is that an advertiser is not denied his rights simply because a single media organ declines his copy, so long as other avenues of publication are available and there has been no state suppression of his views. This is not to say that there could not be a case for printing the ad; only that the case cannot rest on a supposed First Amendment obligation. One might argue, for example, that printing the ad would foster healthy debate or that lies are more likely to be shown up for what they are if they are brought to the light of day, but these are precisely the arguments the editor *disclaims* in her eagerness to take a "principled" free speech stand. By running the First Amendment up the nearest flagpole and rushing to salute it, the editor and her staff short-circuited their thought processes and threw away the opportunity to take the serious measure of a complicated issue. They allowed First Amendment slogans to blur the distinction between the positive effects of the exchange of ideas and the harm done—a harm to which they contribute—when flat-out lies are able to merchandise themselves as ideas. They rented the dignity of their publication to a hatemonger masquerading as a scholar because they were bamboozled by the invocation of a doctrine that did not really apply and was certainly not dispositive. In this case, at least, the First Amendment did bad work, first in the mouth (or pen) of Mr. Smith and then in the collective brain of the student editors.

Let me be clear. I am not saying that First Amendment principles are inherently bad (they are *inherently* nothing), only that independent of some particular partisan vision, they have no necessary content; and if the vision by which they have been appropriated is hostile to your interests, you would be well advised not to rely on them. This does not mean that you would be better off if they were not available; like any other formulas embedded in the process by which decisions are made, free speech principles function to protect society against over-hasty outcomes; they serve as channels through which an argument must pass on its way to ratification. But the channels are not, as they are sometimes said to be, merely and reassuringly procedural. They have as much content as the contents they "filter," and therefore one must be alert to the content they presently bear and not look to them for a deliverance from politics, for it is politics, either your own or someone else's, that is responsible for the form free speech principles now have. My counsel is therefore pragmatic rather than draconian: so long as so-called "free speech principles" have been fashioned by your enemies, contest their relevance to the issue at hand; but if you manage to refashion them in line with your purposes, urge them with a vengeance.

It is a counsel that follows from the thesis that there is no such thing as free speech, which is not, after all, a thesis as startling or corrosive as may first have seemed. It merely says that there is no class of utterances separable from the world of conduct, and that therefore the identifications of some utterances as members of that nonexistent class will always be evidence that a political line has been drawn rather than a line that denies politics entry into the form of public discourse. It is the job of the First Amendment to mark out an area in which competing views can be considered without state interference; but if the very marking out of that area is itself an interference (as it always will be), First Amendment jurisprudence is inevitably self-defeating and subversive of its own aspirations. That's the bad news. The good news is that precisely *because* speech is never "free" in the two senses required—free of consequences and free from state pressure—speech always matters, is always doing work; because everything we say impinges on the world in ways indistinguishable from the effects of physical action, we must take responsibility for our verbal performances—*all* of them—and not assume that they are being taken care of by a clause in the Constitution. Of course, with responsibility come risks, but they have always been our risks and no doctrine of free speech has ever insulated us from them. They are the risks of either allowing or policing the flow of discourse. They are the risks, respectively, of permitting speech that does obvious harm and of shutting off speech in ways that might deny us the benefit of Joyce's *Ulysses* or Lawrence's *Lady Chatterly's Lover* or Titian's paintings. Nothing, I repeat, can insulate us from those risks. (If there is no normative guidance in determining when and what speech to protect, there is no normative guidance in determining what is art—like free speech a category that includes everything and nothing—and what is obscenity.) And, moreover, nothing can provide us with a principle for deciding which risk in the long run is the best to take. I am persuaded that at the present moment, right now, the risk of not attending to hate speech is greater than the risk that by regulating it we will deprive ourselves of valuable voices and insights or slide down the slippery slope toward tyranny. This is a judgment for which I can offer reasons but no guarantees. All I am saying is that the judgments of those who would come down on the other side carry no guarantees either since the abstractions that usually accompany such guarantees are malleable political constructs. It is not that there are no choices to make or means of making them; it is just that the choices as well as the means are inextricable from the din and confusion of partisan struggle. There is no safe place.

4

The Campus: "An Island of Repression in a Sea of Freedom"

Chester E. Finn, Jr.

Two weeks before the Supreme Court held that the First Amendment protects one's right to burn the flag, the regents of the University of Wisconsin decreed that students on their twelve campuses no longer possess the right to say anything ugly to or about one another. Though depicted as an antidiscrimination measure, this revision of the student-conduct code declares that "certain types of expressive behavior directed at individuals and intended to demean and to create a hostile environment for education or other university-authorized activities would be prohibited and made subject to disciplinary sanctions." Penalties range from written warnings to expulsion.

Several months earlier, the University of Michigan adopted a six-page "anti-bias code" that provides for punishment of students who engage in conduct that "stigmatizes or victimizes an indivudal on the basis of race, ethnicity, religion, sex, sexual orientation, creed, national origin, ancestry, age, marital status, handicap, or Vietnam-era veteran status." (Presumably this last bizarre provision applies whether the "victim" is labeled a war hero or a draft dodger.)

Nor are Wisconsin and Michigan the only state universities to have gone this route. In June, the higher-education regents of Massachusetts prohibited "racism, anti-Semitism, ethnic, cultural, and religious intolerance" on their twenty-seven campuses. A kindred regulation took effect on July 1 at the Chapel Hill campus of the University of North Carolina. And in place for some time at the law school of the State University of New York at Buffalo has been the practice of noting a student's use of racist language on his academic record and alerting prospective employers and the bar association.

Not to be outdone by the huge state schools, a number of private universities, like Emory in Atlanta and Stanford in California, have also made efforts to regulate unpleasant discourse and what the National Education Association terms "ethno-violence," a comprehensive neologism that includes "acts of insensitivity."

Proponents of such measures are straightforward about their intentions. Says University of Wisconsin President Kenneth Shaw of the new rule: "It can particularly send a message to minority students that the board and its administration do care." Comments Emory's director of equal opportunity: "We just wanted to ensure that at a time when other universities were having problems that we made it clear that we wouldn't tolerate graffiti on walls or comments in classes." And in Massachusetts, the regents concluded that, "There must be a unity and cohesion in the diversity which we seek to achieve, thereby creating an atmosphere of pluralism."

This "pluralism" is not to be confused with the version endorsed by the First Amendment. Elsewhere we are expected, like it or not, to attend to what Justice Brennan calls the "bedrock principle . . . that the government may not prohibit the expression of an idea simply because society finds the idea itself offensive or disagreeable." Not so for those running universities. "What we are proposing is not completely in line with the First Amendment," a leader of Stanford's student government has acknowledged to a reporter, but "I'm not sure it should be. We . . . are trying to set a standard different from what society at large is trying to accomplish." Explains the Emory official: "I don't believe freedom of speech on campus was designed to allow people to demean others on campus." And a Stanford law professor contends that, "Racial epithets and sexually haranguing speech silences rather than furthers discussion."

Disregard the hubris and the sanctimony. Academics and their youthful apprentices have long viewed their own institutions and causes as nobler than the workaday world and humdrum pursuits of ordinary mortals. Forget, too, the manifest evidence of what some of the nation's most esteemed universities are teaching their students about basic civics. Consider only the two large issues that these developments pose, each freighted with a hefty burden of irony.

The first can still evoke a wry smile. We are, after all, seeing students pleading for controls to be imposed on campus behavior in the name of decency and morality. Yet these same students would be outraged if their colleges and universities were once again to function *in loco parentis* by constraining personal liberty in any other way. What is more, faculties, administrators, and trustees are complying with the student demands; they are adopting and—one must assume—enforcing these behavior codes. By and large, these are the same campuses that have long since shrugged off any serious responsibility for student conduct with respect to alcohol, drugs, and promiscuity (indeed, have cheerily collaborated in making the last of these behaviors more heedless by installing condom dispensers in the dorms). These are colleges that do not oblige anyone to attend class regularly, to excercise in the gym, to drive safely, or to eat a balanced diet. A student may do anything he likes with or to his fellow students, it appears, including things that are indisputably illegal, unhealthy, and dangerous for everyone concerned, and the university turns a blind eye. But a student may not, under any circumstances, speak ill of another student's origins, inclinations, or appearance.

The larger—and not the least bit amusing—issue is, of course, the matter of freedom of expression and efforts to limit it. That the emotionally charged flag-burning decision emerged from the Supreme Court the same month as authorities in China shot hundreds of students (and others) demonstrating for democracy in the streets of Beijing is as stark an illustration as one will ever see of the gravity and passion embedded in every aspect of this question.

In the Western world, the university has historically been the locus of the freest expression to be found anywhere. One might say that the precepts embodied in the First Amendment have applied there with exceptional clarity, and long before they were vouchsafed in other areas of society. For while private colleges are not formally bound by the Bill of Rights, they, like their public-sector counterparts, are heirs to an even older tradition. The campus was a sanctuary in which knowledge and truth might be pursued—and imparted—with impunity, no matter how unpopular, distasteful, or politically heterodox the process might sometimes be. That is the essence of academic freedom and it is the only truly significant distinction between the universities of the democracies and those operating under totalitarian regimes. Wretched though the food and lodging are for students on Chinese campuses, these were not the provocations that made martyrs in Tiananmen Square. It was the idea of freedom that stirred China's students and professors (and millions of others, as well). And it was the fear of allowing such ideas to take root that prompted the government's brutal response.

Having enjoyed almost untrammeled freedom of thought and expression for three and a half centuries, and having vigorously and, for the most part, successfully fended off efforts by outsiders (state legislators and congressional subcommittees, big donors, influential alumni, etc.) to constrain that freedom, American colleges and universities are now muzzling themselves. The anti-discrimination and anti-harassment rules being adopted will delimit what can be said and done on campus. Inevitably, this must govern what can be taught and written in lab, library and lecture hall, as well as the sordid antics of fraternity houses and the crude nastiness of inebriated teenagers. ("The calls for a ban on 'harassment by vilification' reached a peak last fall" at Stanford, explained the New York *Times* "after two drunken freshmen turned a symphony recruiting poster into a black-face caricature of Beethoven and posted it near a black student's room.")

Constraints on free expression and open inquiry do not, of course, depend on the adoption of a formal code of conduct. Guest speakers with controversial views have for some years now risked being harassed, heckled, even shouted down by hostile campus audiences, just as scholars engaging in certain forms of research, treading into sensitive topics, or reaching unwelcome conclusions have risked calumny from academic "colleagues." More recently, students have begun to monitor their professors and to take action if what is said in class irks or offends them.

Thus, at Harvard Law School this past spring, Bonnie Savage, the aptly named leader of the Harvard Women's Law Association (HWLA), sent professor Ian Macneil a multicount allegation of sexism in his course on contracts. The first offense cited was Macneil's quoting (on page 963 of his textbook) Byron's well-known line, "And whispering, 'I will ne'er consent,'—consented." This, and much else that he had said and written, the HWLA found objectionable. "A professor in any position at any school," Savage pronounced, "has no right or privilege to use the classroom in such a way as to offend, at the very least, 40 percent of the students. . . ."

This was no private communication. Savage dispatched copies to sundry deans and the chairman of the faculty-appointments committee because, she later explained, "We thought he might be considered for tenure." The whole affair, Macneil responded in the *Harvard Law Record,* was "shoddy, unlawyerlike, reminiscent of Senator McCarthy, and entirely consistent with HWLA's prior conduct." As for the Byron passage, it "is in fact a perfect summary of what happens in the Battle of Forms" (a part of the contract-making process).

Macneil is not the only Harvard professor to have been given a hard time in recent years for writing or uttering words that upset students, however well-suited they might be to the lesson at hand. Not long ago, the historian Stephan Thernstrom was accused by a student vigilante of such classroom errors as "read[ing] aloud from white plantation owners' journals 'without also giving the slaves' point of view.' " Episodes of this kind, says Thernstrom, serve to discourage him and other scholars from even teaching courses on topics that bear on race and ethnicity.

Nor is Harvard the only major university where student allegations, unremonstrated by the administration, have produced such a result. At Michigan last fall, the distinguished demographer, Reynolds Farley, was teaching an undergraduate course in "race and cultural contact," as he had done for the previous ten years, when a column appeared in the Michigan *Daily* alleging racial insensitivity on his part, citing—wholly out of context, of course—half a dozen so-called examples, and demanding that the sociology department make amends. Farley was not amused and, rather than invite more unjust attacks, is discontinuing the course. Consequently 50 to 125 Michigan students a year will be deprived of the opportunity to examine issues of ethnicity and the history of race relations in America under the tutelage of this world-class scholar. And to make matters even worse, Farley notes that several faculty colleagues have mentioned that they are dropping any discussion of various important race-related issues from their courses, lest similar treatment befall them.

This might seem perverse, not least from the standpoint of "aggrieved" students and their faculty mentors, because another of their major goals is to oblige everyone to take more courses on precisely these topics. "I would like to see colleges engage all incoming students in mandatory racial-education programs," writes William Damon, professor of psychology and chairman of the education department at Clark University, in the *Chronicle of Higher Eduation.* And his call is being answered on a growing number of campuses, including the state colleges of Massachusetts, the University of Wisconsin, and the University of California at Berkeley.

Ironies abound here, too, since the faculties and governing boards adopting these course requirements are generally the very bodies that resist any suggestion of a "core curriculum" or tight "distribution requirements" on the ground that diverse student preferences should be accommodated and that, in any case, there are no disciplines, writings, or ideas of such general importance that everyone should be obliged to study them. Curricular relativism can be suspended, though, when "pluralism" is itself the subject to be studied. "It is important to make such programs mandatory," Professor Damon explains, "so that they can reach students who otherwise might not be inclined to participate."

Save for the hypocrisy, this may appear at first glance to be part of an ancient and legitimate function of college faculties; deciding what subjects are of sufficient moment as to require students to examine them. If a particular university has its curricular priorities askew, requiring the study of racism rather than, say, mathematics, one can presumably enroll elsewhere (there being about 3,400 institutions to choose from).

A second glance is in order, however, before conceding legitimacy. What is commonly sought in these required courses, and the non-credit counterparts that abound on campuses where they have not yet entered the formal curriculum, is not open inquiry but, rather, a form of attitude adjustment, even ideological indoctrination. Thus Professor Damon:

> Such programs should emphasize discussions in which trained instructors explore students' beliefs concerning racial diversity and its societal implications. . . . They should cover, and *provide clear justification for, any racially or ethically sensitive admissions or hiring criteria that students may see on campus.* [Emphasis added]

Along similar lines, the Massachusetts regents insist that each campus provide "a program of educational activities designed to enlighten faculty, administrators, staff and students with regard to . . . ways in which the dominant society manifests and perpetuates racism." So, too, the Berkeley academic senate last year voted (227 to 194) to begin requiring all undergraduates to sign up for new courses in "American cultures" in which they will explore questions like "How have power relations between groups been manifested in such matters as racism, economics, politics, environmental design, religion, education, law, business, and the arts in the United States?"

In response to Professor Damon's description of the instructional goals of the mandatory course he is urging, Harvard's Thernstrom wrote in a letter to the *Chronicle of Higher Education*:

> Justification? Is that what educators are supposed to provide? For "any" criteria that omniscient administrators choose to adopt? . . . How about a mandatory course providing "a clear justification" for American foreign policy since 1945? Or one justifying the Reagan administration's domestic policies? . . . True, Professor Damon declares that such courses should "avoid preaching and indoctrination," but it seems to me that providing "justification" for highly controversial social programs cannot be anything but indoctrination.

Whether this bleak assessment will prove accurate hinges in large part on who ends up teaching these courses and the intellectual norms to which they hew. With scholars of the stature of Farley and Thernstrom already deterred—coerced into self-censorship—it is likely that colleges will enlist as instructors people who agree that the purpose of these "education" efforts is more political than intellectual. Such individuals are not hard to find in the curricular domain now known as "cultural studies." In this field, acknowledged Professor Donald Lazere at the 1988 conference of the Modern Language Association (MLA), "politics are obviously central." Indeed, the agenda of the field itself was defined by Richard Johnson, an Englishman who is one of its leading figures, as

> a series of critiques of innocent-sounding categories of innocent-sounding practices, obviously culture, and art and literature, but also communication, and consumption, entertainment, education, leisure, style, the family, femininity and masculinity, and sexuality and pleasure, and, of course, the most objective-sounding, neutral-sounding categories of all, knowledge and science.

It is not far from MLA discussions to campus staffing decisions. Here is how the historian Alan C. Kors of the University of Pennsylvania describes the organization of a dorm-based program to educate students at his institution about "racism, sexism, and homophobia":

> [W]hat the administration has done, in fact, is turn this education of the students over to ideologically-conscious groups with ideological and political agendas, namely, the "Women's Center" and the Office of Affirmative Action. . . . These are people who have been granted, in effect, to use a term they like, the "privileged ideological position" on campus. Now the notion that the Penn Women's Center speaks for Penn women is absurd, since it obviously doesn't speak for more than a very small minority of a diverse, individuated female population. . . . But the university's administration has an easy way of buying off certain pressure groups, and it consists of giving those in possession of privileged ideologies the responsibility for reeducating students and faculty with improper attitudes. As a result, you really have the foundations of a University of Beijing in Philadelphia.

These additions to the formal and informal curricula of American colleges and universities, like the behavior codes and anti-harassment policies the institutions are embracing, are invariably promulgated in the name of enhancing "diversity" on campus. This has become the chief purpose of present-day affirmative-action hiring and admissions policies, too. It has, after all, been a while since one could observe prospective students or instructors turned away in any numbers at the campus gates because they were women or minority-group members or because of their religion or handicap. The one exception in recent years has been Asian students, whose dazzling academic performance led some universities to impose admission quotas lest this group become "overrepresented" in the student body. Asians, in fact, recently won a victory at Berkeley, when the chancellor apologized for admissions policies that had held down their numbers and announced a new one. The changes include raising from 40 to 50 percent the fraction of Berkeley undergraduates who will be admitted on the basis of academic merit alone; the other half must be "underrepresented minorities." (The likely impact of this new policy will be to maintain the enrollment shares of black and Hispanic students, to boost the numbers of Asians admitted, and to cause a drop in white matriculations, who plainly will not make it as a minority and who may be trounced by the Asians in the merit competition.)

With these few exceptions, however, affirmative action in the late '80s has nothing to do with invidious discrimination on grounds of race, gender, etc. Most colleges and universities would kill for more blacks and Hispanics in their student bodies and for more of the same minorities, as well as more women, in their faculties. (The only reason they are not equally eager for additional female *students* is that women today constitute a clear majority of the nation's 12.8 million higher-education enrollees.) "Diversity," then, is now the goal.

That we have generally grown used to this in matters of campus admission and employment does not mean that the academy lacks the capacity to surprise and dismay. These days that capacity usually entails a faculty-hiring decision where the race or gender or ideology of the candidate is entangled with his academic specialty. In recent months, I have run into several outstanding young (white male) political scientists who are finding it impossible to land tenure-track teaching posts at medium- and high-status colleges because, as one of them wryly explained to me, their scholarly strengths lie in the study of "DWEMs." When I confessed ignorance of the acronym, he patiently explained that it stands for "Dead White European Males." Had they specialized in revolutionary ideologies, the politics of feminism and racism, or trendy quantitative social-science methodologies, they could perhaps have transcended their inconvenient gender and mundane color and have a reasonable shot at academic employment. But to spend one's hours with the likes of Aristotle, Machiavelli, Hobbes, and Burke is to have nothing very important to offer a political science department today, whatever one's intellectual and peda-gogical accomplishments.

One can, by contrast, get wooed by the largest and most prestigious of academic departments, no matter how repugnant one's own views, provided that one offers the right blend of personal traits and intellectual enthusiasms. Richard Abowitz recently recounted the efforts by the University of Wisconsin to attract June Jordan, a radical black activist (and poet), from Stony Brook to Madison. After examining her writings and orations spanning the previous fifteen years, Abowitz concluded that if Jordan remained true to form, "her courses at the University of Wisconsin would do nothing more than propagate the crudest forms of social, po-litical, and economic prejudice," exactly the attitudes that the university had dedicated itself to wiping out through such measures as the new stu-dent conduct code. Yet with but a single abstention, Madison's English department voted unanimously to offer her a tenured position with a gen-erous salary. (Berkeley's offer must have been even more attractive, for that is where Jordan now teaches.)

Esoteric forms of affirmative action are by no means confined to the professoriate. Last year the editors of the *Columbia Law Review* adopted a new "diversity" program that will reserve special slots on the editorial board for individuals who qualify by virtue of their race, physical handi-cap, or sexual orientation. Law-review boards, of course, have customar-ily been meritocracies, with membership gained through outstanding aca-demic achievement. With Columbia in the lead, one must suppose this will no longer be the rule, even though the New York *Post* commented, "No one has yet stepped forward . . . to explain why sexual orientation, for instance, would keep a student from performing well enough in law school to compete for the law review on the same basis as everyone else."

Diversity and tolerance, evenhandedly applied, are estimable precepts. But that is not how they are construed in the academy today. Nor do the narrowing limits of free expression lead only to penalties for indi-viduals who engage in "biased" talk or "hostile" behavior. They also leave little room for opinion that deviates from campus political norms or for grievances from unexpected directions. During Harvard's race-awareness week last spring, when a white student dared to complain that she had experienced "minority ethnocentrism" on campus—black and Hispanic stu-dents, it seems, often ignored her—she was given short shrift and no sym-pathy by the speaker (who had already suggested that Harvard and Dartmouth were "genocidal" institutions).

More commonly, however, it is rambunctious student newspapers and magazines that get into trouble with academic authorities for printing something that contravenes the conventional wisdom. Given the predominant campus climate, it is not surprising that these are often publications with a moderate or right-of-center orientation. Sometimes, clearly, they do mischievous, stupid, and offensive things, but for such things the degree of toleration in higher education seems to vary with the ideology of the perpetrator. (Acts of discrimination and oppression based on political views, it should be observed, are *not* among the categories proscribed in the new codes of behavior.) In addition to a much-reported sequence of events at Dartmouth, there have been recent efforts to censor or suppress student publications, and sometimes to discipline their staff members, at Brown, Berkeley, UCLA, Vassar, and California State University at Northridge.

The last of these prompted one of the most extraordinary media events of 1989, a joint press conference on May 16 featuring—no one could have made this up—former Attorney General Edwin Meese III and the director of the Washington office of the American Civil Liberties Union (ACLU), Morton Halperin. What brought them together was shared outrage over what Halperin termed the "double standard" on campus. "Our position," he reminded the attending journalists, "is that there is an absolute right to express views even if others find those views repugnant." He could cite numerous instances, he said, where campus authorities were making life difficult for outspoken conservative students, yet could find "no cases where universities discipline students for views or opinions on the Left, or for racist comments against non-minorities."

Meese, not surprisingly, concurred, as did James Taranto, the former Northridge student journalist whose lawsuit settlement afforded the specific occasion for the press conference. In 1987, Taranto, then news editor of his campus paper, had written a column faulting UCLA officials for suspending a student editor who had published a cartoon mocking affirmative action. Taranto reproduced the offending cartoon in the Northridge paper, whereupon his faculty adviser suspended *him* from his position for two weeks because he had printed "controversial" material without her permission. The ACLU agreed to represent him in a First Amendment suit—"We were as outraged as he was by the attempt to censor the press," Halperin recalled—and two years later a settlement was reached.

While we are accumulating ironies, let it be noted that the ACLU, the selfsame organization in which Michael Dukakis's "card-carrying membership" yielded George Bush considerable mileage in the 1988 election campaign, has been conspicuously more vigilant and outspoken about campus assaults on free expression in 1989 than has the Bush administration. The secretary of education, Lauro Cavazos (himself a former university president), has been silent. The White House has been mute. During an incident at Brown in May, when an art professor cancelled a long-planned screening of the classic film *Birth of a Nation* because the Providence branch of the NAACP had denounced it, the local ACLU affiliate was the only voice raised in dismay. "University officials," declared its executive director, "have now opened the door to numerous pressure groups who may wish to ban from the campus other films they too deem 'offensive.' " Indeed. A colleague of mine recently revived a long-lapsed membership in the ACLU on the straightforward ground that no other national entity is resisting the spread of attitude-adjustment, censorship, and behavior codes in higher education.

All this would be worrisome enough even if the academy were doing well with respesct to actual education for the minority students whose number it is so keen to increase and whose sensibilities campus administrators are so touchy about. But that is simply not the case.

Black and Hispanic students are less likely to enroll in college to begin with. This is not because admission offices turn them away—to the contrary—and not because too little student aid is available to help them defray the costs. (In any event, 80 percent of all students attend state institutions, in which tuitions average about $1,200 per year.) The largest reason more minority students do not matriculate is that so many attended wretched elementary and secondary schools in which they took the wrong courses, were poorly taught, had little expected of them, skipped class a lot, never learned much, and may well have dropped out.

Minority youngsters are not, of course, the only victims of our foundering public-education system, but they are the ones whose life prospects are most blighted by it, the ones for whom a solid basic education can make the biggest difference. Academic leaders know this full well, just as they understand that shoddy schools are major producers of ill-prepared college students. Yet for all its protestations and pieties, and notwithstanding its ardor for enhancing "diversity" on campus, the higher-education system has done essentially nothing to strengthen the schools that serve as its feeder institutions. It has not even taken the straightforward steps that are well within its purview—such as a complete overhaul of the education of teachers and principals. It has not reached down into the schools to begin the "admissions-counseling" process with disadvantaged fifth- and sixth-graders. And it most certainly has not made the tough decisions that over time could have a profound influence on the standards of the entire elementary-secondary system, such as announcing well in advance that beginning in, say, 1998 no student will be admitted to college who has not actually attained a specified level of knowledge and skills.

Such strong medicine is resisted with the argument that it must surely be bad for minority youngsters. That has been precisely the response to the NCAA's attempts to curb exploitation of minority athletes by requiring them to meet minimum academic standards in order to play intercollegiate sports or receive athletic scholarships. Georgetown's basketball coach staged a well-publicized one-man "strike" to protest this, claiming that the rules are discriminatory. The NCAA is expected to recant, heedless of the warning by the black tennis champion Arthur Ashe that, "Black America stands to lose another generation of our young men unless they are helped to learn as well as play ball."

Getting more adequately prepared students inside the campus gates might also help to boost the egregiously low proportion of minority matriculants who end up with a degree. The college dropout rate is a problem for everyone, and has been rising over the past decade, but it is manifestly worse for black and Hispanic students. According to the U.S. Department of Education, among the 1980 high school graduates who immediately enrolled full-time in college, 50 percent of the Asians and 56 percent of the white students earned their bachelor's degrees within five-and-a-half years, but this was true for only 31 percent of black students, and for 33 percent of Hispanics. (For minority *athletes,* the dropout rate is higher still. "It's no secret," Ashe writes, "that 75 percent of black football and basketball players fail to graduate from college.")

One has got to conclude that if the colleges and universities put as much effort into high-quality instruction, vigorous advising, extra tutoring, summer sessions, and other suppplementary academic services as they do to combating naughty campus behavior and unkind words—and maximizing fieldhouse revenues—they could make a big dent in these numbers. But, of course, it is easier to adopt a behavior code for students than to alter faculty-time allocations and administration priorities. Symbolic responses to problems are always quicker and less burdensome, at least in the short run, than hard work.

Completing the degree, regrettably, does not end the matter, either. While possessing a college diploma will indisputably help a person get ahead in life even if he is still ignorant and intellectually inept, for a variety of public and private reasons it is desirable that college graduates also be well-educated. For minority graduates, it may be especially important that any plausible grounds for doubt be erased—from the minds of prospective employers, among others—as to the actual intellectual standards that their degrees represent.

Today, unfortunately, one cannot equate the acquisition of a bachelor's degree with possession of substantial knowledge and skills. When the Department of Education examined literacy levels among young adults in 1985, it accumulated data that enable us to glimpse the cognitive attainments of college graduates, as well as those with less schooling. The good news is that the former had generally attained a higher level than the latter. The bad news is that degree-holders did none too well.

Three scales were used, representing "prose literacy," "document literacy," and "quantitative literacy." At the highest level of the scales, white college graduates were to be found in proportions of 47, 52, and 48 percent, respectively—not really very laudable considering that the intellectual challenges to be mastered at these levels entailed such tasks as discerning the main point of a newspaper column, coping with a bus schedule, and calculating the change due and tip owed on a simple lunch. Among black college graduates, however, these levels were reached by only 18, 11, and 14 percent respectively. (The number of Hispanic college graduates in the sample was too small for statistical reliability.)

The higher-education system, in short, is awarding a great many diplomas to individuals whose intellectual attainments are meager, even at the end of college, and for minority graduates this is happening so often that the academy may be faulted for massive deception. It is giving people degrees which imply that they have accomplished something they have not in fact achieved. Like driving a new car home from the dealer only to discover that it is a lemon, the owners of such degrees are likely one day to think themselves cheated rather than aided by the hypocrisy and erratic quality control of the academic enterprise. The taxpayers who now underwrite most of that enterprise are apt to feel much the same. Over time this can only diminish the support, the respect, and the allure of higher education itself, as well as further depleting its tiny residuum of moral capital.

Some academic leaders understand this. A few also have the gumption to say it. "The alternatives I see ahead for our higher-education system are reform from without or reform from within," Stephen J. Trachtenberg, the new president of George Washington University, predicted in a recent address to the American Association of University Administrators. "The present situation cannot hold because too many Americans are coming to regard it as incompatible with ethics, values, and moral imperatives."

Reform from within would surely be preferable. It nearly always is. But in 1989 the most prominent forms of spontaneous change on many of our high-status college and university campuses are apt instead to exacerbate the gravest problems the academy faces. Creating more complex and onerous rituals as they worship at the altar of "diversity," they concurrently provide the putative beneficiaries of their efforts so feeble an education as to suggest a cynical theology indeed. Meanwhile, in the realms of intellectual inquiry and expression, they permit ever less diversity, turning the campus (in the memorable phrase of civil rights scholar Abigail Thernstrom) into "an island of repression in a sea of freedom."

Part Three

Cultural Diversity, The Politics of Race and Sex on Campus, and the Western Intellectual Tradition

5

The Challenge of Diversity
and Multicultural Education

The President's Task Force on
Multicultural Education and Campus Diversity

I. EXECUTIVE SUMMARY

This document envisions and seeks to initiate a process which leads to a profound appreciation and celebration of our diversity as an academic community and nation, a process which is collaborative and supportive of sustained discourse and exchange. In this context of appreciated and celebrated diversity, we can and must create and promote an environment in which: (a) all members have equal opportunity; (b) respect, mutual regard for cultural and gender differences, and full democratic participation and partnership are the norm; (c) the diversity of communities we serve are reflected, thus enhancing our ability to serve and teach in a collaborative process; and (d) the quality of campus life is intellectually nurtured by university policies and practices.

Reprinted with permission of California State University, Long Beach.

II. INTRODUCTION

The President's Task Force on Multicultural Education and Campus Diversity was established in the summer of 1990 by Provost and Academic Vice President Karl Anatol in response to President Curtis McCray's challenge to the university to identify and institute ways to recognize and respond creatively to its diversity. The general charge for the Task Force was to initiate a process leading to the establishment of a truly multicultural, democratic institution which cherishes, builds on, and celebrates its diversity. The Task Force envisioned its charge to:

A.   explore the intellectual underpinnings of a multicultural university, including defining multiculturalism as an intellectual and practical project;

B.   draw upon faculty resources in the exploration of the intellectual rationale and educational imperative of the multicultural university;

C.   assess the institutional environment, analyzing that which is good and essential and that which needs to be improved;

D.   identify related issues of concern for study and action;

E.   collaborate with academic bodies, executive offices, faculty and staff organizations, and student groups to move with insight, commitment, and speed toward policies and practices to implement the charge;

F.   create and nurture an environment which fosters a process of mutual engagement in and challenge to realize and expand the educational mission and enhance the quality of campus life; and

G.   produce a document which provides both an intellectual framework and inspiration for the initiation and achievement of the above process and task.

III. BACKGROUND TO THE PROJECT

The formation of the Task Force responds to several basic developments in American higher education in general and to developments at California State University, Long Beach in particular. First, in recent years a major debate has emerged in American universities and colleges and in the larger society over the content and purpose of a liberal education and the need for curricula to reflect the realities of American culture and society. This essentially requires moving from a monocultural model of education to a multicultural one which stresses the rich complexity and diversity of social and human reality. Second, the multicultural project has its historical roots in the social and academic struggles of various racial and ethnic groups. Women and the many faculty members who have been historically sensitive to issues of race, ethnicity, gender, and class view a multicultural and inclusive curriculum as indispensible to educational excellence.

The University Mission Statement adopted in Spring 1990 recognizes the need for multicultural education, stating that, "A fundamental goal of all the university's programs is to prepare students to function effectively in a culturally diverse society, by developing an understanding of our diverse heritage(s), including essential contributions of women and ethnic (groups)." President McCray has also emphasized repeatedly in various contexts that multiculturalism is a fundamental part of CSULB's educational mission.

Finally, the increasing diversity of the student body in terms of race, ethnicity, gender, language, and class has encouraged a search not only for ways of accommodation, but also for ways to utilize this diversity creatively to enhance and expand the educational experience. The increasing diversity among the students reflects an increasing diversity in society and, thus, requires a similar proactive response to the university's service communities.

IV. RATIONALE

The university poses for itself the project of becoming truly a multicultural community which embraces, builds on, and celebrates its diversity. This project is a morally, intellectually, and socially grounded one. Its moral justification is rooted first in its commitment to respect for the human person. This respect is and must be for the person not simply as an abstracted individual but also as a concrete person-in-community or a person in a defining group. Thus, the University Mission Statement is correct to state that "instruction emphasizes the ethical and social dimensions in all disciplines, as well as their applications to contemporary world issues." The hinge upon which the ethical and social turn(s), is the fundamental and inviolable respect for each person in all her/his diverse expressions. Without such a respect, the humanistic mission of the university is undermined and unfulfilled. Also, our constant historical concern and quest for a just and good society is informed and undergirded by moral concerns about the quality and meaning of human relations in the full sense of the word human, i.e., in its rich and complex diversity.

Multicultural education is intellectually grounded on several levels. It is a necessary corrective for the conceptual and content inadequacy of the exclusive curriculum which omits or diminishes the rich variety of human culture. Likewise, multicultural education is a necessary corrective for racist, sexist, classist, and chauvinist approaches to knowledge and education, again enriching and expanding the educational enterprise. Multicultural education envisions and encourages, moreover, a curriculum reflective of the society and world in which we live, thus providing an intellectual and social competence otherwise diminished or denied and is an effective response to the global economy as well as societal changes and demands.

Multicultural education is socially grounded in its role as a just response to current demographic changes. While the U.S. and California cultural landscape has always been diverse, with the recent increased arrivals of immigrants from Southeast Asia, Central and South America, and other countries, our campus and societal community have become even more varied. Across all age groups in the state, the population of people of color is expected to become the majority shortly after the next century. Among the K-12 population, people of color are already the majority. Within the service area of CSU, Long Beach and, in particular, the population of Long Beach Unified School District, there has been a dramatic demographic shift during the past two decades. This shift requires an adequate multicultural educational response which prepares for a diverse society through a curriculum which teaches social and human diversity and is grounded in it.

Social grounds for multicultural education are also found in the related area of preparing a youthful population of color (Latino, Asian, African, Native American) for what David Hayes-Bautista calls the "burden of support" of an older Euro-American population. Such an anticipated burden of support requires not only knowledge of its imminence but the cultivation of a quality of relations which appreciates diversity, mutuality, and interdependence of ethnic and age groups. A multicultural education, moreover, is part and parcel of the thrust to create the just and good society, to avoid civil strife, and to enhance the quality of social life through cultivation of democratic values of and for civility, cooperativeness, mutuality, mutual respect, equality, justice, and interdependence.

V. GOALS OF A MULTICULTURAL EDUCATION

The goals of multiculturalism emerge from the diversity of our historical experience and expand to include appreciation of our global interdependence. They aim at an education grounded in a diversity more reflective of the reality of American life than the monochromatic and monocultural versions often projected. These goals also reach beyond the mistaken image of U.S. society as a melting-pot in which diversity is dissolved and beyond the common but erroneous view of society as color and gender blind. Multiculturalism does not deny, ignore, or demean such fundamental expressions of diversity. On the contrary, it recognizes and respects them and utilizes them creatively to enrich and enhance the educational experience. It realizes that respect for the human person requires respect for people in all the diversities in which they are encountered.

The goals of multicultural education are thus practical as well as moral. Such an education prepares students for present-day American society by equipping them with a variety of skills and attitudes that will be useful and necessary for living in and contributing to the present and the emerging future. An important task of the university, then, is to create an environment in which students can learn *to think critically* about their own lives, to view life around them with a measure of objectivity and reason, and *to assume responsibility* for the world in which they live, which they help to create, and hope to pass on to future generations. Multicultural education aims to educate citizens who are able *to recognize, respect, and appreciate* human diversity and the rights of others, including their right to be different from one another and from us. Such an education aims higher than mere toleration, but accepts the word in at least the minimum sense which does not tolerate intolerance.

A person who has profited from a multicultural education will be able *to communicate* with others in spite of the differences brought by diversity of culture, race, gender, etc., and *to negotiate* with others and *to interact* with them for mutual benefit and the common good. Among many more such skills to be cultivated, a primary one is the civility which enables people to live together with a minimum of friction and the maximum of harmony.

Understanding and respecting diverse groups in the U.S. helps prepare persons for understanding and respecting others in a global context. This too is a fundamental goal of multicultural education. Global interdependence is becoming an increasingly compelling reality, and students and citizens in general must be prepared to respond positively and effectively to this. An essential part of the university's mission is to facilitate such preparation as an intellectual and ethical priority.

Another essential goal of multicultural education is a correct and effective orientation toward our past and future. The past which, in our society, is transmitted by education must be our collective past which includes our history in all of its diversity and cultural uniqueness. To recognize and build on the diversity of our past and present is to prepare ourselves for our future and to face successfully the national and global multicultural challenges which await us. The culture we need to appropriate from the past, then, is one which is respectful of diversity, useful, forward-facing, and of ethical merit.

Finally, to cherish both individuality and interdependence at the same time, and to respect the rights as well as responsibilities of individuals and diverse groups, necessitates a mutual respect, tolerance for difference and ambiguity, and an ability to deal effectively with conflicting claims and needs. This, too, is a major goal of multicultural education. The challenge, then, is not to sacrifice *pluribus* to *unum* or vice versa, but to achieve a synthesis which preserves and builds on both. To pose and achieve such a model of multiculturalism can be a fundamental contribution to the university and society.

VI. DEFINING THE MULTICULTURAL PROJECT

Multiculturalism is a complex and multidimensional phenomenon and project. It is, thus, several things at once. It is, first of all, a *philosophy* or a framework and statement of understanding and commitment. It is also a *methodology,* a definite approach and perspective to achieve stated goals. It is a *process,* that is to say, a series of activities and interactions to achieve identified goals. Finally, it is a *product,* perceptible and definable results, which are open to ongoing refinement and expansion.

Given this many-sidedness, multiculturalism is best defined as an education generated and sustained by a campus environment which genuinely respects and self-consciously builds on the rich diversity of its members. Its definition of diversity is broad and inclusive, and includes defining factors such as race, ethnicity, gender, special need, class, sexual orientation, language, religion, age, and other distinctions historically used to fragment the campus, society, and the human community. Within this document this entire list is implied whenever we refer to human diversity. Limitations of our time and energy require that we give primary attention' to the broadest categories, but this does not mean a lack of concern ,for all. Special care should be taken that no groups be made scapegoats or be abused in any way.

Multicultural education supports the construction of a curriculum which: (1) affirms the concept of diversity as central and indispensable to understanding social reality; (2) provides fundamental grounding in diverse cultures and gender studies as essential to a serious and adequate education; (3) is committed to educational equity for students which translates as equal opportunity and maximum outcome; (4) is directed toward providing students with knowledge, skills, and attitudes necessary to succeed in and contribute to society and the human community; and (5) is committed to furthering the body of knowledge on diversity through research and scholarly debate (e.g., graduate research methods classes, student and faculty research projects).

While clearly dedicated to *educational excellence* in a diversity-respecting environment, multicultural education is also committed to *social responsibility* and *solidarity*. As an essential, even vanguard, institution in society, the university is positioned in a context for cultivating civic values contributive to a multicultural, just, and democratic culture. This means building on our best ideals and values of mutual respect and shared goals of a truly inclusive and diversity-respecting, just, and democratic society. This respect for diversity must not only respect individual difference, but also group difference and the value and right of the continuity of cultural diversity within a common civic culture.

VII. CONCERNS AND CHALLENGES

To achieve such a broad and inclusive process of multicultural education, it is necessary to address successfully the issues of: curriculum, research, social climate on campus, underrepresentation of ethnic groups and women, and community relations including contributing to our service communities.

Curriculum

Reassessment and recrafting of the curriculum to reflect the multicultural reality of the campus, community, and world is essential, indeed indispensable. There is no single model which stands in opposition to the existing curricula. What unites most is their goal of overcoming what may be called the "exclusive" curricula, whether these be Euro-centric, Anglo-centric, or male-centric. The problem with "exclusive" curricula is that they equate the values of a dominant group with "universality," and falsely present the experience of a dominant group as a formula for all other groups. Any exclusive curricula, moreover, masks the rationale for one group's dominance over others and the mechanisms of social control by which this is maintained. Mutual knowledge, opportunity, and understanding and appreciation of difference must now be the foundation for a multicultural campus and for a multicultural society.

Various scholars in multicultural education have noted the negative effects of exclusive curricula on all students. First, such curricula, in ignoring other groups, reinforce a false sense of superiority for European American students by keeping them ignorant of the history, values, and beliefs of other groups and ignorant of the diversity within the so-called majority experience. These students are also robbed of an outsider perspective, i.e., they are denied the opportunity to see themselves as others see them. They fail to develop strategies for communication with individuals from a variety of backgrounds. They fail, furthermore, to develop the skills, knowledge, and attitudes necessary to succeed and contribute to our diverse society. Students from other cultural backgrounds are short-changed too because their own experiences are either ignored or seen from only the dominant perspective. Similar concerns can be raised with respect to male-centric curricula.

At the recent Celebrating Diversity Conference, Carl Grant noted that if we truly want a multicultural society and want to reflect all groups in our curriculum, we are faced with some hard choices in redefining and reconceptualizing the existing curriculum—especially in areas which directly reflect cultural values. James Banks stated, in his address to the CSULB community, that this requires that definitions of multicultural transformation not be considered as "catering to special interests," while the interests of dominant groups are seen as being "universal." Respect for diversity requires that we move beyond the chauvinistic notion that the "exclusive" curricula are synonymous with universalism. As an alternative to the exclusive curricula, we must facilitate what Banks calls "multiple acculturation," that is to say, pursuing multiple models.

Multicultural transformation also requires a greater emphasis on the critical analysis of social problems and inequity. It requires helping students to identify options for decisions and to take actions which implement their decisions. In such a process, students learn to become social critics and reflective agents of change.

The multicultural curriculum requires: (1) respect for human rights and human diversity; (2) recognition of the strengths and values of cultural diversity; (3) support for social justice and equal opportunity for all people; (4) commitment to democratic values of mutual respect, civility, equality, and mutual interdependence; and (5) awareness of the fundamental importance of race, ethnicity, gender, class, special needs, sexual orientation, language, religion, and age in understanding social reality.

Multiculturalism thus requires a complete re-thinking and adaptation of the curriculum to the cultural reality of our university and society. It is a more thorough-going challenge than can be met by a single course or specific requirement. There is presently a proposal under consideration to include multicultural education within the general education program; regardless of how this process develops, we point out that the creation of a multicultural university must be a broader, more radical task.

Social Climate

Another major concern in creating the truly multicultural university is the challenge of creating a social climate on campus where diversity is not simply tolerated, but is embraced and built on to create a rich complexity of educational and social exchanges. This is not possible when physical and verbal incidents of intolerance tear at the social and educational fabric. Insensitivity and lack of respect for cultural and national differences have been increasing in small towns and large cities. Our own university, like other colleges and universities across the nation, is greatly concerned not only with the increase in insensitivity and lack of respect, but also with the growing number of violent acts based on race and gender.

The Office of the Chancellor has directed the CSU system to develop policies that will respond to incidents of racial and sexual abuses in a prompt and just manner. Formal policies alone, however, will not stem the rise of violent incidents in the universities. The institutions must prepare students, faculty, staff, and administrators to live in a society that is increasingly multicultural and multiethnic. Although California is leading the country in demographic diversity, the states of Florida, Illinois, New York, Texas, and most of the nation's largest cities will be equally diverse by the turn of the century.

America has entered a new era in which its previously ignored cultural and national groups and its women are seeking recognition and political power. Universities are the institutions best equipped to study and understand, explain and facilitate this step in the nation's historical development. Indeed, universities throughout the land proclaim this boldly in their mission statements, but have too often failed to prepare their students for the responsibilities and challenges of the America of the twenty-first century.

Universities must begin to fulfill this mission if they are to fulfill their obligations to society. At CSULB, both students and faculty need to learn how to interact with each other, how to be sensitive to cultural, national, and gender differences and how to value this diversity as they value the quest for knowledge, freedom of thought and expression, and democratic principles and ideals.

Finally, to have a university that embraces diversity, a campus community that nurtures all members, requires strong leadership. Although leadership in this clearly rests with the administration and faculty, each person on campus must collaborate in creating a campus community that embraces and builds on diversity. It is, therefore, the responsibility of every person, whether administrator, faculty, student, or staff to avoid and condemn any acts of intolerance or disrespect.

Underrepresentation

Underrepresentation of students, faculty, and staff of diverse groups poses another concern and challenge in the thrust toward the truly multicultural university. This is especially true and difficult for students. Since our university is entrusted with the role of educating tomorrow's leaders, it must exercise leadership to ensure that it is admitting an equitable cross-section of all students in the state, and preparing all students with the knowlege and skills necessary to participate in a multicultural society.

As many multicultural educators have recently pointed out, it is a mistake to cast the problem of equity and the need for multicultural education in terms of a majority/minority of Black/White or Asian formula. Khmer (Cambodians), to cite one example, are broadly labeled "Asians," but they are grossly underrepresented (given their numbers in our state population) at the University of California and within the California State University system. California's increasing diversity, however, is not limited to ethnicity and language background. Increasingly, the gap between rich and poor—in our state and in the nation as a whole—is also widening. The correlation between family income and performance on standardized measures such as the SAT is well documented.

Given the continuing challenge of promoting an equitable representation among all major groups in the state, there is a need for the CSU system to exercise leadership by coming to grips with lingering discrepancies based upon ethnicity, linguistic background, and social class.

Ethnic underrepresentation among the faculty is also a major concern. Our commitment to creating a truly multicultural university requires that we make an active effort to hire qualified faculty members from underrepresented groups. To build for the future, it is also important that the university take an active role in encouraging a more diverse group of students to pursue graduate education and teaching careers. Enhancing and enriching the educational experience requires dealing with the present reality, that the majority of those entering graduate programs and ultimately teaching in higher education, are Anglo- or European American, middle class, mono-cultural, and monolingual.

Regardless of a person's background, it is essential that all faculty members have some knowledge of techniques for teaching students from a wide range of backgrounds. It is necessary that they have some under-standing of the major cultural groups among our students, and also strategies for learning about students who come from smaller and less familiar groups. Hiring a diverse staff is important to the multicultural project for similar reasons.

Community Relations and Service

The university has both an academic and a social mission. These are in-extricably linked. At the heart of the educational mission is the preparation of students for full and effective participation in and contribution to society. As part of the community in which it is located, the university can and must establish collaborative relations with its surrounding communities, to assist them in various kinds of problem-solving and developmental projects. Linkages need to be strengthened with surrounding communities, through partnerships with schools and through field activities and com-munity learning, that broaden learning from mere book knowledge to experiential study.

Some universities have begun to do this already. For example, in the UC system, San Diego and Santa Cruz now provide either general education or major credit through supervised undergraduate community study courses. In UCSD's Third College, undergraduate students with an interest in teaching take a three course field experience track which begins with a focus on a local community, followed by a field experience in a classroom of that school.

Such an approach allows prospective teachers the opportunity to gain a holistic picture of the relationship between community and school and the chance to determine whether they are truly interested in teaching. All too often, those interested in teaching have little exposure to its daily challenges until they fulfill observation and student teaching requirements as part of their postgraduate professional preparation. These requirements are performed—all too frequently—in schools which are not represen-tative of those in which they are most likely to be hired. The UCSD Third College approach overcomes these problems by linking preprofessional with professional training and by linking the university with local communities.

Experiential links with the community should not be limited to teacher education. Within the past fifteen years, California communities have provided a remarkable laboratory for field study in social and demographic change. Immigrant communities have revitalized decaying inner cities and stagnant suburban economies across the state. The recent emergence of these communities recalls the role which immigrant towns have played throughout our history and reinforces the evidence that immigrants contribute to the larger economy by helping themselves. Students in social sciences, the arts, and humanities need to be trained in rudimentary data collection techniques to chronicle the contributions and impact of the new Americans within our communities.

VIII. ANTICIPATED DIFFICULTIES

In pursuit of our objectives, we will, as have other educational institutions, face formidable difficulties. As a community united and committed to creating the best possible educational environment, however, we can overcome these difficulties. Among the first challenges we face are systemic challenges which include: (1) finding and securing adequate funding for the project in a context of shrinking resources; (2) developing a process of rewards for multicultural initiative and innovation; (3) overcoming the conservative nature of the institution as institution, i.e., its slowness and resistance to change; (4) urging, cultivating, and sustaining faculty and administrative leadership who are critical to the formulation and success of the project; and (5) successfully combatting false efficiency of the bureaucratic process which results in marginalization, compartmentalization, and counterproductive packaging.

The Task Force is also sensitive to anticipated faculty concerns which include: (1) apprehension about dealing with unfamiliar issues; (2) concern about new requirements competing for FTE; (3) reluctance to change carefully developed courses; (4) concerns about demands on one's time and energy; (5) concerns that foundational curriculum not be undermined or damaged; (6) concerns about competence and areas of expertise; and (7) adequate attention to the demands of academic freedom.

We are also aware of attitudes which must be challenged and overcome if the project is to succeed. These include: (1) deeply held personal beliefs that are contrary to diversity concerns; (2) prejudices of race, gender, class, and other differences; (3) monocultural intellectual preferences; (4) negative assumptions about the value and quality of multicultural research and scholarship; and (5) incorrect belief that multicultural education is an ethnic or gender project rather than a collaborative and collective project involving and benefitting all.

These concerns are understandable, and we are confident the problems they pose can be overcome in the spirit of collegiality and in the process of collaboration and mutual engagement for the best possible educational environment.

IX. RECOMMENDATIONS

A.   Actions by University-Level Administrators

1. Faculty development

Faculty development activities need to provide assistance to new and continuing faculty members, both full- and part-time, to enable them to meet the needs of the twenty-first century. Some suggestions:

a. include information on the importance of multiculturalism in new faculty orientation;

b. offer workshops in developing teaching strategies that are effective for students with a variety of learning styles reflective of gender and ethnic diversity;

c. offer, in workshops and various other forums, such as school or department faculty meetings, suggestions on sensitivity to classroom language, interactions, and instructional tools, that make all students feel included; and

d. assist newly hired faculty members, both full- and part-time, in understanding university functioning, understanding the expectations of faculty members in instruction, research and scholarly activity, committees and university service assignments, and planning one's work both during the academic year and during summer, to accomplish the tasks.

2. Staff development

A university that embraces diversity, that conveys a sense of inclusion of and respect for all people, must have diversity in the staff and administration as well as in students and faculty. All administrative offices, at all levels, need to continue to make a conscious effort to include diversity.

a. Assure that affirmative action guidelines are followed in recruiting and hiring, and women and members of diverse cultural, racial, and ethnic groups have equitable opportunities for advancement.

b. Offer suggestions and training on sensitivity to language and behavior that demonstrate respect for all individuals, for all people who interact with students.

3. Dissemination of information

a. Identify a location as a central repository for materials on diversity issues, especially for materials and references that can be used by faculty members seeking to modify courses.

b. Gather and publicize information on projects and activities at other campuses that have been effective in helping all students succeed in their education, with special attention to the needs of women and students from diverse cultural, racial, and ethnic groups.

c. Consider distributing a periodic newsletter on diversity issues and on projects intended to improve diversity and multicultural education.

4. Work with the Surrounding Community

Campus administrators should help to develop links between the university and all of its service communities, including the various ethnic communities.

a. Promote interactions in which the university assists the communities in the maintenance, articulation, and development of their respective cultures.

b. Establish an Action Research Center that would serve to match faculty research projects with community interests and needs.

5. Support

Assist faculty members to find support for activities that promote diversity and multicultural education.

a. Provide funding where possible.

b. Solicit outside funding.

c. Assist in finding sources for sponsored research.

B. Actions at the School Level

School deans (or equivalent, for programs that are not within Schools) should be held responsible for fostering diversity by assuring that departments carry out activities leading to inclusion of students and faculty from all groups. In addition to activities specific to the discipline, these should include:

1. recruiting and hiring practices that assure the largest possible pool of qualified candidates who are women and members of various ethnic groups;

2. RTP procedures and standards that reward faculty activities which serve to promote diversity and multicultural education as an essential aspect of educational excellence;

3. encouraging and supporting efforts of faculty to include multicultural content and viewpoints in their teaching and research;

4. encouraging and supporting activities that lead to recruitment and retention of students from groups underrepresented in the discipline; and

5. fostering classroom atmospheres that help all students succeed in meeting the goals of the course, including developing teaching strategies that recognize diverse learning styles; maintaining courtesy to all groups in classroom interactions; including students usually called "nontraditional" in such activities as special projects, research, and others appropriate to the discipline.

C. Ongoing Projects by Departments and Faculty Members

The university should encourage all faculty members to make a conscious effort to include gender and diversity issues in curriculum planning, course content, teaching styles, and research when appropriate.

1. Examine existing courses, and, where appropriate, develop new courses to include diversity of viewpoints.

    a. Incorporate consideration of racial, ethnic, gender, class, and language issues in course materials and discussions.

    b. Recognize and use student diversity in the classroom; use teaching strategies that promote active participation by students from diverse backgrounds and cultures; encourage students to interact with those of different backgrounds in group activities, study sessions, or activities appropriate to the course.

2. Encourage students to develop skills in cooperative work that are essential for effective performance in employment, in social interactions, in participatory democracy, in local communities, and in the nation.

3. Recognizing that education of teachers is a responsibility of the entire university, all departments should be especially attentive to the need to prepare future teachers to work with students from a variety of backgrounds and cultures.

4. Share resource materials, teaching materials, and information relative to diversity issues with other faculty members by providing materials to the central repository, participating in workshops, and assisting faculty members trying to modify courses.

5. Integrate diversity perspectives into research projects.

6. Include work with the surrounding community in research projects and internships.

D.   Miscellaneous Recommendations

Some recommendations need to be referred to various campus offices or to faculty policy bodies.

1. Recruiting

There should be a handbook on recruiting, to be used by all search committees. This handbook should include hiring criteria and procedures, policy on affirmative action, and guidelines for effective recruiting of women and members of various ethnic groups.

2. Student Retention

There needs to be better use of information on student retention in policy decisions.

a. Collect student data in a way that makes it possible to evaluate the effects of programs and policies on student retention.

b. Examine policies, such as arbitrarily established GPA requirements, to see if they are having an inappropriate effect on retention of various ethnic group students.

c. Establish an orientation and advisement program that can recognize and meet the needs of students from diverse backgrounds.

3. Program Review

The Program Review Self-Study questionnaire should be revised to include specific questions on:

a. the program's hiring plan to achieve diversity in faculty and staff composition; and

b. an evaluation of the program's success in achieving multicultural education.

CONCLUSION

To fulfill its mission, the university's goal must be to provide an education which, at its core, has a multicultural foundation. It must do this not simply to respond to current demographic changes but for even more profound and important reasons. First, it must be done because an intellectually and ethnically sound education requires a multicultural foundation; diversity is at the heart of the human experience and there is no adequate intellectual understanding of it or ethical appreciation of it without such a multicultural approach. Second, in doing what is intellectually and ethnically sound, we at the same time respect, retrieve, and utilize the best of our past. Our nation has always had a demography of diversity and due respect was always warranted for it. The current changes merely reaffirm and increase the urgency of such a respect.

The United States, at this critical juncture in its history, is in a position to make a unique contribution to the world in the twenty-first century. This contribution would be a multicultural democracy which recognizes and respects not simply the rights of the individual but also the needs and rights of groups, not simply the person as an ideal or abstract, but the concrete person-in-community and in group. This is the next step in the "great experiment" we call democracy.

In California, we find ourselves with a unique and rare opportunity to create a vision and model of education for effective citizenship and global exchange in a multicultural democracy. Multiculturality is an indisputable part of California history and can be built on to provide a microcosm of national possibility and promise. Our contribution to the nation and the twenty-first century can be our witness to the value and viability of the multicultural university, a dynamic example of human diversity as human richness, productivity, and promise.

6

"Diversity" and "Breaking the Disciplines": Two New Assaults on the Curriculum

Thomas Short

". . . the breaking of the disciplines was an assumption."

"Cultural diversity" in higher education, towards which there is now a nationwide movement, means three things: increased recruitment of minority students and minority faculty, a greater number of "minority studies" or "multicultural studies," and opposition to the alleged hegemony of Western civilization. It is supported by three arguments: the need to combat racism, the injustice of imposing alien cultural norms on minority students, and the purely educational benefit to all students of being exposed to diverse perspectives. In fact, it is felt that the case hardly needs to be argued, for how could "cultural diversity" be anything but good?

Although less prominent at the moment, a parallel movement for increased "interdisciplinary" studies also proposed a good that seems to be beyond question: overcoming the fragmentation of the disciplines. On the one hand, we are urged to seek wholeness of vision, and on the other, cultural diversity. Whether or not these two ideals are compatible, the movements that proclaim them are in fact connected. In this article I contend that each is political in inspiration and intent and that they will not

From *Academic Questions* 1 (Summer 1988): 6–29. Copyright © 1988 by Thomas Short. Reprinted by permission of Transaction.

result either in genuine diversity or in wholeness of vision. Instead, they are linked vehicles for the next great step to be taken in the politicization of the academy.

In the sixties increased enrollment of black students combined with the influence of radical ideas led to the creation of a self-ghettoizing cadre demanding curricular changes in the name of racial justice. Black studies seemed a small exception to the principle that the curriculum should not be determined by political objectives; but before we knew it, feminism was also establishing its claim as a part of the curriculum, and then to all of it. Both proceed on the basis of an enormously damaging lie, namely, that the traditional curriculum "excludes" blacks and women. The legitimate attempt to correct omissions and bias was radicalized into the dogmatic assertion that every part of the curriculum not explicitly devoted to correcting social injustice implicitly defends a racist and sexist status quo. As a result, a new educational principle has become established: in place of the old idea that academic freedom is based on disciplinary competence and entails a responsibility to exclude extraneous political matters from the classroom, we are now told that all education is political and that one can do no better than propound a liberating ideology in each and every course.

As used here, such terms as "the standard curriculum" and "the traditional liberal arts curriculum" designate the undergraduate curriculum that has been common to the best colleges and universities, minus such recent additions to it, inspired by political motives or motives of social reform, as black studies and women's studies. In using this language I do not mean to imply that the curriculum is fixed for all time in unchangeable splendor. Rather, it is traditional in the sense that it conforms to the principle that changes should be made in response to advances in knowledge and intellectual skills, and not at the behest of political imperatives or in response to every shift of intellectual fashion.

That principle does not explain all curricular choices. It leaves room for some selections of topic or emphasis, as dictated by pedagogical strategy or by considerations of social utility or current interest. Also, violations of the principle have occurred and will occur. However, until recently, general acceptance of that principle has *limited* discretion otherwise based, and it has provided a *ground* on which to protest changes that are either politically motivated or frivolous. It is in rejecting this principle, and in effect substituting for it the principle that social reform or political objective ought to dictate part or all of the curriculum, that recent curricular developments depart from tradition. Defenders of the traditional curriculum are usually ridiculed as ossified pedants who do not even know their own disciplines have evolved over time and are still evolving, or as political conservatives whose aim is to defend the social status quo. Neither charge is fair. Curricular conservatives are not necessarily political conservatives, and they are certainly not less knowledgeable or less sophisticated than their trendier colleagues.

As in the 1960s and 1970s, so also now: the easier path will be to accept at face value the reasons given for proposed curricular innovations, without inquiring too deeply either into the plausibility and coherence of those reasons or into the political motivations behind them. If, however, we take time to look, we will see that those reasons *are* incoherent, and that what lies behind them is the now familiar impetus of radical politics. The question is whether we have learned sufficiently from past experience to take action in time to stop politicization's further progress. In my opinion, higher education, already deeply undermined, is in greater danger now than ever before.

"CULTURAL DIVERSITY"

I am not against a culturally pluralistic society. The issue I shall discuss is confined to higher education and does not pertain to programs in the lower schools intended to preserve ethnic subcultures or to foster the pride and self-respect of various ethnic groups. The motive and likely effect of adding minority studies to college curricula is something else altogether, no matter how much the rhetoric of cultural pluralism is adapted to the purpose.

I also agree that higher education ought to be extended to more minority students, although this does not necessarily mean proportional representation of selected minorities on all campuses. Schools differing in religious, ethnic, or sexual composition, such as Brandeis, Notre Dame, and Vassar, have done outstanding jobs of educating their students and promoting respect for the groups—Jews, Catholics (especially Irish Catholics), and women—they represent or did represent. However, black institutions have not done as well, for special reasons having little to do with their students' generally lower levels of preparation.[1] There is, therefore, good reason why efforts should be made to bring more black students to predominantly white colleges. And the same conclusion might be reached for different reasons in the case of Hispanic-American students.

What I contend is that minority recruitment and minority presence have no curricular implications. Specifically, minority students do not require minority studies. Nor is there any other reason to institute such studies. Hence, I also oppose one of the reasons given for minority recruitment, namely, to promote minority studies. I further argue against some of the proposed means of minority recruitment, namely any that would result in recruiting students unable to succeed in the traditional curriculum. (This does not preclude recruiting the scholastically disadvantaged, but there must be reason to suppose that the particular students recruited can benefit from special programs designed to help them catch up on the others—and those programs must be provided. Otherwise, recruiting the disadvantaged does no good to anyone, and least of all to the disadvantaged.)

One last prefatory note. I use the term "majority" in quotes to designate all those not considered to be among minorities. The reason for the quotes is that there is no longer an ethnic majority in the United States and the term "minority" is not always applied to the same minority groups. Thus, Jews and people of Italian, Irish, Polish, or Greek descent are rarely counted as minorities by those who urge minority studies. For purposes of this discussion, then, people of those groups belong to the "majority." The minorities that proponents of minority studies usually have in mind are blacks (i.e., Americans with a noticeable fraction of Negro ancestry), Chicanos (or other Hispanic Americans), American Indians, and sometimes Orientals.

ARGUMENTS FOR MINORITY RECRUITMENT

Two reasons are given for increased recruitment of minority students. One reason is beyond question right: a college education will benefit them, and society as a whole will benefit from their enhanced knowledge and ability. A second reason frequently heard in the last few years is that minority students are needed on "majority" campuses to correct "majority" students' racial or ethnic stereotypes, giving each group a chance to appreciate the cultures and viewpoints of the others. This sounds good and is in line with the rationale of a residential college, which is that students have much to learn from one another outside of formal course work. However, this second reason is often combined with proposals for minority studies and "multicultural courses." The idea is that minority students are needed in those courses to help convey "minority perspectives" to the "majority." The use of minorities to help in the formal education of "majority" students is objectionable at first glance, and it is even worse when looked at more closely. We will return to that point after we have examined the case made for minority studies.

Apart from their proposed role in minority studies, will the mere presence of minority students on predominantly "majority" campuses help combat prejudice? Possibly. But the opposite effect is made more likely by policies that encourage self-ghettoization and the adoption of ethnically indefinite courses that are both less demanding than the rest of the curriculum and highly political. While some black students have competed successfully in the most demanding courses and have formed friendships with whites, the overall impression gained by most white students of their black peers is that of an angry group that keeps to itself and avoids the academic mainstream.

ARGUMENTS FOR MINORITY STUDIES

Two reasons are also given for minority studies. One is that they are needed for minority students, and the other is that they are needed for "majority" students. Both arguments proceed from the same underlying assumption, that the traditional liberal arts curriculum represents the culture of "majority," a culture that is an *alternative* to the ethnic cultures of the black Americans, Chicanos, etc. The first argument is that by imposing the traditional liberal arts on minority students we are depriving them of their cultural heritage; and since that is unjust, we should balance the curriculum by the addition of courses in minority cultures. The second argument is that this same balance is required for the well-rounded education of any student. Every student should become acquainted with a diversity of cultures and perspectives. In addition, this will help "majority" students appreciate the values and perspectives of other groups in their society, and, consequently, the cultural arrogance and prejudices of the "majority" will crumble.

Before we consider these two arguments *seriatim,* let us examine their common premise. In what sense can the liberal arts be said to represent "the culture" of America's "majority" or dominant group, to which minority group cultures are alternatives?

CRITIQUE OF THE ASSUMPTION
UNDERLYING MINORITY STUDIES

The liberal arts are nothing like an ethnic culture. They are a growing body of scientific and historical knowledge and intellectual skills, an accumulated treasury of music, art works, and literature in many languages, and a continuing debate over basic principles. They cannot be learned without disciplined study, usually under the guidance of teachers. Greeks do not come to college knowing Plato nor Italians, Dante. Nor do Plato and Dante have much to do with the Episcopalian Sunday School and country club culture of affluent WASPs. Plato, Dante, Milton, fugue and sonata forms, Latin, the Calculus, genetics, supply and demand curves, English constitutional history, and Marxist theory—all are a struggle equally for affluent WASPs and for Americans of other backgrounds. Ethnic background makes no difference to these studies, though rigor of previous schooling does. An ethnic culture, by contrast, is something one grows up with: with few exceptions (such as the biblical study that is part of some Jewish subcultures), formal study is not necessary to acquiring one's ethnic heritage—and it would never suffice. The liberal arts are no one's ethnic culture.

If not as an ethnic culture, then in what other sense could the liberal arts be the culture of the "majority" and an alternative to the cultures of other groups? In fact, the liberal arts are the product of an enormous diversity of people from around the world over thousands of years. They contain borrowings from peoples who had no idea of liberal education, and they contain additions made by nations that learned those arts first from other nations. Obviously, then, the liberal arts do not belong to one group only. How could such a view have arisen? There are several errors that explain its origin and which, if uncorrected, will cause that mistaken view to persist. Let us identify and dispel four of these errors.

First, there is the familiar charge that the traditional curriculum unjustly neglects the contributions of women, black Americans, and other ethnic groups. This charge is much weakened by the current celebration of inferior works chosen simply on the basis of the race or sex of their authors. Better works by women and blacks have long been included in the traditional curriculum. However, the real error lies in the inference that is drawn. The alleged neglect of the contributions of women and blacks does not entail charges that the traditional curriculum represents a culture peculiar to white men. If that curriculum were the culture of white men, then there would be no injustice in its excluding works by women and blacks. It could not be true to itself unless it did so. But neglect of important contributions by women and blacks, to the extent that it has occurred, *is* a mistake, and therefore the curriculum is not essentially white or male. It follows that such oversights should be corrected by adding the omitted items to the standard curriculum. Housing those omissions in black studies or women's studies is exactly the wrong thing to do; it institutionalizes bias.

Second, the idea that the liberal arts tradition "excludes" blacks and women because (even with all neglected contributions added) it has in fact been created mainly by white men, confuses source with use, origin with destination. Origin is not destiny. What has an origin in one place may be of greater service or value in another. What one person or group creates is there for another person or group to use, if they see any value in it. There is no limitation of a good idea to the race or sex or ethnic group of the person who happened to think of it first. In history, we see again and again that a spark from one place lit a torch in another. Christian ideas of charity and humility, originating in the Near East, tamed the Vikings; the Muslim science of algebra became the language of mathematics throughout the world. Had the ancient Celts rejected all ideas from abroad as alien to themselves, there would still be people in Britain practicing human sacrifice and seeking to cure toothache by incantation. What could be more racist or sexist than the supposition that what has been created by white men cannot be understood or appreciated or used or further developed equally well or better by women and blacks? There is nothing in the liberal arts that excludes blacks and women, even though white males have had up to the present the larger part in developing those subjects.

Third, as soon as the second error has been dispatched, we will be told that we have missed the real point, which is that the liberal arts, *because* they have been created by white men, embody a white and male and (as is often added) heterosexual point of view. This is a point of view, the argument continues, from which white patriarchy is seen as inevitable and as right. To impose that point of view on women, blacks, Hispanic Americans, homosexuals, etc., is to make them internalize the rationale for their own domination by white male heterosexuals. The black man who is "white" inside willingly cooperates in his own exploitation by white society, just as women have been taught, and therefore sincerely believe, that their rightful role is subordinate to men. And so on. It is a remarkable symptom of the present extraordinary situation in higher education that one segment of the academic community regards such views, so far as they are acquainted with them at all, as sheerest nonsense, and refuses to believe that anyone, least of all any of their colleagues could take that nonsense seriously, or that it will be taken seriously long enough or by enough people to pose a real threat, while another rapidly growing segment is busily elaborating these ideas and teaching them to their students. Those in the former camp are urged to glance through the assigned readings in the women's studies courses on their campuses or read through some of the treatises written on black studies pedagogy.

The views just summarized—and, if anything, understated—are "supported" by the recent flood of politicized and shoddy scholarship which serious scholars do not want to dignify by reasoned reply. Unfortunately, reply is now urgently needed. For this "scholarship" has been given spurious legitimacy by the creation of academic journals that print it and academic specialties that teach it, by the book lists of reputable publishers, and by page-counting administrators who grant tenure on the basis of such publications. There is no room here for critical examination of that literature. However, even a quick review reveals that its pretensions are not borne out by its accomplishments. It pretends to show that white patriarchy is a deeply buried presupposition of all the sciences and all the various departments of traditional scholarship. To establish this, it relies sometimes on abstract argument and sometimes on examples of racist or sexist bias. The abstract argument is inevitably circular; it consists of restating the conclusion in one or another of the trendy and obfuscatory jargons of the present day, e.g, the writings of the French feminists relying on Lancanian psychoanalysis and deconstruction. As for the examples of bias that have been cited, they are few in number, though endlessly repeated, and fall into three classes. First, there are those that are just as dubious as the generalizations they are supposed to support. Second, there are utterly trivial examples. That Virgil mistook the queen bee for a king may indicate his proclivity for patriarchy, but it does not show any blinding prejudice anywhere; even male apiarists can identify eggs. Third, there are serious examples of bias, but they are just where one might expect them—in areas of research that impinge directly on social policy, such as theories and measurements of intelligence. Biased conclusions of those types are identified and corrected by the usual methods of science and scholarship, and have been identified and corrected mostly by white males. Hence, no prejudices built into the very nature of scholarship are demonstrated.

The theories these shoddy arguments are supposed to support are in any case implausible. It is their implausibility that makes them seem to some people to be exciting, sophisticated, or profound. However, this same implausibility puts the burden of proof on those who subscribe to these doctrines, and that burden, as we have just seen, has not been borne. Excitement is not reason enough to justify the view that there is a racist or sexist bias in subjects having nothing to do with either sex or race. And where we could plausibly expect a racially or sexually conditioned perspective to make a difference, as in the parts of literature that probe social relations, there the contributions of blacks and women have been particularly noted. Finally, the history of the liberal arts is inconsistent with the idea that they front for white patriarchy (much less, as is often suggested, capitalist "exploitation"). The liberal arts have been the creation of people of all sorts of complexions, including many women and a relatively high percentage of homosexuals, working and writing under the greatest possible variety of political regimes, and, in the case of political theorists, poets, and philosophers, often writing against political oppression. If there is one theme underlying the liberal arts, it is liberation.

The fourth and last error is the claim that the traditional curriculum is "Eurocentric" or, even nastier, represents the "hegemony of Western Europe." This is a canard of the same class as allegations that the curriculum is "white" or "male." The liberal arts curriculum owes more to Europe than to any other continent, but there are at least three respects in which it is not exclusively Western. First, it, and European civilization, too, incorporate contributions from around the globe, albeit more from the Near than from the Far East and more from Muslim North Africa than from sub-Saharan Africa. Second, the subjects studied are of universal significance, and for that reason they have been taken up everywhere. Science is no longer exclusively Western, and neither are the opposed political ideals that originated in the West, viz., liberal democracy and communism. Even the idea of a university is in origin Western, though there are now universities throughout Asia and Africa and the island nations of the Pacific. Third, the variety of ethnic cultures and great civilizations is itself a subject of universal interest and has long formed part of the liberal arts curriculum. The joke is on those who suppose that by introducing Asian studies or the study of Eastern religions they are doing something new or are escaping the dread hegemony of the West. The very idea of studying other cultures is typically Western, going back at least to Herodotus. It is one of the gifts of ancient Greece to the world. This openness of the West to new ideas and other perspectives makes talk of this "hegemony" a mere solecism.

In any case, arguments for non-Western studies, Third World studies, and so on do not bear on the question of minority studies. I have nevertheless dwelt on this topic, because many people do in fact conflate these disparate things. Even though black Americans have grown up in an industrial democracy and know no African language, it is assumed that they must possess an African "sensibility" and share with black Africans a peculiarly "black" set of values. Again, it is frequently assumed that the culture of Hispanic Americans is essentially a Third World culture. These assumptions are racist. They imply the essential doctrine of racism, that race determines culture. Their racism can be evaded only by restating them in an overtly political manner.

Thus it is said that black Americans and Hispanic Americans are exploited by Western, white capitalism, just as blacks in Africa and as Latin Americans are exploited by American capitalists. Both at home and abroad, blacks and Hispanics are "colonized" peoples. Hence, American blacks and Hispanics share essentially the same culture with Africans and others in the Third World: that is to say, the culture of the oppressed. We are now back in the labyrinth of fantasy I described above, wherein the traditional liberal arts are portrayed as the culture of the oppressor— except that this is the converse, an equally frantic effort to invent ("discover") a culture of the oppressed, which is "caring," nonexploitive, and egalitarian. Ironically, this requires one to ignore the actual richness of cultural diversity among the many peoples of the world.

So much for the assumptions common to both of the arguments for minority studies. Let us now consider those arguments *seriatim*; for each reveals something about the appeal that the "cultural diversity" movement has for well-meaning people.

DO MINORITY STUDENTS
NEED MINORITY STUDIES?

What can we say about the experience of minority students at "majority" colleges? Perhaps two things. On the one hand, minority students find few, if any, contributions from their own minority groups represented in the standard curriculum. This accentuates the insecurities natural to all beginning students and particularly to those who identify with groups that have suffered from negative stereotyping by the rest of society. On the other hand, black and Hispanic students have complained that at "majority" colleges they acquire ways of speaking and thinking that set them apart from their families and friends at home. They are frequently viewed by people at home as having affected the manners of those from whom they and their ancestors have suffered injury, injustice, and insult. How neatly symmetric, how deplorable: minority students fear failure in traditional studies, but if they succeed, they suffer guilt.

By adopting the opinion that the standard curriculum is a cultural imposition, minority students can excuse their failures, actual or feared, and turn injured pride into principled defiance. At the same time, they can insulate themselves from the manners and attitudes that, if adopted, cause them problems at home. Minority studies and self-ghettoization are the refuge of the beleaguered minority student. Unfortunately they are no solution to the real problem the student faces.

In the first place, minority studies interfere with the education for which minority students come to college. The standard curriculum, re-member, is in fact not a cultural imposition but imparts knowledge and skills that benefit anyone who receives them. That knowledge and those skills are not a part of any ethnic culture. Time spent on minority stud-ies is time taken away from those traditional studies that prepare the stu-dent for a fuller participation in our society. Minority studies for minority students is a way of ensuring that minorities remain on—or get pushed out to—the margins of life, both in academia and in our society.

In addition, the false idea that the traditional curriculum is somebody else's "culture" increases minorities' fear of failure and their fear of feel-ing guilty when successful, and these fears are themselves a major contrib-uting cause of failure. You do not have to be black or Hispanic to recall the times when your fear of not being able to understand something pre-vented you from concentrating on it or caused you to give up the struggle prematurely, or the times when your convenient conviction that it was not worthwhile rationalized not trying. Faculty and administrators who tolerate or encourage the myth of cultural imperialism make themselves partly responsible for the continued high failure rate of minority students and the continued marginality of some of America's minorities.

But what of the "invisibility" of minorities in the curriculum? In the long history of mankind, the past three thousand years is a brief period. The civilization misleadingly called "Western" began in the countries of Asia Minor, northern Africa, and southern Europe that border the Medi-terranean. It took more than a thousand years for that civilization to reach the rude tribes of Germany and Scandinavia (classical learning did not exist in Sweden until its conversion to Christianity in the eleventh cen-tury, fifteen hundred years after the death of Socrates). Accidents of history, geography, climate, economy, and social organization explain that delay, as they do the additional delay of eight hundred years that it has taken the same civilization to reach central Africa. There is no evidence here of racial inferiority.

The attempt to denigrate Western civilization as merely one cultural alternative is as patronizing as it is foolish, and it cannot be expected to fool all the minority students it patronizes. Their self-esteem must come to be based on their ready grasp of standard subjects, and not on some fantasy of a suppressed Afro-American or Hispanic-American culture. This, of course, is to shift the focus of attention away from group and onto individual achievement, which is contrary to the current orthodoxy of radi-cal academics.

Significant contributions by black Americans, other minorities, and women should of course be added to the curriculum in cases where they have been omitted. However, it does no one's self-esteem any good to be made to study inferior works by people of one's own sex or race or ethnic group in place of superior works by others. No one of any intelligence who reads both is going to agree that Alice Walker is as profound or as artful as Shakespeare, yet it is possible that Walker's black lesbian saga is now assigned more often in college courses than all of Shakespeare's plays combined.[2] In any case, correcting omissions has nothing to do with minority studies. To suppose otherwise is to confuse the culture of an ethnic group with what persons of that group have created.

Studying the works of black American poets, novelists and essayists, the rhythms of jazz, or the political ideas of the black civil rights movement is not the same thing as studying the subculture of black Americans. These are contributions black Americans have made to the general culture of all educated people. The best of those contributions belong in the curriculum for the same reason that the political experiences of the Greek city-states or the teaching and poetry of the Bible belong in it. It is not a matter of equal representation for anyone's subculture. It is a matter of recognizing something that has value for us all. Rather than being a source of black pride within the standard curriculum, the contributions of black Americans are relegated to black studies; this is patronizing and demeaning. It is racism all over again. Many of those contributions have roots in black subculture (or one of the black subcultures), but their value transcends their origins, just as the value of the Ten Commandments transcends the tribal circumstances of the ancient Hebrews. They belong, now, to us all.

I do not mean to minimize the problems of minority students. College tends to alienate all students from folks back home, and this is particularly the case for first generation college students regardless of ethnic background. When the ethnic background is strong, when a difference in language is also involved, and when the older generation cannot comprehend the differences a college education makes, then, as in the case of many Chicanos, the wrench is particularly painful.[3] It is still worse in the case of black students, because black Americans have learned long ago to hear injustice in the tones of white speech and to see hypocrisy in their manners. Reluctance to find oneself adopting those tones and manners is heightened by yet another factor: just as the anti-Semitic Jew is a familiar type, so too, as E. Franklin Frazier and other black scholars have pointed out, is the tendency of some educated blacks to adopt anti-black prejudices.[4] Thomas Sowell describes blacks who prefer an inept performance of Chopin's lost minor works to the best rendition of jazz: they do not want to admit, even to themselves, that they enjoy "Negro" music.[5] It is easy to understand, then, why black students fear becoming "white on the inside."

However, neither Frazier nor Sowell blames the curriculum for the faults of some middle class blacks. Their sin lies not in enjoying Chopin but in aping a prejudiced rejection of jazz. Learning to enjoy Chopin or to do trigonometry is not becoming "white on the inside." It is just becoming educated. Anyone capable of appreciating serious music who rejects either Chopin or jazz is someone insisting on remaining ignorant and limited. Nor is affecting a dislike of jazz becoming "white on the inside"; rather, it is becoming anti-black. The expression, "white on the inside," obscures the distinction between learning the good things some whites have discovered or created and adopting the foul prejudices by which many whites have been disfigured. It is a distinction that should be of enormous importance to black students. The problems with which all minority students must struggle are not solved—they are multiplied many times over—by wrongly calling the curriculum "white" or "WASP." And since that libel is precisely the premise of minority studies, minority studies hurt and do not help minority students.

DO "MAJORITY" STUDENTS NEED MINORITY STUDIES?

Let us turn, then, to the second argument for minority studies, that they are needed for "majority" students. One reason given is that everyone needs to become acquainted with a diversity of perspectives. But a diversity of perspectives is already contained within "the Western tradition," no matter how narrowly construed. In addition, the standard curriculum contains courses on other civilizations and on ethnic cultures. There is nothing limiting about study limited to the standard curriculum.

Another reason given is that by studying the cultures of ethnic minorities, "majority" students will shed their prejudices. There is no basis for this conclusion, but murkiness in the concept of minority studies makes discussion of the point difficult. Are minority studies a study of ethnic subcultures? Plenty of ethnographers have maintained an attitude of superiority to the cultures they studied—and defined as primitive. Are minority studies a celebration of contributions to our society by persons belonging to minority groups? By relegating those contributions to a curricular ghetto, a counterproductive tendency is, in fact, encouraged. Because the works are chosen on the basis of the race or ethnicity of their creator, rather than on the basis of quality, the "majority" student will tend to see those works as merely ethnic and of no real personal importance.

Are minority studies a sociological analysis of the problems of minorities? There can be no guarantee that the results of that analysis will weaken prejudice, unless genuine inquiry has been replaced by ideology. In fact, minority studies do tend to have a large component of that kind of ideological commitment. Nathan Glazer, on the basis of extensive research, reports that it was assumed in the design of most ethnic studies programs that they were "to advocate instead of analyzing, exploring, considering. What they were designed to advocate was commitment to the group as well as a distinctive view of its history. . . . Advocacy has become the predominant theme of these programs."[6] Nor is that fault easily avoided: it is the direct result of the intent to overcome prejudice by academic instruction. Academic neutrality is thereby foresworn and instruction made suspect. Paradoxically, such instruction is less effective in correcting false stereotypes than instruction that has no such intent.

Far more than dabbling in subcultures, exposure to the traditional liberal arts teaches all of us humility and respect for people of both sexes and all races and nations. For these courses expose students to subjects of universal significance, in which wealth and social class and race and sex and nationality and age and physical handicap matter not a whit. There is no such thing as differences of "perspective" on the truths of mathematics or (despite occasional uncertainty about what is law or fact) on the laws of physics or the facts of history. They are the same for all. And where there are disputable points, as in historical explanation, literary interpretation, or philosophy, the perspectives one may adopt are not conditioned by biology or by social background. You cannot deduce a person's sex or race or social origin from what he believes about the causes of the Civil War or from his being a philosophical idealist or a materialist. The liberal arts liberate us from the particularities of our condition, and from perspectives narrowed by private experience and self-interest, precisely because they transcend those particularities and study what is of universal significance.

But now all of that is under relentless attack. In the name of freedom and tolerance, the curriculum is being divided along lines of race and sex, class and ethnicity, turning superficial differences (or, in the case of sex, differences that are not superficial but are irrelevant to matters of the mind) into basic principles, obscuring our common humanity, and guaranteeing continued animosity.

THE MISUSE OF MINORITY STUDENTS AND FACULTY

That minority students should be recruited to help convey minority "perspectives" to the "majority" reverses the direction of the argument that minority studies are needed for minority students. Now it is the students who are needed for the studies. Urban blacks are to be enticed to rural colleges like my own not for the sake of their education but so that they may be used to educate our already overprivileged and overindulged affluent white students. Having tried to teach the latter myself, I think that is an unfair burden to put on black students—who just might be seeking an education for themselves. One can reply that the education of minority students need not be scanted; but the real motive for their recruitment will have its inevitable effect. Recruited as representatives of minority cultures and minority viewpoints and experiences (always assuming that there is a distinctive viewpoint of experience for each minority group), they will be regarded as such by their teachers and fellow students. Being used, they will feel used and isolated, treated as exhibits and not as persons. Black students on my own campus have complained of exactly that experience.

Worse may be in store for them, since some white faculty at Kenyon College (and, I am sure, elsewhere as well) have declared forthrightly and in public that in seeking greater "cultural diversity" they do *not* want minorities who are middle class. What they do want are representatives of an oppressed underclass. These whites, and their radicalized black allies, their radicalized Chicano allies, etc., will see to it that minority students and faculty do not follow whatever may be their natural bent, but remain or become exponents of "the perspective of the oppressed." The movement for "cultural diversity" will not end racial stereotyping, it will promote it. Only now the stereotyping is to be politically charged. Blacks and other minorities are to be kept on the margins, but as self-consciously oppressed people demanding radical changes—a potentially revolutionary body, a lumpen proletariat that, in league with white academics, will fulfill Marcuse's, not Marx's, prescription for revolution.

In this connection, notice the contradiction between the idea that black students need black faculty as role models and the idea that black faculty are needed to express a black point of view. Granting the racist fiction that there is something properly called "the black point of view," black students hardly need black faculty to model it for them. If the idea of role models makes any sense at all, its sense must be that black students studying traditional subjects need to see some black faculty in *those* subjects, in order to be reassured that they, too, can succeed in areas formerly the exclusive or nearly exclusive province of whites. For them to find black faculty teaching black studies only or primarily, conveys exactly the wrong message. The same applies to other minorities.

FROM "DIVERSITY" TO TRYANNY

The real objective of the "cultural diversity" movement is to swell the chorus of complaint against the supposed hegemony of Western civilization. This turns out to mean not Western civilization as a whole (which, after all, includes Marxism) but the political, economic, and social principles of liberal democracy.

Amidst all the talk of a diversity of "lifestyles," of the "straight" and "gay," the alleged diversity of "values" of black Americans and white, the different ways in which men and women are said to "experience" the same objects (or objects that really are not the same, because experienced so differently), and so on, there is the unmistakable promise of an absolute uniformity of opinion: women's studies teaches that Western civilization is patriarchal and oppresses women, that its emphasis on objectivity and rationality excludes women's experience; black studies teaches that racism and slavery were built into the very origins of Western philosophy and into the founding of this nation; Third World studies shows how world hunger is induced by Western capitalism; and so on.

Such courses do not have to be that way, but that is the way most are. Thus, we should be leery of promises that more courses of the same type will be unbiased. The very nature of these courses as already taught should be warning enough about the political motives that lie behind them and behind the ready acceptance of arguments patently bad. "Diversity" is the mask a monolithic mentality has donned. "Diversity" will be limited strictly to appearances: in a variety of colors, styles, and accents the message will be the same.

And what sort of world does this uniform point of view promise us? When we consider that Western Europe is the source of the principles of liberty and respect for the individual, of rational inquiry and tolerance for varied opinion, of democracy and limitations on majority power, then we begin to see that a world freed from the hegemony of "Western" civilization is a world made safe for totalitarianism, albeit that this totalitarianism will also be Western in origin.

There is a perfect agreement between the pedagogical strategy and its ultimate practical effect. I do not mean to suggest that all or even very many of those calling for "diversity" intend bringing about a totalitarian form of government. Surely they believe they are doing just the opposite. I am only suggesting that what lies behind their efforts is an animus against their own society and its institutions and principles, and that this animus, if unchecked, will lead, eventually, to a form of education in which rational inquiry and variety of opinion sink from sight together, pointing to a form of government similarly totalitarian.

"BREAKING THE DISCIPLINES"

The introduction of politically motivated "diversity" runs into discipline-based resistance. Every attempt to staff new courses in Third World studies, minority studies, peace studies, nuclear age studies, and so on is met by the competing needs of departmental staffing. Each department has its structure of courses that majors are required to take and other courses that serve the non-major, and those courses must be taught. With some exceptions, the nature of the discipline, rather than political considerations, determines what those courses are to be. It becomes necessary, therefore, to attack the discipline-based curriculum. Hence, the attempt to break the disciplines.

The con man's favorite trick is to gain your confidence by warning you against con men, and that is how attacks on disciplinary education proceed. We all fear being suckered by narrow, blinkered perspectives, and students, in their relative ignorance, rightly fear this most of all. Thus they readily believe what they are told, when what they are told is that the curriculum is biased towards the West, that its departmentalization serves only to protect the turf of tired pedants, and that disciplinary divisions prevent insights into vital connections that interdisciplinary studies will provide. They are also told that their own boredom and malaise are due to the fragmentation of society reflected and sustained in the fragmentation of the curriculum.

What, thereby, they miss is that disciplined inquiry is the best possible means of discovering facts, generating new ideas, and exposing the limitations of narrow perspectives, and that the "interdisciplinary" courses that are being offered very often present a political message without the discipline-based knowledge necessary to its critical examination. At Kenyon a new interdisciplinary program and major in international studies was introduced a few years ago, "for the students who wish to gain exposure to a non-Western culture, compare it to the Western culture, and analyze complex global problems such as underdevelopment, nuclear weapons, and human rights." Only by dint of hard arguing and adroit maneuvering by one of my colleagues was the Economics Department's basic course made part of this program—and even then as only one of a set of five units from which students could choose three. Arguments that underdevelopment is due to capitalist exploitation—or any other view of Third World economic problems—were to be, and may still be, assessed by students with no background in economics.

The idea that a study can be interdisciplinary at an undergraduate level, where students have rarely acquired the rudiments of any discipline, is mistaken. The mistake is compounded at Kenyon and no doubt many other places when those teaching these courses also lack the relevant disciplines. One "interdisciplinary" study here this year is entitled "Sexuality and Homosexuality." Its official description explains that it will examine *all* of sexuality by "focusing" on homosexuality. Anyone swallowing that may go on to read that the "disciplines involved include history, anthropology, psychology, religion, and literature"—though the instructor is a classicist. The gimlet-eyed watchdog committee that must approve interdisciplinary courses approved that course again for next year and also another course by the same instructor, on "Men and Masculinity." Topping that, they also approved a course by a plant biologist on how Indo-European languages oppress women. Its title? "Wimmin, Language, and Reality." Her qualifications? *One* course in linguistics and some women's studies courses. Nor will any of the assigned readings make up for her deficiencies: she lists no basic text in linguistics, whether theoretical or historical, but only feminist screeds of the type of Mary Daly's *Wickedary*.

The new assault on the discipline-based curriculum is not unique to Kenyon. In the October 14, 1987, issue of *The Chronicle of Higher Education*, an article by Hunter R. Rawlings III, the vice president for academic affairs at the University of Colorado at Boulder, appeared under the title, "The Basic Mission of Higher Education Thwarted by Academic Departments." The basic mission is "to see things whole," and "the academic department structure makes that goal almost impossible to achieve."[7]

The romantic quest for wholeness of vison is inescapable, but it must either sail over seas of specialist knowledge or come to grief in shallow waters on the mud of boredom. The malaise of today's students is less the result of fragmentary education than of being taught so little that they have nothing with which to occupy their minds. Between automatic partying and spasms of protest against the injustices of American society, their lives pass away in dreariness. At Kenyon they often complain of being told about sexism over and over again in various courses. But most have had little experience of any other sort of education and, so, do not know what to seek in its place. Although intellectual discipline is increasingly difficult to impart to students, they must be made to understand that fresh ideas are impossible apart from discipline and apart from depth in a specialty, but that those ideas are rewarding and, despite their limited origins, open one to the world. Furthermore, interdisciplinary connections are not precluded by specialization; on the contrary, such connections are viable only when they develop naturally out of work within disciplines. Of course, disciplinary boundaries will change in response to advances in knowledge, and there is a danger of disciplinary divisions being arbitrarily enforced. But meaningful connections cannot be forced on disciplines from the outside.

It seems to be forgotten that academic freedom presupposes the departmentalization of the academy. Academic freedom is not free speech for professors: in particular, it is not freedom for political speech. It is the freedom to do research and to teach as one sees fit to teach *within* the discipline or disciplines in which one has proven competence. The AAUP has emphasized that controversial material extraneous to one's subject should not be introduced into one's courses. Some of these "interdisciplinary" courses are entirely extraneous in this sense.

Another aspect of academic freedom is faculty control of the curriculum. Faculty recruitment and retention decisions, as well as most curricular decisions, are entirely or largely in the hands of individual departments, and ought to be. For within these confines decisions can be made on the basis of the requirements of the discipline. However, as interdisciplinary and transdisciplinary courses proliferate, personnel and curricular decisions must be made increasingly on the basis of other than disciplinary considerations. What considerations will those be? And who is best qualified to make decisions on the basis of such considerations?

If the faculty as a whole makes these decisions, there will be a tendency toward a uniform curriculum determined by majority sentiment rather than a curriculum based on the state of knowledge in particular disciplines. The faculty is thereby in no better position than are administrators to make curricular choices and personnel decisions. The erosion of discipline-based instruction increases the already clear and present danger that colleges will become dominated by the political sentiments of those who have the administration's support. Think only of the extent to which radical feminism has taken over many of the best campuses.

THE POLITICAL BACKGROUND

In 1981 Professor Jane Dickie of Hope College addressed a conference on women's studies in this vein:

Rather than dealing with the separate issues in oppression, or inserting women's studies material on gender, race, class in small doses, we must fundamentally change the way we look at liberal education. Rather than saying, "Today we are going to deal with racism," and then dismissing race as irrelevant for the rest of the course, we would encourage continual critique of racist methodologies and content in all subject areas.[8]

Several things may be learned from this passage representative of the views of academic feminists. First, women's studies is not about women, particularly; rather, it is about the alleged oppressiveness of our society. It makes common cause with those who complain of racism and with those who, most implausibly in the United States, complain of class oppression. U.S. resistance to Third World "liberation" movements and all the other agenda items are dragged in by other women's studies specialists. And they do more than make common cause with these other radical critiques; they make them all a part of their women's studies courses, as women's studies syllabi make clear. Second, oppression, whether based on sex, race, or class is assumed to pervade every part of the traditional curriculum. Third, it follows that the fight against oppression, valiantly carried out in women's studies courses, is an attack on every part of the curriculum that is not similarly politicized.

At another women's studies conference, Professor Paul Lauter of S.U.N.Y./Old Westbury, said:

Feminism, from my point of view, is an ideology designed to change society. The idea, after all, is not to describe the world but to change it— including college. Anybody who thinks that feminism can be integrated into the university and the college organization in anything like the way these exist today is deluding herself or himself, in my judgment.[9]

And at yet another conference, Professor Johnella E. Butler, representing black studies at Smith College, discussed with feminists the question of how to bring down "the master's house" and quoted with approval Audre Lorde's statement that the "master's tools [i.e., the standard curriculum] will never dismantle the master's house."[10] At still a fourth conference, Professor Eva Hooker, C.S.C., Saint Mary's College, described how, when she had been invited to the conference, it was described to her as:

taking on the transformation of the academy. Not just a piece, not just women's studies, but the whole working and studying place of the profession.[11]

Then she described the impact of the women's studies syllabi that were displayed at the conference: "the breaking of the disciplines was an assumption." "Breaking the Disciplines" was also the title of one of the conference sessions.

Despite these ambitions and declarations and despite their enormous success to date, the women's studies movement and the radical impulse for which it has served as a vehicle have gone about as far, in present circumstances, as they can go. Although successfully "mainstreamed" into a variety of the traditional departments, women's studies' impetuous career is checked by the remaining disciplinary requirements. It is true that some disciplines—English literature especially—are awash with the politicized scholarship of radical feminism. Yet even so, there remains a strong argument that a person majoring in English should take a certain structure of courses, from Chaucer and Milton to the elements of prosody; and many of those topics resist "feminization." Students can see, and are complaining, that the insistently feminist study of Milton and Twain (two examples that have been mentioned to me by women students) leaves a great deal out. And then there are all those other majors, such as mathematics and chemistry, in which radical feminism can make little headway.

Thus we find radical feminists debating two alternatives, both already tested in practice and neither fully satisfying. One is to "ghettoize" women's studies, as black studies has been ghettoized, by making it a separate discipline. The other is to "mainstream" women's studies into already established disciplines, which, they feel, has had the unintended consequence of ideological dilution.[12] But there is a way out of this distressing dilemma: it is to eliminate the established disciplines altogether. Only in this way can the academic imperialism championed by Professor Dickie be satisfied. Every course will be Oppression Studies. Academic feminists have joined with other radical academics to bring about a further radicalization of the curriculum, partly in the name of "diversity" and partly in the name of "interdisciplinary studies."

The following quotation testifies to the degree to which the politically committed are consciously willing to plot strategies intended to deceive their colleagues. In this passage, Professor Penny S. Gold of Knox College addresses a 1985 women's studies conference on the question of whether women's studies should be renamed "gender studies":

> If the goal is to reach as many people as possible, Gender Studies may
> be the best name. It is not immediately identifiable with a particular political
> movement. . . . Similarly, a program at the University of Wisconsin run
> by Marxist sociologists is called the "Class Analysis" program rather than

"Marxist Studies," although it clearly is the latter in both intent and practice. Related to wider student appeal is also, of course, wider faculty and administrative appeal. It may be easier to get Gender Studies through faculty committees.[13]

And at Miami University of Ohio, "some 300 administrators and faculty members, mostly from state universities and small colleges," attended a conference "organized by faculty members of an interdisciplinary studies program," as we learn from *The Chronicle of Higher Education*. Even the *Chronicle* reporter, though he should be used to this sort of thing by now, seemed amazed by what was said. Yet he did not mention that any of the 300 in attendance objected. The report contains these remarks:

[T]he scholars said, higher education—and the liberal arts in particular— should address broad social issues, encourage student activism, and stop pretending that teaching is not a political act.

Several called for the empowerment of students through collaborative classroom experience.

A number of speakers . . . cited the women's studies movement as a successful example of how higher education has incorporated new ways to teach as part of a progressive political endeavor.

[Some speakers] cited liberation theology as a guide to what higher education could achieve in the future.[14]

Meanwhile, a candidate for the Democratic presidential nomination, Jesse Jackson, has involved himself in a campaign by organized minority groups at Stanford University against the year-long freshman course, "Western Culture." This campaign included a march led by Jackson, chanting "Hey! Hey! Ho! Ho! Western Culture has got to go!" As everyone knows, Stanford faculty has changed that course to one in which the core reading list of classics is greatly reduced in size and supplemented to include works by women and minorities.[15]

Here is how Paula Goldsmid, in 1979, at that time an associate dean at Oberlin College, but since then the dean of the faculty at Scripps College, Claremont, California, explained to other feminists how they could transform their own institutions:

No college is going to say it values things remaining the same or believes in a static definition of intellectual inquiry. Look in your mission statements and catalogs, your archives, statements of purpose by Boards of Trustees, and find statements on which you can hang your objectives.

[At Oberlin] we do not have any faculty hired as women's studies faculty.

We do not have courses called Women's Studies, but we *claimed* [emphasis in the original text] many courses and quite a few faculty; so we submitted catalog copy when the deadline came, and our words were printed in the catalog. There we are. We have a new kind of legitimacy.[16]

The entire seven pages of Dean Goldsmid's remarks serve as a guide to how a dedicated minority can achieve curricular innovations while evading open debate of the merits of those innovations.

When seeking ways to go beyond the gains won by radical feminists, what better strategy than to call for the introduction of more minority students? And then with stepped-up minority recruitment it will be claimed that we must introduce more courses in "minority studies." If we do not, then the newly recruited minorities will be informed that they are being denied their cultural heritage, while the majority students will be told that they are being denied the experience of other cultures. And the pressure will be on again.

SOMETHING TO DO

In my opinion, the curriculum, already in perilously weakened condition, faces its gravest challenge yet. In order to meet the challenge we shall have to do what is extremely difficult to do, and that is to say forthrightly that we are in favor of disciplinary-based education and against the new efforts to introduce more "cultural diversity" into colleges. This is difficult to do because the appearance of goodness is all on the side of interdisciplinary studies and making students appreciate cultural diversity. To oppose these changes is to appear to be protecting one's own narrow academic turf and a societal status quo; it is to appear to be attempting to keep students from learning certain things that we ourselves will be accused of fearing. But if we let those impressions stand it is our own fault. They have been created by the well-chosen rhetoric of radical academics. It is up to us to find the language in which the truth may be effectively represented.

I know from experience that many of my allies will maintain that we cannot stop this juggernaut by meeting it head-on, that we cannot win by saying we are for departmentalization and against diversity. They will maintain that we have to agree with the aims of interdisciplinary inquiry and "cultural diversity," but then try to keep the pursuit of these aims moderate and reasonable. That has not worked in the past, with respect to black studies and women's studies, and it will not work now. Even when sound principles are included in faculty legislation that creates or permits these new curricular initiatives, the enthusiasts who carry out those initiatives will do things in their own way. And the principles enshrined in practice will be of greater weight than those that exist only on paper. Moderate faculty simply do not have the energy or the will to make their colleagues keep their promises, especially when that requires an attention to what actually goes on in their courses—an attention too easily described as "McCarthyite."

What we must do, then, is to explain how "cultural diversity" is a sham that fronts for a politically motivated attack on liberal democracy. We shall have to distinguish this sham diversity from the genuine diversity of ideas that is in fact being edged out of the curriculum. We shall have to give a positive account of the intellectual diversity that *is* essential to liberal education. And we shall have to explain how Western civilization, rather than being racist, sexist, classist, and ethnocentric, is actually the source of those principles and ideals by which diversity of opinion is sought, diversity of cultures honored, and individuals of all types respected.

In addition, we shall have to expose the fraudulence of most "interdisciplinary" studies in the undergraduate curriculum: studies that are uninformed by any discipline and organized under no other unifying impulse than political passion. We shall have to state the obvious: that you cannot engage in an interdisciplinary study when you have not yet begun to acquire any one intellectual discipline. And we shall have to give a positive account of the virtues of immersing oneself in a single discipline before sallying forth to establish connections to the disciplines. We shall have to explain how individual disciplines are the source of those factual discoveries and detailed arguments and new ideas that give life to the life of the mind. We must be careful to add that disciplinary study does not foreclose the possibility of interdisciplinary connections but actually leads to them. And we shall have to point out that in the absence of discipline-based testing of theories, there is no check on the political dogmas propounded in "interdisciplinary" courses.

Finally, we shall have to confront the facts of politicization and call them by name. For without establishing the political ligaments that bind them all into one dangerously thrashing limb, our fears about these various academic innovations will seem exaggerated. We will be told that we have nothing to worry about, since those curricular experiments will surely be abandoned as soon as they are found unworkable. We will have to explain that they will not be abandoned, since they never were intended to work by the generally accepted standards of the academy.

It is necessary to "talk the issue up," to make a noise so as to create an intellectual context in which the issue can be seen as such. We need to help students and others see through the sophistries that support demands for "cultural diversity" and "breaking the disciplines." Perhaps more importantly, we need to present the alternative in a positive light. Without an intense awareness of the issue, of there being two sides to the question, the academy will be politicized almost without anyone noticing. For the model for change will not be exactly the confrontational one of the black studies movement in the 1960s. Not at least at first, prior to the formation of a critical mass of radicalized students. Instead, the techniques employed will be borrowed from the women's studies movement. These often consist in taking small, seemingly uncontroversial steps in order to prepare the way for larger steps later on. Thus, in order to put those small steps in the right context, we need to heighten awareness of what is really happening.

Our concerns will need to be presented to alumni, parents, and the general public as well as to our colleagues in faculty meetings and to student bodies. For within our institutions we are not outgunned. It is not that we do not have the better arguments on our side, but only that too few of our colleagues are willing to make them, perhaps because the rest are unwilling to listen. Students' minds have been deadened by miseducation, many faculty have already learned the easy pleasures of politicization, and administrators are now dependent on winning the foundation support that is available only for curriculum innovations (often involving, as an added incentive, the expansion of administrative offices to manage extradepartmental programs). The public needs to be made to understand that politicization is occurring, that it is dangerous to a democracy, and that it helps to account for the rising cost and declining quality of American education at all levels. In our society money talks no louder anywhere than on college campuses, and it is about time for those who are paying the bills to take an interest in what their money is buying. We who are trying to stop the politicization of higher education can use their support.

NOTES

1. Thomas Sowell, *Black Education: Myth and Tragedies* (New York: McKay, 1972), chapter 10. This book, eye-opening and invaluable, is not found in the Black Studies Library either at Kenyon College or at Ohio State University, despite its title, despite its author's being black, and despite his strong defense of extending quality education to more black Americans.

116   Part Three: Diversity, Politics of Race and Sex on Campus . . .

2. This was a "guess" hazarded by Professor Christopher Clausen of the English Department of Pennsylvania State University, in an essay on p. A52 of the January 13, 1988, *Chronicle of Higher Education*. I can add that at Kenyon, Walker's book was assigned in at least three different courses in three different departments in one semester, and a video edition of the much tamer movie version of the novel is also frequently shown on campus.

3. Richard Rodriguez, *Hunger of Memory* (Boston: Godine, 1981). This excellent book should be more widely read. It presents an autobiographical account of the Chicano intellectual and is at once sensitive and anti-ideological.

4. E. Franklin Frazier, *Black Bourgeoise* (New York: Collier, 1962).

5. Sowell, ibid., p. 121.

6. Nathan Glazer, *Ethnic Dilemmas* (Cambridge, Mass.: Harvard University Press, 1983), p. 113.

7. *Chronicle of Higher Education*, October 14, 1987, p. B2. Of course this is not an isolated article. Interdisciplinary studies is being "talked up." For example, the preceding issue of the *Chronicle* had a front page article, "Interdisciplinary Research: How Big a Challenge to Traditional Fields?"

8. *Proceedings* of the Seventh Annual Great Lakes Colleges Association's (GLCA) Women's Studies Conference, "Toward a Feminist Transformation of the Academy: III," 1981, p. 66.

9. *Proceedings* of the Fourth Annual GLCA Women's Studies Conference, "The Structure of Knowledge—A Feminist Perspective," 1978, pp. 53–54.

10. Keynote Address, *Proceedings* of the Ninth Annual GLCA Women's Studies Conference, "Feminist Pedagogy and the Learning Climate," 1983, pp. 115–17.

11. *Proceedings* of the Sixth Annual GLCA Women's Studies Conference, 1980, p. 77.

12. See, e.g., p. 20 of the *Proceedings* of the Tenth Annual GLCA Women's Studies Conference, "Looking Back: A Celebration of Sources," 1984: ". . . projects that focus on mainstreaming run the risk of losing their clear crystalline substance in the large muddy river that they volunteer to join." I.e., their simplistic dogmas might be challenged by facts and alternative ideas. Margaret McIntosh is characteristically bolder: in "A Note on Terminology," *Women's Studies Quarterly* XI, Summer 1983, pp. 29–30, she argues that rather than seeing women's studies as a tributary feeding into the mainstream, the aim of the former should be to "rechannel" the latter.

13. *Proceedings* of the Eleventh Annual GLCA Women's Studies Conference, "Looking Forward: Women's Strategies for Survival," 1985, p. 14.

14. *Chronicle of Higher Education*, November 11, 1987, pp. A13, A21.

15. *The New York Times*, January 19, 1988, p. 1. For more information on the role of organized minority groups and the role of Jesse Jackson, see *The Stanford Daily*, January 22, 1988.

16. *Proceedings* of the Fifth Annual GLCA Women's Studies Conference, 1979, pp. 55–56.

Bibliographical Note: the *Proceedings* of the annual GLCA Women's Studies conferences, from which I have quoted, are not widely distributed and were probably never expected to be read by any but true believers. They represent what proponents of women's studies, not only from GLCA faculties but also the leading lights of the movement nationwide, such as Florence Howe, Elizabeth Minnich, and Margaret McIntosh, say to one another. No one sampling these documents can remain in any doubt about the intellectual level and political intensity of women's studies. They are available, or were, from the central offices of the GLCA, 2929 Plymouth Road, Suite 207, Ann Arbor, Michigan 48105.

7

Meno's Boy:
Hearing His Story—& His Sister's

Catharine R. Stimpson

Today, on our changing campuses, the relations among multiculturalism, freedom of speech, and academic freedom are contentious. This situation demands that faculty serve as peacemakers, not wound-pickers. Offered in a spirit of peacemaking, my paper links multiculturalism and freedom. Its title is "Meno's Boy," in reference, not to a situation comedy, but to a Platonic dialogue.

In *The Meno,* Socrates is talking to Meno, a younger man. Their subjects are virtue, knowledge, and education, the process through which we learn what virtue is. Their conversation also has its flirtatious moments, some homoerotic winks that the more strait-laced advocates of the Western tradition have preferred to ignore. "I know," Socrates tells Meno, "that all pretty young gentlemen like to have pretty similes made about them."[1] When Socrates wishes to demonstrate that knowledge is inherent in our souls, he summons one of Meno's uneducated slave boys and leads the boy through a dialogue about mathematics. For Socrates, the uneducated boy's ability to talk about mathematics at all is proof that his knowledge was always, already there, an innate possession, not an acquisition.

This urbane drama of Socrates, Meno, and Meno's boy embodies

From *Academe,* Bulletin of the American Association of University Professors, November–December 1991. Reprinted by permission of the publisher and the author.

some of the steamiest issues in the academy today. One of the most complex, with an old history, is epistemological. How do we know what we know? More narrowly, what role does language play? Is language a tool that helps us to uncover and discover the self and the world it inhabits? Or, alternatively, is language the master tool that creates meaning for the self and the world it inhabits? Are we neo-realists or neo-nominalists? To a surprising extent, these epistemological questions have infiltrated our discussions about multiculturalism and freedom of speech. Some of our most serious thinkers argue that language is a master tool that constructs and interprets our world. Not only do words hurt—words give sticks and stones their meaning. These thinkers, however, march off in different directions from this epistemological starting block. For Paul Chevigny, in *More Speech,* the freer the speech, the more reliable and solid an architect of the world it is.[2] In contrast, for Richard Delgado, in "Campus Anti-racism Rules," a recent essay, racist speech paints a "stigma-picture of disfavored groups."[3] Because such pictures painfully control a group, they must themselves be regulated.

Far more vulgar commentators than Chevigny and Delgado have concocted a weird syllogism that links proponents of multiculturalism with proponents of deconstruction, the name for a cluster of sophisticated theories of rhetoric that doubt the existence of a meaningful world *a priori* to language. The syllogism asserts first that deconstruction gleefully destroys academic standards and values; next, that proponents of multiculturalism are the beneficiaries of lax standards and values; and finally, that deconstruction and multiculturalism are therefore allies. Moreover, these vulgar commentators cry, multiculturalists and deconstructionists are both barbarians, a linguistic turn comparable to confusing a New York City or Miami or Los Angeles neighborhood with a European château.

Plato, Meno, and Meno's boy point to another issue: the general content of our collective memories, or history, and the more specific content of the Western tradition. How will we remember Plato, his predecessors, his contemporaries, and his lineal descendents? Shaping any historical narrative is an intricate task. Shaping those of the West today may be unusually so. For the very word "West" is a swamp of connotations. My *Shorter Oxford English Dictionary* gives it a full column of closely printed entries. Moreover, multiculturalism is challenging our traditional historiography. In *The Meno,* the boy's last words are deferential and polite, "Certainly, Socrates." The boy then disappears, vanishing from the stage of the dialogue. Today, however, Meno's boy is speaking for himself, about himself. He is claiming the status of historical subject. So is his sister. So is Meno's sister. Their voices often lack deference, but, as they speak more and more freely, they promise to provide a Socrates and a Plato for the twenty-first century.

Meno's boy, the boy's sister, and Meno's sister are also creating new academic programs and curricula. I think, for example, of black studies (with its several names), of women's studies (with its several names), or of post-colonial studies. A multicultural curriculum differs significantly from the new "centricities"—such as Afrocentrism. Properly done, the former is a descriptive enterprise that shows the complex relations among cultures; the latter is a more normative enterprise that focuses on one culture and that tends either to romanticize or to denigrate it. These multicultural programs are another testing ground for academic freedom. They ask if established institutions will permit new voices to flourish. Then new programs must ask themselves if they will nurture the academic freedom that has enabled them to emerge. For the most part, they do respect academic freedom, but each of us must object when they do not. I winced, for example, when I read of a women's studies instructor who refused to let an ROTC student wear his military fatigues to her class.

One peculiar charge against such programs as black studies is that they "fragment" the curriculum. Educators, of course, fragment and divide up the curriculum all the time. We split it along disciplinary lines. We have philosophy and physics, literature and civil engineering, history and histology. We split the curriculum along national lines. We have Irish studies, Italian studies, and Hungarian studies. We split the curriculum along regional lines. We have Asian studies and urban studies. Splitting seems to become "a problem," dividing up "divisive," when Meno's boy, the boy's sister, or Meno's sister is the organizing principle. Crucially, none of them is a whiz-bang, back-flipping cheerleader for the West. All of them have grievances about their historic lack of full standing in Western political structures and their deep association with the irrational in Western cultural structures. They bring, in brief, a critical perspective.

The unreflective charge about "fragmentation" occurs simultaneously with the debates about the place of the West in the curriculum. These debates can be as vulgar as those about epistemology. At their sorriest, they set up coldly polar oppositions. Academic freedom fails to guarantee either a joyous receptivity to criticism or the intelligent recognition of complexities. In one such position, Plato is a plaster saint and multiculturalism the devilish enemy of intellectual freedom and reason. Here, multicultural orthodoxy putatively insists that "race is the determinant of a human being's mind."[4] In a second but dissimilar binary opposition, multiculturalism is potentially a land of plenty and pleasure, but for millennia, the West has served as a hard-boiled Army of Occupation. Here,

Plato is a corpse, but with ghostly powers, in the military graveyard of Dead White Men.

The complex reality that the academy has inherited is that history tells a multicultural story. Cultures attract and repel each other; they conquer, colonize, accommodate, and resist each other. The *Satires* of Juvenal in the first and second centuries dramatize a cosmopolitan, multicultural Rome in which some voices express their keen resentment of rising classes of ex-slaves and foreigners. Moreover, the history of the United States is a multicultural story in which we have learned, no matter how erratically and unevenly, to accept cultural pluralism.

Most commonly, multiculturalism has referred to racial and ethnic pluralism. Today, the concept is expanding.[5] Our thinking about diversity is more diverse. Multiculturalism now includes a range of groups, each of which thinks of itself as a minority and as different from the norm. Most of these groups are still racial and ethnic. One, gays and lesbians, is sexual. Some are religious. Some, like feminism, are political and cultural. Some are economic. A powerful way in which individuals construct their identity is through claiming membership in one or more groups. If these groups are in conflict with each other, an individual can either feel as if she or he has melded ordinary categories to create an extraordinary identity or as if she or he lives with ongoing psychological conflicts. In brief, a multicultural identity can either be a whole new psychic world or a struggle among fragments of the old—or both at once. A few years ago, a speaker at a panel on contemporary culture at the annual meeting of the Modern Language Association was decrying the radical Christian right and its attacks on multiculturalism, expansively defined. At the end, a woman spoke from the floor. "I am black," she said, with firmness and humor, "and a feminist and a lesbian and an Evangelical Christian. You have just tried to wipe out my identity."

The audibility of the voices of Meno's boy, the boy's sister, or Meno's sister is one feature of cultural democracy, a social vision that incorporates multiculturalism and that can influence education. In the 1970s, European debates about cultural policy produced the term. However, like the United States itself, cultural democracy has many parents. The Bill of Rights of 1791 established the constitutional principle of free speech. The antislavery movement of the nineteenth century taught us to respect the rights, minds, and humanity of African-Americans. The women's movement of the nineteenth century taught us to respect the rights, minds, and humanity of women. The expansion of education in the nineteenth century—the founding of more liberal arts colleges, the women's college, the black college, the land-grant and research university—opened up cultural opportunities for many. Finally, the academic disciplines of history, anthropology, and literature urge us to understand the otherness of others.

Today, two demographic developments intensify the need for a cultural democracy. The first is national, the sheer social and cultural diversity of the United States. Our lives are the raw material of a multicultural curriculum. The 1980 census found that one out of every five Americans had a minority background. The 1990 census found nearly one out of every four claiming African, Hispanic, Asian, or American Indian ancestry. The other three out of four are themselves a motley crew.

The second development is international. "Minorities" in the United States are the majority of the world's citizens. If the population of the world were figured as a village of one thousand people, there would be 546 Asians, 210 Europeans, 86 Africans, 80 South Americans, and 60 North Americans.[6] The global village has many different languages, streets, and neighbors. In turn, this geography engenders a "new cultural politics of difference."[7] It is small wonder that 49 percent of all college and university presidents who responded to a recent survey found "greater understanding and awareness of racial/ethnic diversity" a "very important" topic. Significantly, 82 percent of the presidents of research and doctorate-granting institutions did so. These are large, heterogeneous places that bring together—for the first time—international students and a variety of United States students, many from provincial backgrounds.[8]

Cultural democracy asks us to act on these principles:

• Each of us—no matter what our race, class, gender, ethnicity, religion, sexuality—deserves access to literacy, education, arts and letters, and public speech. Clearly, some of us have more talent than others. I am no Spike Lee, no Patricia Shroeder. Nevertheless, each of us has a voice that should get some training. As clearly, some cultural works are more valuable than others, some traditions more productive than others. The job of scholars and critics is to say which and to detail how they have come to judgment.

• Each of us must have access to our own historical and cultural traditions. Our libraries, schools, and mass media must respect our individual cultural and multicultural identities. I am fiercely proud of the grandfather who was born in England, who arrived in New York when he was eight, who then worked his way across America as a cowherd, janitor, and baggage handler. I am just as fiercely proud of the grandmother who had to leave her rural school in Iowa when she was twelve and go into domestic service. I want to root my pride in these ancestors in the soil of public knowledge.

• Nevertheless, our pride in our own cultural identities is not an end in itself, but the home from which we travel in order to meet others. I must move from learning the story of my grandfather and grandmother to learning the story of other families. My orthodoxies are not a single truth for others to swallow, but a perspective for their use. Preferably, we will exchange stories and perspectives in conversations, the term William James deploys in *Pragmatism* for the process of building a consensual view of reality. After such exchanges, history is not simply the story of my culture, but the grand narrative of all our cultures, sometimes at peace with each other, sometimes at each other's throats.

These conversations can be hard work. Negotiations can be no fun. One of the many educational contributions of women's studies is the patient effort it has devoted to creating a classroom where multicultural conversations can go on. Our conversations will not flourish without free speech. I must listen to Senator Jesse Helms sneer at homosexual and feminist art. Senator Helms and his ilk must, of course, listen to me. A legal scholar writes, "A strong freedom of expression is not an impediment to the integration of a multicultural nation. Rather, it is essential, not just for the tolerance of hateful ideas, but for the day-to-day, one-to-one personal interchanges on which the sense of belonging to a national community ultimately depends."[9] We badly need, however, new protocols of listening as well as our constitutionally protected protocols of speaking. We must be able to hear a buzzing swarm of stories. We must also be able to exercise our moral imagination and try to hear ourselves as others hear us. How do sound waves splash on other shores? With such exercise, we might become less careless and hurtful.

• No community can exist without some commonalities. In the United States today, we share an economy; a mass culture; criminal codes; and a political system, structured by the Constitution and the Bill of Rights. However, we have no common moral, religious, and artistic culture. Our energetic pluralism renders this commonality impossible. Our political values bind us together in diversity. One obligation of education is to teach the sources of both unity and differences.

"Hate speech," openly expressed, is one of the ugliest citizens of a cultural democracy. Severely chastising my utopianism, hate speech is a vicious sign of our capacities for cruelty, our incapacities for accepting "the other." Hate speech is also a tragic sign of the gap between our campuses as they are and the campus as an ideal citadel of wisdom, civility, and fairness. Since the 1970s, the campus has focused on two grammars of hate speech: first, sexual harassment, and second, the verbal abuse of racial, religious, ethnic, or sexual groups. Stimulating our attention to the second has been the rise in the euphemistically named "racial incidents" that began in the mid-1980s. Although I do not exculpate smaller institutions, these incidents seem to be "most acute at large research and doctorate institutions."[10] Although I do not exculpate women, men seem more apt to give offense than women, especially young men in groups.

To deal with diversity and its difficult tensions, the academy has supported curricular change (a social justice requirement, for example), extracurricular programs (dormitory workshops on diversity, for example), and anti-harassment, pro-civility codes, abbreviated to "speech codes." All of these efforts have spurred a reaction, the best of it a reasoned defense of free speech. All of these efforts have been, unhappily, labelled "PC." Indeed, the label of PC has been applied so ferociously that it has obscured the fact of hate speech, the number of racial incidents, and the presence of censorship elsewhere in education. I think, for example, of the punishments religious institutions have inflicted on heterodox theologicians. Because speech codes might intrinsically seem to veer toward restrictions, and because at least one speech code, from the University of Michigan, has been thrown out in court, speech codes have been the most controversial and litigious of campus efforts to make diversity work.[11]

I am aware of the request of Charles Lawrence that we describe the controversy over speech codes fully and eschew a binary opposition in which "the liberty of free speech is in conflict with the elimination of racism."[12] Any accurate description must map several festering sites of conflict: between a person's freedom to speak, no matter how hatefully, and another person's freedom from hate speech; between a picture of a community as a group of free persons with rights and a picture of a community as a group of free persons with responsibilities toward each other; between a pragmatism that says that restrictions on speech will not do away with racism and a pragmatism that claims the opposite; between a theory that the best remedy for historical injustice is relief for an individual and a theory that the best remedy for historical injustice is relief for a class. Although I am no lawyer, my amateur's reading of legal literature takes in still more conflicts: between the First Amendment, with its devotion to freedom, and the Fourteenth Amendment, with its devotion to equality,[13] between "categorization," a form of legal reasoning that permits "content-based restrictions only of speech that falls into one of a few, narrow categories" and "contextualization," a form of legal reasoning that balances competing interests.[14]

Given the number and intensity of these conflicts, it is inevitable that the legal writing about hate speech stretches out along a spectrum of opinion. Representing one end are articles by Floyd Abrams or Benno C. Schmidt, Jr., each of which offers a classical defense of freedom of speech. Correctly, Abrams fears the breakdown of a general consensus that the government cannot touch the content of speech. He places interference with "offensive expression . . . in the areas of sexist and racist speech" in a context with Supreme Court dissents from the decision that allowed flag-burning and the Supreme Court decision that permitted the Federal Communications Commission to "punish radio broadcasts of 'indecent' but not obscene words."[15] Schmidt is far more agitated about the campus than about the government as a censor. Despite the work of the Supreme Court and various legislators, he improbably believes that, "The most serious problems of freedom of expression in the U.S. today exist on our campuses . . . there is little resistance to growing pressure to suppress and to punish . . . speech that offends notions of civility and community." This is egregious to Schmidt because the "paramount obligation of an academic community" is not to maintain civility and harmony but to defend freedom. Indeed, the more "diverse, pluralistic, and contentious" a society, the more it needs "freedom of speech and freedom of religion."[16]

At the other end of the spectrum is "Public Response to Racist Speech," an article by Mari J. Matsuda, indebted to Richard Delgado. Persuasively, she fills in the blanks in the arguments of a Schmidt. She pleads for us to listen to the story of the victim of hate speech. She is aware of how difficult it is for a victim to answer back, to fight bad speech with good. Because of such difficulties, she calls for "outsider jurisprudence —jurisprudence derived from considering stories from the bottom."[17] An outsider's jurisprudence argues that the United States does restrict certain kinds of speech now. For example, we have defamation laws. Why, then, can the state not extend restrictions to include racist speech? Actionable racist speech would deliver a persecutorial, hateful, and degrading message of racial inferiority against a historically oppressed group. If the United States were to establish such an extension, it would not be breaking new ground but following an international path.

Although I respect Matsuda's integrity and loathe hate speech, I find her ideas impossible. Plausibly enough, she wants the law to anesthetize the terrible pain of groups and individuals. However, she freezes the complex movements of history that the law must confront into two monolithic blocks: the racially dominant pain-givers and the racially subordinate pain-receivers. She then writes as if every member of the racial majority possessed an equivalent capacity for loutish, knavish behavior and as if every member of the racial minority were equivalent in their victimization. This dissolution of the individual into the class permits her to think that hate expressed against a class is hate expressed against an individual. Her sense of the helplessness of the oppressed also permits her to dismiss too easily the power of good speech—from majority and minority alike. Moreover, she argues that a historically oppressed group can say hateful things about the dominant group. For example, an African-American rap group can denigrate white women. The oppressed group will, however, lose the privilege of insult if and when it becomes equal to the oppressors. But who is to figure out this calculus of power? And who is to say when this calculus has changed and equality now rules?

Fortunately, a middle zone is evolving in which cultural democrats can both defend freedom of speech and hear the victim's story.[18] In this zone, we recognize that hate speech happens on the campus. We do not plug our ears by burying our heads in the bucket of sand meant to put out social fires. Our responses are two-fold. First, we are obliged to assert the crucial values of freedom of inquiry and speech. Among these values is, paradoxically, the expression of hate speech so that we hear and then work against it. We cannot answer and fight against a sulky silence. The good campus will also listen and respond to the victim's story. Indeed, the accurate classroom will transmit the victim's story—the hardships of Meno's boy, his sister, and Meno's sister. Next, we can establish an equitable process through which the good campus democratically designs and administers sanctions against hate speech. However, a campus can do so only under the narrowest, clearest, and tightest of conditions. Constitutionally protected speech is inviolable. Hate speech is actionable only when it is so repetitively and patently hostile, dangerous, threatening, and intimidating to an individual that it stops work and campus life. X could, I fear, say "All faggots are sinful." X could, I fear, tell Y that he is a sinful faggot. However, X or X and his friends could not go to Y's room night after night, batter the door, and yell, "Faggot, we're going to drive you out of here. Faggot, we're going to kill you." Surely, the campus must deflect an arrow of speech dipped in the curare of hate before it strikes and paralyzes a student.

Because of the principles and practices at stake, the debate about hate speech in academic and legal circles has been hard. It has, however, been genuine. Too often, in contrast, the wider public debate has been scuzzy, effluent with polarities, scare tactics, half-truths, and cartoonish exaggerations. Some professors of all ideological persuasions have bought into the scuzziness with their own paranoia, self-pity, hallucinations, and media handouts. On the one hand, they have compared the University of Pennsylvania to the University of Beijing and declared that academic freedom is in greater jeopardy than it was in the 1950s during the reign of Joseph McCarthy. On the other hand, a professor has hammered at Europeans as the People of Ice and burnished Africans as the People of the Sun.

One treatment of speech codes exemplifies the passage from good to lousy debate. In 1990, the Carnegie Foundation for the Advancement of Teaching published *Campus Life: In Search of Community.* It reported that 60 percent of the chief student affairs offices of 355 institutions had said that their campus had a "written policy on bigotry, racial harassment, or intimidation." Eleven percent said that their campus was working on one. Obviously, such policies would vary widely—from simple statements denouncing bigotry to more complex efforts to define harassment or intimidation. Then, on March 12, 1991, Representative Henry J. Hyde, to some fanfare, entered the arena of private education and muscularly introduced "A Bill to amend Title VI of the Civil Rights Act of 1964 to protect the free speech rights of college students" (House Resolution 1380). If passed, it would forbid private educational institutions (except for religious institutions) from making or enforcing "any rule subjecting any students to disciplinary sanctions based solely on the basis of conduct that is speech." The "Briefing Paper" that accompanied the bill put the Carnegie findings under the headline, "How many universities have codes that discipline students for 'offensive' speech?" On the same day, the American Civil Liberties Union, supporting Hyde, shoved out a press release that cited a recent Carnegie survey that had allegedly shown that "about 70 percent of colleges and universities have tried to design inhibitions on First Amendment activity."[19] Thereafter, editorialists—in print and visual media—breathlessly announced that 70 percent of our colleges and universities had codes that banned insulting speech.

Where, in this hurly-burly, is academic freedom? Like freedom itself, it demands constant vigilance. Like advocates of every cultural movement, some advocates of multiculturalism are more interested in gaining adherents than in providing such vigilance. Obviously, however, academic freedom and multiculturalism are compatible allies. The danger is not in the principles of either but in abandoning the principles of both. We walk away from these principles under a number of contradictory conditions: when we forget that freedom of thought enables thought; when we believe that multiculturalism has but a single story; when we believe that only the members of a group can teach about that group; when, in contrast, we assume, no matter how subconsciously, that minority faculty are faculty only because they are minority; when we look askance at faculty and students who want to investigate questions of race, gender, or sexuality and to enter the world of Socrates and Meno, of Meno's sister, of Meno's boy and his sister.

We also abandon our principles when we ignore the historic relation between academic freedom and responsibility. The 1940 *Statement of Principles on Academic Freedom and Tenure* refers succinctly to "duties correlative with rights" and declares firmly that the professoriate should "at all times be accurate, should exercise appropriate restraint, should show respect for the opinions of others." In the time of social anxiety that multiculturalism provokes; in a time of scuzzy public debate for which multiculturalism provides an excuse; it is necessary for us to demonstrate the virtues of accuracy, restraint, and respect for the opinions of others. In brief, we must offer a model of speaking and listening. We can still be theatrical, dramatic, ironic, playful or intense. We must, however, represent a deliberate etiquette of consciousness and an alternative to decadent public discourse.

We must also recall an injunction that is so hoary that we treat it as if it were an old relative doddering away in front of reruns of the Loretta Young show. The injunction, simply, is "Professor, know thyself." We must know our capacities for prejudice as well as for objectivity, for thoughtfulness as well as for thought. We gain such knowledge through an incessant private and public self-interrogation. This process will help us say more confidently than we now can that a negative response to a gay man's book is not homophobic; that a negative response to an African-American student's bluebook is not racist; and that a negative response to a course in European writers is not multiculturalism turned sour.

The next few years will be difficult for the academy. Scandal has touched us. Fiscal constraints rope us in. Fights over resources will be ugly. A renewed commitment to free speech and responsibility will counsel our quest for the moral unity and gravity we need in austerity. So believing, I follow a tradition that construes academic freedom as a promissory note. That is, we promise, for good reasons, that academic freedom will enrich scholarship, teaching, and the civility of our communities. This conviction reflects an enlightened trust in our moral, social, and intellectual capabilities. Now it is multiculturalism that permits us to convey our faith in this hopeful, self-trusting tradition.

NOTES

1. Plato. *The Dialogues of Plato*. Vol. 1, Trans. B. Jowett with Intro. by Daphne Demos. New York: Random House, 1937.
2. Paul Chevigny. *More Speech: Dialogue Rights and Modern Liberty*. Philadelphia: Temple University Press, 1988.
3. Richard Delgado, "Campus Antiracism Rules: Constitutional Narratives in Collision." *Northwestern University Law Review* 85 (1991): 343–87.
4. "Derisory Tower." *New Republic* 204, 7 (February 18, 1991): 5.
5. Articles in *Academe* (November–December 1990), on multiculturalism, show awareness of this expansion.
6. Donald Stewart. "Building on Diversity: An American Tradition," Remarks before the Woodrow Wilson National Fellowship Foundation Board of Trustees, Institute for Advanced Study, Princeton, New Jersey, October 18, 1990.
7. Cornell West. "The New Cultural Politics of Difference." *October* 53 (Summer 1990): 93–109.
8. *Campus Life: In Search of Community*. With "Foreword" by Ernest L. Boyer. Princeton, N.J.: Carnegie Foundation for the Advancement of Teaching, 1990: Table A-4, n.p.
9. Kenneth L. Karst. "Boundaries and Reasons: Freedom of Expression and the Subordination of Groups." *University of Illinois Law Review* (1990): 149.
10. *Campus Life*, 17.
11. Robin Wilson. "Colleges' Anti-Harassment Policies Bring Controversy Over Free-Speech Issues." *The Chronicle of Higher Education* 36, 5 (October 1, 1989). Wilson describes some of the controversies.
12. Charles R. Lawrence III. "The Debates Over Placing Limits on Racist Speech Must Not Ignore the Damage It Does to Its Victims." *The Chronicle of Higher Education* 36, 8 (October 25, 1989): B1.
13. See Susan M. Finegan. "Anti-Harassment Disciplinary Policies: A Violation of First Amendment Rights on the Public University Campus?" *Boston College Third World Law Journal* 11 (Winter 1991): 107–35.
14. "Recent Cases, First Amendment-Racist and Sexist Expression on Campus-Court Strikes Down University Limits on Hate Speech." *Harvard Law Review* 103:6 (April 1990): 1397–1402.
15. Floyd Abrams. "Book Review." *Harvard Law Review* 103:5 (March 1990): 1170–71.
16. Benno C. Schmidt, Jr. "Universities Must Defend Free Speech." *Wall Street Journal* (May 6, 1991): A-16.
17. Mari J. Matsuda. "Public Response to Racist Speech: Considering the Victim's Story." *Michigan Law Review* 87:8 (August 1989): 2323.
18. Influencing my picture of such a middle zone have been the 1991 AAUP "Preliminary Statement on Freedom of Expression and Campus Harassment Codes" (*Academe* May–June 1991); the 1990 Rutgers University revised "Uni-

versity Student Life Policy Against Insult, Defamation, and Harassment"; and articles by Mary Ellen Gale, Jens B. Koepke, John T. Shapiro, and David S. Tatel.

19. *ACLU News.* Washington, D.C.: ACLU Offices (March 12, 1991): 1.

8

The Value of the Canon

Irving Howe

I.

Of all the disputes agitating the American campus, the one that seems to me especially significant is that over "the canon." What should be taught in the humanities and social sciences, especially introductory courses? What is the place of the classics? How shall we respond to those professors who attack "Eurocentrism" and advocate "multiculturalism"? This is not the sort of tedious quarrel that now and then flutters through the academy; it involves matters of public urgency. I propose to see this dispute, at first, through a narrow, even sectarian lens, with the hope that you will come to accept my reasons for doing so.

Here, roughly, are the lines of division. On one side stand (too often, fall) the cultural "traditionalists," who may range politically across the entire spectrum. Opposing them is a heterogeneous grouping of mostly younger teachers, many of them veterans of the 1960s, which includes feminists, black activists, Marxists, deconstructionists, and various mixtures of these.

At some colleges and universities traditional survey courses of world and English literature, as also of social thought, have been scrapped or diluted. At others they are in peril. At still others they will be. What replaces them is sometimes a mere option of electives, sometimes "multicultural" courses introducing material from Third World cultures and thinning out an already thin sampling of Western writings, and sometimes courses geared especially to issues of class, race, and gender. Given the notorious lethargy of academic decision-making, there has probably been more clamor than change; but if there's enough clamor, there will be change.

University administrators, timorous by inclination, are seldom firm in behalf of principles regarding education. Subjected to enough pressure, many of them will buckle under. So will a good number of professors who vaguely subscribe to "the humanist tradition" but are not famously courageous in its defense. Academic liberalism has notable virtues, but combativeness is not often one of them. In the academy, whichever group goes on the offensive gains an advantage. Some of those who are now attacking "traditionalist" humanities and social science courses do so out of sincere persuasion; some, from a political agenda (what was at first solemnly and now is half-ironically called P.C.—politically correct); and some from an all-too human readiness to follow the academic fashion that, for the moment, is "in."

Can we find a neutral term to designate the antitraditionalists? I can't think of a satisfactory one, so I propose an unsatisfactory one: Let's agree to call them the insurgents, though in fact they have won quite a few victories. In the academy these professors are often called "the left" or "the cultural left," and that is how many of them see themselves. But this is a comic misunderstanding, occasionally based on ignorance. In behalf of both their self-awareness and decent clarity of debate, I want to show that in fact the socialist and Marxist traditions have been close to traditionalist views of culture. Not that the left hasn't had its share of ranters (I exclude Stalinists and hooligans) who, in the name of "the revolution," were intent upon jettisoning the culture of the past; but generally such types have been a mere marginal affliction treated with disdain.

Let me cite three figures. Here is Georg Lukacs, the most influential Marxist critic of the twentieth century:

> Those who do not know Marxism may be surprised at the respect for *the classical heritage of mankind* which one finds in the really great representatives of that doctrine. (Emphasis added.)

Here is Leon Trotsky, arguing in 1924 against a group of Soviet writers who felt that as the builders of "a new society" they could dismiss the "reactionary culture" of the past:

If I say the importance of *The Divine Comedy* lies in the fact that it gives me an understanding of the state of mind of certain classes in a certain epoch, this means that I transform it into *a mere historical document*. . . . How is it thinkable that there should not be a historical but *a directly aesthetic relationship* between us and a medieval Italian book? This is explained by the fact that in class society, in spite of its changeability, there are certain common features. Works of art developed in a medieval Italian city can affect us too. What does this require? . . . That these findings and moods shall have received such broad, intense, powerful expressions as to have raised them above the limitations of the life of those days. (Emphasis added.)

Trotsky's remarks could serve as a reply to those American professors of literature who insist upon the omnipresence of ideology as it seeps into and perhaps saturates literary texts, and who scoff that only "formalists" believe that novels and poems have autonomous being and value. In arguing, as he did in his book *Literature and Revolution,* that art must be judged by "its own laws," Trotsky seems not at all P.C. Still less so is Antonio Gramsci, the Italian Marxist, whose austere opinions about education might make even our conservatives blanch:

Latin and Greek were learnt through their grammar, mechanically, but the accusation of formalism and aridity is very unjust. . . . In education one is dealing with children in whom one has to inculcate certain habits of diligence, precision, poise (even physical poise), ability to concentrate on specific subjects, which cannot be acquired without the mechanical repetition of disciplined and methodical acts.

These are not the isolated ruminations of a few intellectuals; Lukacs, Trotsky, and Gramsci speak with authority for a view of culture prevalent in the various branches of the Marxist (and also, by the way, the non-Marxist) left. And that view informed many movements of the left. There were the Labor night schools in England bringing to industrial workers elements of the English cultural past; there was the once-famous Rand School of New York City; there were the reading circles that Jewish workers, in both Eastern Europe and American cities, formed to acquaint themselves with Tolstoy, Heine, and Zola. And in Ignazio Silone's novel *Bread and Wine* we have a poignant account of an underground cell in Rome during the Mussolini years that reads literary works as a way of holding itself together.

My interest here is not to vindicate socialism or Marxism—that is another matter. Nor is there anything sacrosanct about the opinions I have quoted or their authors. But it is surely worth establishing that the claims of many academic insurgents to be speaking from a left, let alone a Marxist, point of view are highly dubious. Very well, the more candid among them might reply, so we're not of the left, at least we're not of the "Eurocentric" left. To recognize that would at least help clear the atmosphere. More important, it might shrink the attractiveness of these people in what is perhaps the only area of American society where the label of "the left" retains some prestige.

What we are witnessing on the campus today is a strange mixture of American populist sentiment and French critical theorizing as they come together in behalf of "changing the subject." The populism provides an underlying structure of feeling, and the theorizing provides a dash of intellectual panache. The populism releases anti-elitist rhetoric, the theorizing releases highly elitist language.

American populism, with its deep suspicion of the making of distinctions of value, has found expression not only in native sages (Henry Ford: "History is bunk") but also in the writings of a long line of intellectuals— indeed, it's only intellectuals who can give full expression to anti-intellectualism. Such sentiments have coursed through American literature, but only recently, since the counterculture of the 1960s, have they found a prominent place in the universities.

As for the French theorizing—metacritical, quasi-philosophical, and at times a stupefying verbal opacity—it has provided a buttress for the academic insurgents. We are living at a time when all the once-regnant world systems that have sustained (also distorted) Western intellectual life, from theologies to ideologies, are taken to be in severe collapse. This leads to a mood of skepticism, an agnosticism of judgment, sometimes a world-weary nihilism in which even the most conventional minds begin to question both distinctions of value and the value of distinctions. If you can find projections of racial, class, and gender bias in both a Western by Louis L'Amour and a classical Greek play, and if you have decided to reject the "elitism" said to be at the core of literary distinctions, then you might as well teach the Western as the Greek play. You can make the same political points, and more easily, in "studying" the Western. And if you happen not to be well informed about Greek culture, it certainly makes things still easier.

I grew up with the conviction that what Geroge Lukacs calls "the classical heritage of mankind" is a precious legacy. It came out of historical circumstances often appalling, filled with injustice and outrage. It was often, in consequence, alloyed with prejudice and flawed sympathies. Still, it was a heritage that had been salvaged from the nightmares, occasionally the glories, of history, and now we would make it "ours," we who came from poor and working-class families. This "heritage of mankind" (which also includes, of course, Romantic and modernist culture) had been denied to the masses of ordinary people, trained into the stupefaction of accepting, even celebrating, their cultural deprivations. One task of political consciousness was therefore to enable the masses to share in what had been salvaged from the past—the literature, art, music, thought—and thereby to reach an active relation with these. That is why many people, not just socialists but liberals, democrats, and those without political tags, kept struggling for universal education. It was not a given; it had to be won. Often, winning proved to be very hard.

Knowledge of the past, we felt, could humanize by promoting distance from ourselves and our narrow habits, and this could promote critical thought. Even partly to grasp a significant experience or literary work of the past would require historical imagination, a sense of other times, which entailed moral imagination, a sense of other ways. It would create a kinship with those who had come before us, hoping and suffering as we have, seeking through language, sound and color to leave behind something of enduring value.

By now we can recognize that there was a certain naïveté in this outlook. The assumption of progress in education turned out to be as problematic as similar assumptions elsewhere in life. There was an underestimation of human recalcitrance and sloth. There was a failure to recognize what the twentieth century has taught us: that aesthetic sensibility by no means assures ethical value. There was little anticipation of the profitable industry of "mass culture," with its shallow kitsch and custom-made dreck. Nevertheless, insofar as we retain an attachment to the democratic idea, we must hold fast to an educational vision somewhat like the one I've sketched. Perhaps it is more an ideal to be approached than a goal to be achieved; no matter. I like the epigrammatic exaggeration, if it is an exaggeration, of John Dewey's remark that "the aim of education is to enable individuals to continue their education."

This vision of culture and education started, I suppose, at some point in the late eighteenth century or the early nineteenth century. It was part of a great sweep of human aspiration drawing upon Western traditions from the Renaissance to the Enlightenment. It spoke in behalf of such liberal values as the autonomy of the self, tolerance for a plurality of opinions, the rights of oppressed national and racial groups, and soon, the claims of the women's movements. To be sure, these values were frequently violated—that has been true for every society in every phase of the world history. But the criticism of such violations largely invoked the declared values themselves, and this remains true for all our contemporary insurgencies. Some may sneer at "Western hegemony," but knowingly or not, they do so in the vocabulary of Western values.

By invoking the "classical heritage of mankind" I don't propose anything fixed and unalterable. Not at all. There are, say, seven or eight writers and a similar number of social thinkers who are of such preeminence that they must be placed at the very center of this heritage; but beyond that, plenty of room remains for disagreement. All traditions change, simply through survival. Some classics die. Who now reads Ariosto? A loss, but losses form part of tradition too. And new arrivals keep being added to the roster of classics—it is not handed down from Mt. Sinai or the University of Chicago. It is composed and fought over by cultivated men and women. In a course providing students a mere sample of literature, there should be included some black and women writers who, because of inherited bias, have been omitted in the past. Yet I think we must give a central position to what Professor John Searle in a recent *New York Review of Books* article specifies as "a certain Western intellectual tradition that goes from, say, Socrates to Wittgenstein in philosophy, and from Homer to James Joyce in literature. . . . It is essential to the liberal education of young men and women in the United States that they should receive some exposure to at least some of the great works of this intellectual tradition."

Nor is it true that most of the great works of the past are bleakly retrograde in outlook—to suppose that is a sign of cultural illiteracy. Bring together in a course on social thought selections from Plato and Aristotle, Machiavelli and Rosseau, Hobbes and Locke, Nietzsche and Freud, Marx and Mill, Jefferson and Dewey, and you have a wide variety of opinions, often clashing with one another, sometimes elusive and surprising, always richly complex. These are some of the thinkers with whom to begin, if only later to deviate from. At least as critical in outlook are many of the great poets and novelists. Is there a more penetrating historian of selfhood than Wordsworth? A more scathing critic of society than the late Dickens? A mind more devoted to ethical seriousness than George Eliot? A sharper critic of the corrupting effects of money than Balzac or Melville?

These writers don't necessarily endorse our current opinions and pieties—why should they? We read them for what Robert Frost calls "counterspeech," the power and brilliance of *other minds,* and if we can go "beyond" them, it is only because they are behind us.

What is being invoked here is not a stuffy obeisance before dead texts from a dead past, but rather a critical engagement with living texts from powerful minds still very much "active" in the present. And we should want our students to read Shakespeare and Tolstoy, Jane Austen and Kafka, Emily Dickinson and Leopold Senghor, not because they "support" one or another view of social revolution, feminism, and black self-esteem. They don't, in many instances; and we don't read them for the sake of enlisting them in a cause of our own. We should want students to read such writers so that they may learn to enjoy the activity of mind, the pleasure of forms, the beauty of language—in short, the arts in their own right.

By contrast, there is a recurrent clamor in the university for "relevance," a notion hard to resist (who wishes to be known as irrelevant?) but proceeding from an impoverished view of political life, and too often ephemeral in its excitements and transient in its impact. I recall seeing in the late 1960s large stacks of Eldridge Cleaver's *Soul on Ice* in the Stanford University bookstore. Hailed as supremely "relevant" and widely described as a work of genius, this book has fallen into disuse in a mere two decades. Cleaver himself drifted off into some sort of spiritualism, ceasing thereby to be "relevant." Where, then, is *Soul on Ice* today? What lasting value did it impart?

American culture is notorious for its indifference to the past. It suffers from the provincialism of the contemporary, veering wildly from fashion to fashion, each touted by the media and then quickly dismissed. But the past is the substance out of which the present has been formed, and to let it slip away from us is to acquiesce in the thinness that characterizes so much of our culture. Serious education must assume, in part, an adversarial stance toward the very society that sustains it—a democratic society makes the wager that it's worth supporting a culture of criticism. But if that criticism loses touch with the heritage of the past, it becomes weightless, a mere compendium of momentary complaints.

Several decades ago, when I began teaching, it could be assumed that entering freshmen had read in high school at least one play by Shakespeare and one novel by Dickens. That wasn't much, but it was something. These days, with the disintegration of the high schools, such an assumption can seldom be made. The really dedicated college teachers of literature feel that, given the bazaar of elective courses an entering student encounters and the propaganda in behalf of "relevance," there is likely to be only one opportunity to acquaint students with a smattering—indeed, the merest fragment—of the great works from the past. Such teachers take pleasure in watching the minds and sensibilities of young people opening up to a poem by Wordsworth, a story by Chekhov, a novel by Ellison. They feel they have planted a seed of responsiveness that, with time and luck, might continue to grow. And if this is said to be a missionary attitude, why should anyone quarrel with it?

II.

Let me now mention some of the objections one hears in academic circles to the views I have put down here, and then provide brief replies.

By requiring students to read what you call "classics" in introductory courses, you impose upon them a certain world view—and that is an elitist act.

In some rudimentary but not very consequential sense, all education entails the "imposing" of values. There are people who say this is true even when children are taught to read and write, since it assumes that reading and writing are "good."

In its extreme version, this idea is not very interesting, since it is not clear how the human race could survive if there were not some "imposition" from one generation to the next. But in a more moderate version, it is an idea that touches upon genuine problems.

Much depends on the character of the individual teacher, the spirit in which he or she approaches a dialogue of Plato, an essay by Mill, a novel by D. H. Lawrence. These can be, and have been used to pummel an ideological line into the heads of students (who often show a notable capacity for emptying them out again). Such pummeling is possible for all points of view but seems most likely in behalf of totalitarian politics and authoritarian theologies, which dispose their adherents to fanaticism. On the other hand, the texts I've mentioned, as well as many others, can be taught in a spirit of openness, so that students are trained to read carefully, think independently, and ask questions. Nor does this imply that the teacher hides his or her opinions. Being a teacher means having a certain authority, but the student should be able to confront that authority freely and critically. This is what we mean by liberal education—not that a teacher plumps for certain political programs, but that the teaching is done in a "liberal" (open, undogmatic) style.

I do not doubt that there are conservatives and radical teachers who teach in this "liberal" spirit. When I was a student at City College in the late 1930s, I studied philosophy with a man who was either a member of the Communist Party or was "cheating it out of dues." Far from being the propagandist of the Party line, which Sidney Hook kept insisting was the necessary role for Communist teachers, this man was decent, humane, and tolerant. Freedom of thought prevailed in his classroom. He had, you might say, a "liberal" character, and perhaps his commitment to teaching as a vocation was stronger than his loyalty to the Party. Were such things not to happen now and then, universities would be intolerable.

If, then, a university proposes a few required courses so that ill-read students may at least glance at what they do not know, that isn't (necessarily) "elitist." Different teachers will approach the agreed-upon texts in different ways, and that is as it should be. If a leftist student gets "stuck" with a conservative teacher, or a conservative student with a leftist teacher, that's part of what education should be. The university is saying to its incoming students: "Here are some sources of wisdom and beauty that have survived the centuries. In time you may choose to abandon them, but first learn something about them."

Your list of classics include only dead, white males, all tied in to notions and values of Western hegemony. Doesn't this narrow excessively the horizons of education?

All depends on how far forward you go to compose your list of classics. If you do not come closer to the present than the mid-eighteenth century, then of course there will not be many, or even any, women in your roster. If you go past the mid-eighteenth century or reach the present, it's not at all true that only "dead, white males" are to be included. For example—and this must hold for hundreds of other teachers also— I have taught and written about Jane Austen, Emily Brontë, Charlotte Brontë, Elizabeth Gaskell, George Eliot, Emily Dickinson, Edith Wharton, Katherine Anne Porter, Doris Lessing, and Flannery O'Connor. I could easily add a comparable list of black writers. Did this, in itself, make me a better teacher? I doubt it. Did it make me a better person? We still lack modes of evaluation subtle enough to say for sure.

The absence of women from the literature of earlier centuries is a result of historical inequities that have only partly been remedied in recent years. Virginia Woolf, in a brilliant passage in *A Room of One's Own,* approaches this problem by imagining Judith, Shakespeare's sister, perhaps equally gifted but prevented by the circumstances of her time from developing her gifts:

Any woman born with a great gift in the sixteenth century would certainly have gone crazed, shot herself, or ended her days in some lonely cottage outside the village, half witch, half wizard, feared and mocked at. . . . A

highly gifted girl who had tried to use her gift of poetry would have been
so thwarted and hindered by other people, so tortured and pulled asunder
by her own contrary instincts, that she must have lost her health and sanity.

The history that Virginia Woolf describes cannot be revoked. If we
look at the great works of literature and thought through the centuries
until about the mid-eighteenth century, we have to recognize that indeed
they have been overwhelmingly the achievements of men. The circumstances
in which these achievements occurred may be excoriated. The achievements
remain precious.

*To isolate a group of texts as the canon is to establish a hierarchy of
bias, in behalf of which there can be no certainty of judgment.*
There is mischief or confusion in the frequent use of the term "hierarchy" by the academic insurgents, a conflation of social and intellectual
uses. A social hierarchy may entail a (mal)distribution of income and power,
open to the usual criticisms; a literary "hierarchy" signifies a judgment,
often based on historical experience, that some works are of supreme or
abiding value, while others are of lesser value, and still others quite without value. To prefer Elizabeth Bishop to Judith Krantz is not of the same
order as sanctioning the inequality of wealth in the United States. To
prefer Shakespeare to Sidney Sheldon is not of the same order as approv-
ing the hierarchy of the nomenklatura in Communist dictatorships.

As for the claim that there is no certainty of judgment, all tastes
being historically molded or individually subjective, I simply do not believe that the people who make it live by it. This is an "egalitarianism"
of valuation that people of even moderate literacy know to be false and
unworkable—the making of judgments, even if provisional and historically modulated, is inescapable in the life of culture. And if we cannot
make judgments or demonstrate the grounds for our preferences, then
we have no business teaching literature—we might just as well be teaching advertising—and there is no reason to have departments of literature.

*The claim that there can be value-free teaching is a liberal deception or
self-deception; so too the claim that there can be texts untouched by social and political bias. Politics or ideology is everywhere, and it's the better part of honesty to admit this.*
If you look hard (or foolishly) enough, you can find political and
social traces everywhere. But to see politics or ideology in all texts is to
scrutinize the riches of literature through a single lens. If you choose, you
can read all or almost all literary works through the single lens of reli-

gion. But what a sad impoverishment of the imagination, and what a violation of our sense of reality, this represents. Politics may be "in" everything, but not everything is politics. A good social critic will know which texts are inviting to a given approach and which it would be wise to leave to others.

To see politics everywhere is to diminish the weight of politics. A serious politics recognizes the limits of its reach; it deals with public affairs while leaving alone large spheres of existence; it seeks not to "totalize" its range of interest. Some serious thinkers believe that the ultimate aim of politics should be to render itself superfluous. That may seem an unrealizable goal; meanwhile, a good part of the struggle for freedom in recent decades has been to draw a line beyond which politics must not tread. The same holds, more or less, for literary study and the teaching of literature.

Wittingly or not, the traditional literary and intellectual canon was based on received elitist ideologies, the values of Western imperialism, racism, sexism, etc., and the teaching of the humanities was marked by corresponding biases. It is now necessary to enlarge the canon so that voices from Africa, Asia, and Latin America can be heard. This is especially important for minority students so that they may learn about their origins and thereby gain in self-esteem.

It is true that over the decades some university teaching has reflected inherited social biases—how, for better or worse, could it not? Most often this was due to the fact that many teachers shared the common beliefs of American society. But not all teachers! As long as those with critical views were allowed to speak freely, the situation, if not ideal, was one that people holding minority opinions and devoted to democratic norms had to accept.

Yet the picture drawn by some academic insurgents—that most teachers, until quite recently, were in the grip of the worst values of Western society —is overdrawn. I can testify that some of my school and college teachers a few decades ago, far from upholding Western imperialism or white supremacy, were sharply critical of American society, in some instances from a boldly reformist outlook. They taught us to care about literature both for its own sake and because, as they felt, it often helped confirm their own worldviews. (And to love it even if it didn't confirm their worldviews.) One high school teacher introduced me to Hardy's *Jude the Obscure* as a novel showing how cruel society can be to rebels, and up to a point, she was right. At college, as a fervent anti-Stalinist Marxist, I wrote a thoughtless "class analysis" of Edmund Spenser's poetry for an

English class, and the kindly instructor, whose politics were probably not very far from mine, suggested that there were more things in the world, especially as Spenser had seen it, than I could yet recognize. I mention these instances to suggest that there has always been a range of opinion among teachers, and if anything, the American academy has tilted more to the left than most other segments of our society. There were of course right-wing professors too; I remember an economics teacher we called "Steamboat" Fulton, the object of amiable ridicule among the students, who nonetheless learned something from him.

Proposals to enlarge the curriculum to include non-Western writings —if made in good faith and not in behalf of an ideological campaign— are in principle to be respected. A course in ancient thought might well include a selection from Confucius; a course in the modern novel might well include a work by Tanizaki or García Márquez.

There are practical difficulties. Due to the erosion of requirements in many universities, those courses that survive are usually no more than a year or a semester in duration, so that there is danger of a diffusion to the point of incoherence. Such courses, if they are to have any value, must focus primarily on the intellectual and cultural traditions of Western society. That, like it or not, is where we come from and that is where we are. All of us who live in America are, to some extent, Western: it gets to us in our deepest and also our most trivial habits of thought and speech, in our sense of right and wrong, in our idealism and our cynicism.

As for the argument that minority students will gain in self-esteem through being exposed to writings by Africans and black Americans, it is hard to know. Might not entering minority students, some of them ill-prepared, gain a stronger sense of self-esteem by mastering the arts of writing and reading than by being told, as some are these days, that Plato and Aristotle plagiarized from an African source? Might not some black students feel as strong a sense of self-esteem by reading, say Dostoyevsky and Malraux (which Ralph Ellison speaks of having done at a susceptible age) as by being confined to black writers? Is there not something grossly patronizing in the notion that while diverse literary studies are appropriate for middle-class white students, something else, racially determined, is required for the minorities? Richard Wright found sustenance in Dreiser, Ralph Ellison in Hemingway, Chinua Achebe in Elliot, Leopold Senghor in the whole of French poetry. Are there not unknown young Wrights and Ellisons, Achebes and Senghors in our universities who might also want to find their way to an individually achieved sense of culture?

In any case, is the main function of the humanities directly to inculcate self-esteem? Do we really know how this can be done? And if done by bounding the curriculum according to racial criteria, may that not perpetuate the very grounds for a lack of self-esteem? I do not know the answers to these questions, but do the advocates of multiculturalism?

One serious objection to "multicultural studies" remains; that it tends to segregate students into categories fixed by birth, upbringing, and obvious environment. Had my teachers tried to lead me toward certain writers because they were Jewish, I would have balked—I wanted to find my own way to Proust, Kafka, and Pirandello, writers who didn't need any racial credentials. Perhaps things are different with students today—we ought not to be dogmatic about these matters. But are there not shared norms of pride and independence among young people, whatever their race and color?

The jazz musician Wynton Marsalis testifies: "Everybody has two heritages, ethnic and human. The human aspects give art its real enduring power. . . . The racial aspect, that's a crutch so you don't have to go out into the world." David Bromwich raises an allied question: Should we wish "to legitimize the belief that the mind of a student deserves to survive in exactly the degree that it corresponds with one of the classes of socially constructed group minds? If I were a student today I would find this assumption frightening. It is, in truth, more than a license for conformity. It is a four-year sentence to conformity."

What you have been saying is pretty much the same as what conservatives say. Doesn't that make you feel uncomfortable?

No, it doesn't. There are conservatives—and conservatives. Some, like the editor of *The New Criterion,* are frantic ideologues with their own version of P.C., the classics as safeguard for the status quo. This is no more attractive than the current campus ideologizing. But there are also conservatives who make the necessary discriminations between using culture, as many have tried to use religion, as a kind of social therapy and seeing culture as a realm with its own values and rewards.

Similar differences hold with regard to the teaching of past thinkers. In a great figure like Edmund Burke you will find not only the persuasions of conservatism but also a critical spirit that does not readily lend itself to ideological coarseness. Even those of us who disagree with him fundamentally can learn from Burke the disciplines of argument and resources of language.

Let us suppose that in University X undergoing a curriculum debate there is rough agreement about which books to teach between professors of the democratic left and their conservative colleagues. Why should that trouble us—or them? We agree on a given matter, perhaps for different reasons. Or there may be a more or less shared belief in the idea of a liberal education. If there is, so much the better. If the agreement is momentary, the differences will emerge soon enough.

A LITTLE EPILOGUE

A *New Republic* reader: "Good lord, you're becoming a virtuoso at pushing through open doors. All this carrying on just to convince us that students should read great books. It's so obvious . . .."

I reply: "Dear reader, you couldn't be more right. But that is where we are."

9

Western Civ—and Me:
An Address at Harvard University

Allan Bloom

Fellow Elitists:

If I were E. D. Hirsch, of "cultural literacy" fame—people do tend to mix us up—I might ask, "What is the literary influence on my salutation?" The answer is Franklin D. Roosevelt's salutation to another select audience, the Daughters of the American Revolution. He began his address, "Fellow Immigrants."

Roosevelt was gently ridiculing those ladies for believing that in America old stock constitutes any title whatsoever to privilege. That notion is a relic of the aristocratic past which this democracy supplanted in favor of equality, or of privilege based on merit. Roosevelt was urbane and witty, this century's greatest virtuoso of democratic leadership. We, the immigrants or the children of immigrants, loved his act; he was on our side. Our enjoyment of his joke was enhanced by the acid of vengeance against those who thought they were better than we. F. D. R. knew how to manipulate such sentiments, and his slap at the D.A.R. was not entirely disinterested insofar as there were a lot more of us than there were of them.

Moreover, Roosevelt's enjoyment was quite different from ours. He was really one of them. His family's claims to antiquity, wealth, and distinction were as good as practically anyone's. It was certainly more pleasant to poke fun at his equals or inferiors than to show resentment toward his superiors. His was an aristocratic condescension. He condescended to rule in a democracy, to be, as was often said about him at the time, "a traitor to his class"—a neat mixture of man's personal striving to be first and the demands of a society where all are held to be equal. The psychology of democracy is complex and fascinating.

That psychology determined the very unusual intensity of the response to my book, *The Closing of the American Mind,* focusing on my alleged elitism. I was suspect as an enemy of our democratic regime. And the first and loudest voices in this chorus came from the Ivy League, particularly from those with some connection to Harvard. Everybody knows that Harvard is in every respect—its students, its faculty, its library, and its endowment—the best university in the world. Long ago when I, a Middle Westerner, taught for a year at Yale, I was amazed at the little Harvard worm that was eating away at the souls of practically all of the professors and students there, except for the ones who had turned down the opportunity to be at Harvard. Elite is not a word I care for very much—it is imprecise and smacks of sociological abstraction—but if any American institution of any kind merits that name, it is Harvard, and it lends that tincture to everyone associated with it.

Why, then, this passion to accuse others of the crime of elitism? One is tempted to attribute it to simple self-protectiveness. "If we say *he* is one, they won't notice *us.*" But I suspect some, or many, acted from a more tortuous, more ambiguous motive—guilt. The leading principle of our regime is the equal worth of all persons, and facts or sentiments that appear to contradict that principle are experienced by a democrat as immoral. Bad conscience accompanies the democrat who finds himself part of an elite. He tries to suppress or deny to himself whatever covert feelings he might experience—I am sure that none of you has had them —of delight or superiority in the fact that he has been distinguished by Harvard, that he is much better off than the poor jerks at Kalamazoo College, even that he deserves it, that superior gifts merit superior education, position, and esteem. A few might consciously believe such things, but since they would be at odds with the egalitarian opinions of democracy, they tend to become spiritual outlaws, hypocrites, and cynically indifferent to the only American principle of justice. The rest, to soothe their consciences, have to engage in casuistry, not to say sophistry.

The simple democratic answer would be open admissions, just as there would be if Harvard were located in Europe, where such elitism is less tolerated. But nobody here really considers that. Harvard, I gather, intends to remain adamantly exclusive, implying thereby that there are significant natural differences among human beings. President Derek Bok's way of squaring such elitism with democratic right-thinking has been, apparently, to teach that the Harvard person is a doer of good works for society as a whole. This is in the spirit of Harvard's own political philosopher, John Rawls, who permits people to possess and cultivate superior talents if they can be proved to benefit the most disadvantaged part of society. Whether this solution is reason or rationalization is open to discussion.

All this suggests the intricate psychology of the democrat, which we must be aware of in order to know ourselves and which we are not likely to be aware of without the help of significant thinkers like Tocqueville, Burke, and Plato, who see us from the outside and judge us in terms of serious alternatives to democracy. The charge of elitism reflects the moral temper of our regime, as the charge of atheism would have done in an earlier age. You couldn't get much of a response in a university today by saying that Allan Bloom doesn't believe in God. But you can get a lot of people worked up by saying that Allan Bloom doesn't believe in equality. And this tells us a lot about our times, and explains how tempting a career is offered to egalitarian Tartufferie. "Elitist" is not a very precise charge; yet compared with the Ivy League, I would have at worst to be called a moderate elitist, and by persons other than those who are now making the charge.

But the real disagreement concerns the content of today's and tomorrow's elite education. We are now witnessing in our universities the introduction of a new "nonelitist," "nonexclusionary" curriculum in the humanities and in parts of the social sciences, and with it a program for reforming the human understanding. This is an extremely radical project whose supporters pass it off as mainstream by marching under the colors of all the movements toward a more equal society which almost all Americans endorse. Not recognized for what it is, this radicalism can thus marshal powerful and sometimes angry passions alongside its own fanatic ones. The American Council of Learned Societies—upset by "the disturbing success" of my book, which is attributed to "American anti-intellectualism" —has even issued a report ordering us to believe that there is now a scholarly consensus, nay, a proof, that all classic texts are expressions of the unconscious class, gender, or race prejudices of their authors. The calling of the humanities in our day, it seems, is to liberate us from the sway of those authors and their prejudices—Shakespeare and Milton, among others, are mentioned in the report. This puts humanists at the cutting edge of the battle against "Eurocentrism." (Clearly, the characters who wrote this report were sent by central casting for the movie version of *The Closing of the American Mind.*)

The battle is not primarily, or even at all, scholarly but moral and political, and members of the reactionary rear guard are the object of special fury, the enemies of historic destiny. Consequently, *The Closing of the American Mind,* which takes an entirely different view of the classic texts and of the humanities in general—a view fundamentally at odds with the radical reform being imposed on us—has been brought before this Inquisition and condemned to banishment from the land of the learned.

People's angers reveal much about what concerns them. Anger almost always disguises itself as moral indignation and, as Aristotle teaches, is the only one of the passions that requires speech and reason—to provide arguments which justify it and without which it is frustrated and withers. Anger proves man's rationality while it obscures and endangers reason. The arguments it adduces always lead back to a general principle of morality and then issue in blame. Here is an example, as reported by Richard Bernstein in the New York *Times* (September 25, 1988):

> In some respects, the scene in North Carolina last weekend recalled the daily "minute of hatred" in George Orwell's *1984,* when citizens are required to rise and hurl invectives at pictures of a man known only as Goldstein, the Great Enemy of the state.
>
> At a conference on the future of liberal education sponsored by Duke University and the University of North Carolina at Chapel Hill, speaker after speaker denounced what they called "the cultural conservatives" who, in the words of a Duke English professor, Stanley Fish, have mounted "dyspeptic attacks on the humanities."
>
> There were no pictures of these "cultural conservatives" on the wall, but they were derided, scorned, laughed at.

Such sentiments—and I appreciate the *Times's* making explicit the resemblance to Stalinist thought control—represent the current establishment in the humanities, literature, and history. These professors are from hot institutions like Stanford and Duke which have most openly dedicated themselves to the new educational dawn called *openness,* a dawn whose rosy fingers are currently wrapped tightly around the throat of the curriculum in most universities.

In *The Closing of the American Mind* I offer a description of the young people of today as they have been affected by the times into which they were born and the failure of liberal education, dominated as it now is by doctrinaire forms of historicism and relativism, to obliterate them from the clichés of the age. Contrary to what some have alleged, I feel sorrow or pity, not contempt, for these young people whose horizon has become so dark and narrow that, in this enlightened country, it has begun to resemble a cave. Self-consciousness, self-awareness, the Delphic "Know thyself" seems to me to be the serious business of education. It is, I recognize, very difficult even to understand what that means, let alone to achieve it. But one thing is certain. If one's head is crammed with ideas that were once serious but have become clichés, if one does not even know that these clichés are not as natural as the sun and moon, and if one has no notion that there are alternatives to them, one is doomed to be the puppet of other people's ideas. Only the search back to the origins of one's ideas in order to see the real arguments for them, before people became so certain of them that they ceased thinking about them at all, can liberate us.

Our study of history has taught us to laugh at the follies of the whole past, the monarchies, oligarchies, theocracies, and aristocracies with their fanaticism for empire or salvation, once taken so seriously. But we have very few tools for seeing ourselves in the same way, as others will see us. Each age always conspires to make its own way of thinking appear to be the only possible or just way, and our age has the least resistance to the triumph of its own way. There is less real presence of respectable alternatives and less knowledge of the titanic intellectual figures who founded our way. Moreover, we are also affected by historicism, which tells us one cannot resist one's way, and relativism, which asks, "What's the use, anyway?" All this has the effect of crippling the natural longing to get out.

In *The Closing of the American Mind* I criticized doctrinaire historicism and relativism as threats to the self-awareness of those who honestly seek it. I pointed to the great sources of those serious ideas which have become dogmas and urge that we turn to the study of them in order to purge ourselves of our dogmatism. For this I have been violently attacked as nostalgic, ideological, and doctrinaire myself. The real meaning is: "Don't touch our belief structure; it hurts."

Yet we ought to recognize, on the basis of historical observation, that what epochs consider their greatest virtue is most often really their greatest temptation, vice, or danger—Roman manliness, Spanish piety, British class, German authenticity. We have to learn to put the scalpel to our virtues. Plato suggests that anyone born in a democracy is likely to be a relativist: it goes with the territory. Relativism may be true, but since we are by birthright inclined to it, we especially had better think it over. Not for the sake of good morals or good social order, at least in any usual sense of those terms, but for the sake of our freedom and our self-awareness.

Since I first addressed the issue of relativism, I have learned with what moral fervor it is protected. For example, the celebrated liberal, Professor Arthur M. Schlesinger, Jr., says that (in contrast to my own alleged absolutism) the authentic American tradition is relativist. To support this latter contention he cites—*mirabile dictu*—the Declaration of Independence's "We hold these truths to be self-evident, that all men are created equal and are endowed by their creator with certain inalienable rights." Professor Schlesinger takes this statement of fundamental principle to be evidence of the American Founders' *relativism*. He made this astounding argument in a commencement address at Brown University, where he apparently thinks the students will believe anything.

It is a waste of time to defend myself when the charges allege that I said things I did not say, but it is perhaps useful to instruct Professor Schlesinger about the real question. I never stated, nor do I believe, that man is, or can be, in possession of absolutes. I tried to teach, evidently not very successfully in his case, that there are two threats to reason, the opinion that one knows the truth about the most important things and the opinion that there is no truth about them. Both of these opinions are fatal to philosophy; the first asserts that the quest for the truth is unnecessary, while the second asserts that it is impossible. The Socratic knowledge of ignorance, which I take to be the beginning point of all philosophy, defines the sensible middle ground between two extremes, the proofs of which demand much more than we know. Pascal's formula about our knowing too little to be dogmatists and too much to be skeptics perfectly describes our human condition as we really experience it, although men have powerful temptations to obscure it and often find it intolerable.

Socrates' way of life is the consequence of his recognition that we can know what it is that we do not know about the most important things and that we are by nature obliged to seek that knowledge. We must remain faithful to the bit of light which pierces through our circumambient darkness.

The fervor with which relativism is protected is matched by the zeal with which its contemporary opposite, "Eurocentrism," is attacked (though in this attack Professor Schlesinger, perhaps a little inconsistently, does not join). This fervor does not propose an investigation but a crusade. The very idea that we ought to look for rational standards by which to judge ourselves is scandalous. One simply has to believe in the current understanding of openness if one is to believe in democracy and be a decent person.

This openness dogma was epitomized by one intellectual who, unencumbered by acquaintance with my book, ridiculed me for not simply accepting that all cultures are equal. He said that this opinion must be standard equipment for all those who expect to cope with "the century of the Pacific" which is upon us.

His formulation set my imagination in motion. I decided it might be interesting to experience a Gulliver's travel to Japan to see whether we really want to set our bark on the great Pacific with a relativist compass and without a "Eurocentric" life jacket. We can weigh anchor at the new, new Stanford, whose slogan has in effect become "Join Stanford and see the world." When we arrive in Japan we shall see a thriving nation. Its success clearly has something to do with its society, which asks much of itself and gets it. It is a real community; its members have roots. Japanese society is often compared to a family. These characteristics are in tune with much of current liberal thought in America. (Remember Governor Mario Cuomo's keynote speech on this very theme to the Democratic convention in 1984.)

But the family in general is inclusive. There is an iron wall separating insiders from outsiders, and its members feel contrary sentiments toward the two. So it is in Japanese society, which is intransigently homogeneous, barring the diversity which is the great pride of the United States today. To put it brutally, the Japanese seem to be racists. They consider themselves superior; they firmly resist immigration; they exclude even the Koreans who have lived for generations among them. They have difficulty restraining cabinet officers from explaining that America's economic failings are due to blacks.

Should we open ourselves up to this new culture? Sympathize with its tastes? Should we aim for restrictiveness rather than diversity? Should we experiment with a more effective racism? All these things could be understood as part of our interest in keeping up with the Japanese economic miracle. Or they could, in a tonier vein, help us in our search for community and roots.

Of course, we recoil in horror at even having such thoughts. But how can we legitimate our horror? It is only the result of our acculturation, excess baggage brought with us on such voyages of discovery. If there are no transcultural values, our reaction is Eurocentric. And the one thing we know absolutely is that Eurocentrism is bad. So we have painted ourselves into a corner.

Condemning Eurocentrism is frequently a sign of intellectual, although not necessarily moral, progress. But it is only a first step. To recognize that some of the things our culture believes are not true imposes on us the duty of finding out which are true and which are not, a business altogether more difficult than the wholesale jettisoning of all that one thought one knew. Such jettisoning always ends up with the selective and thoughtless return to old Eurocentric ideas on the basis of what one needs right now, of what pleases one, of pure feeling.

This process has been nicely illustrated in recent times by the case of Salman Rushdie, author of the novel *The Satanic Verses,* which insulted the Muslim faith and occasioned the Ayatollah Khomeini's command to have Rushdie killed. There was general shock throughout the Western world at this, and writers, whose ox was being gored, rushed before the TV cameras to denounce so blatant an attack on the inviolable principle of freedom of speech. All well and good. But the kicker was that most of these very same writers had for many years been teaching that we must respect the integrity of other cultures and that it was arrogant Eurocentrism to judge other cultures according to our standards, themselves merely products of our culture. In this case, however, all such reasonings were forgotten, and the Eurocentric principle of freedom of speech was treated as though its claims to transcultural status, its claims to be valid everywhere and always, were true. A few days earlier such claims had been treated as instruments of American imperialism; miraculously they were transformed into absolutes. By now, however, one can already see a softening of the question of Rushdie's innocence among the more modish radical intellectuals.

Leaving aside the intellectual incoherence here, this floating means to say that we do not know from moment to moment what we will do when there are conflicts, which there inevitably will be between human rights and the imperatives of the culturally sacred. The serious arguments that established the right of freedom of speech were made by philosophers —most notably Locke, Milton, and John Stuart Mill—but our contemporaries do not return to them to refresh their memories and to see whether the arguments are really good. And this is due not only to laziness but also to the current attack on the very idea of such study.

From the slogans and the arguments echoed so frequently in the universities and the press one can judge the intentions of the "nonelitist" and "nonexclusionary" curriculum now sweeping the country, and what is at stake. The key word is *canon.* What we are witnessing is the Quarrel of the Canons, the twentieth century's farcical version of the seventeenth century Quarrel Between the Ancients and the Moderns—the greatest document of which is Swift's *Battle of the Books.* Would that he were here to describe ours as he described theirs!

The issue is what food best nourishes the hungers of young souls. The canon is the newly valued, demagogically intended, expression for the books taught and read by students at the core of their formal education. But as soon as one adopts the term, as both sides have done, the nature of the debate has thereby been determined. For canon means what is established by authority, by the powers, hence not by criteria that are rationally defensible. The debate shifts from the content of books to how they become powerful, the motives for which they are used. And since canons are, by definition, instruments of domination, they are there to be overthrown, *deconstructed,* in the name of liberation by those who seek *empowerment.*

Philosophy in the past was about knowing; now it is about power. "Philosophy is the most spiritualized will to power." That is from Nietzsche, as is, more or less, all the current talk about the canon. "It's all about power," as they say, and in a more metaphysical sense than most know. This is the source of the deep drama being played out so frivolously about us. Professor Edward Said of the Columbia English department said at Stanford that the new university reforms were the triumph of post-modernism, meaning, among other things, that the curriculum which taught that the theoretical life is highest has been overcome. Curiously, books are invested with a very great significance in all this. They are the causes, not mere epiphenomena, as Marxism would have it. Change the books, not the ownership of the means of production, and you change the world. "Readers of the world, you have nothing to lose but your canon."

Underlying the tumult over non-Western content, then, is a discussion among Westerners using entirely Western categories about the decline or end of the West. The suicide of the West is, by definition, accomplished by Western hands. The *Times* report of the North Carolina conference gives the flavor of the public discussion:

the conference's participants denounced what they said was a narrow, outdated interpretation of the humanities and of culture itself, one based, they frequently pointed out, on works written by "dead white European males."

That is *the* slogan. Above all the campaign is against Eurocentrism:

The message of the North Carolina conference was that American society has changed too much for this view to prevail any longer. Blacks, women, Latinos, and homosexuals are demanding recognition for their own canons. "Projects like those of [William] Bennett, [E. D.] Hirsch, and [Allan] Bloom all look back to the recovery of the earlier vision of American culture, as opposed to the conception of a kind of ethnic carnival or festival of cultures or ways of life or customs," Professor Fish said.

Replace the old, cold Greek temple with an Oriental bazaar. Overthrow the Waspocracy by means of a Rainbow Coalition. This has more or less plausibility as a political "strategy." Whether it should be the polar star in the formation of young minds is another question. It promises continuing wondrous curricular variations as different specialties and groups vie for power.*

This is the popular surface of the movement, the publicly acceptable principle of everyone's getting a piece of the action in a nation that has bought into group politics. But there is a deeper, stronger, and more revealing side:

> The conference buzzed with code words. When the speakers talked about "the hegemonic culture," they meant undemocratic domination by white men. The scholars particularly scorned the idea that certain great works of literature have absolute value or represent some eternal truth. Just about everything, they argued, is an expression of race, class, or gender.

This is academic jargon, one-third Marxist, two-thirds Nietzschean; but it points toward the metaphysics of the cosmic power struggle in terms of which we interpret everything nowadays. All books have to be reinterpreted to find the conscious or unconscious power motive of their authors. As Nietzsche puts it, "Every philosophy is the author's secret confession."

The other side in this struggle can be found in the words of the black writer and activist W. E. B. Du Bois at the turn of the century:

> I sit with Shakespeare and he winces not. Across the color line I walk arm in arm with Balzac and Dumas, where smiling men and welcoming

---

*During the question period following the lecture from which this article has been adapted, I discovered that this project has been a roaring success with at least some students. A Chinese, a black, an Armenian, and a person speaking for homosexuals wondered whether they were being "excluded," inasmuch as books by members of their "communities" are not represented in curricula in proportion to their numbers in the population. They seemed to think that Greeks and Italians have been in control of the universities and that now their day is coming. One can imagine a census which would redistribute the representation of books. The premise of these students' concerns is that "where you come from," your culture, is more important than where you are going. They are rather like Plato's noble guardian dogs in the *Republic* who love what is familiar, no matter how bad it is, and hate all that is strange or foreign. This kind of demand is entirely new. You do not go to college to discover for yourself what is good but to be confirmed in your origins.

women glide in gilded halls. From out of the caves of evening that swing between the strong-limbed earth and the tracery of the stars, I summon Aristotle and Aurelius and what soul I will, and they come all graciously with no scorn or condescension. So, wed with Truth, I dwell above the veil.

I confess that this view is most congenial to me. Du Bois found our common transcultural humanity not in a canon, but in certain works from which he learned about himself and gained strength for his lonely journey, beyond the veil. He found community rather than war. He used the books to think about his situation, moving beyond the corrosive of prejudice to the independent and sublime dignity of the fully developed soul. He recapitulates the ever-renewed experience of books by intelligent poor and oppressed people seeking for a way out.

But during the recent Stanford curriculum debate, a leader of the black student group declared that the implicit message of the Western civilization curriculum is "nigger go home." From this perspective Du Bois was suffering from false consciousness, a deceptive faith in theoretical liberation offered by the inventors of practical slavery.

Now, obviously books are being used by nations and religions to support their way and to train the young to it. But that is not the whole story. Many books, perhaps the most important ones, have an independent status and bring us light from outside our cave, without which we would be blind. They are frequently the acid which reveals the outlines of abusive power. This is especially true in a liberal society like our own, where it is hard to find a "canonical" book which truly supports our way unqualifiedly. Further, it is at least plausible that the books which have a continuing good reputation and used to be read in colleges have made it on their intrinsic merits. To be sure, traditions tend to ossify and also to aggregate superfluous matters, to be taught authoritatively by tiresome persons who do not know why they are important and who hold their jobs because they are virtuosos of trivia. But this only means that the traditions have to be renewed from time to time and the professors made to give an account of themselves.

One of the most obvious cases of a writer used as an authority to bolster what might be called a structure of power is Aristotle during the Christian Middle Ages. Scholasticism was a stifling force which had to be rebelled against in order to free the mind. But to take that Will Durant-like interpretation as exhaustive would be naive. In the first place, Aristotle is something on his own. He survived the wreckage of scholasticism quite nicely and needed no power structure prior to that time or afterward to insure the continuing interest in his works.

Secondly, Aristotle's accession to power was a result of a revolution in Christianity brought about by the explosion of Greek philosophy into Christian Europe. That philosophy had been preserved and renewed among the Muslims, and the challenge of reason to revelation presented by the Muslim philosophers precipitated a crisis in Christianity that was appeased but not entirely resolved by Thomas Aquinas. Here we have a truly interesting case of the relation between the allegedly Western and the allegedly non-Western.

But this is by no means the only case which shows what a grave error it is to accept that the books of the dead white Western male canon are essentially Western—or any of those other things. The fact that I am doubtful about the non-Western craze suggests automatically, even to sympathetic critics, that I am promoting Western Civ or the like. Yet the very language used reveals how enslaved we have become to the historicist assertion that all thought is decisively culture-bound. When Averroes and Thomas Aquinas read Aristotle they did not think of him as Greek and put him into his historical context. They had no interest in Greek Civ but treated him as a wise man, hence a contemporary at all times.

We smile at this naiveté, but they understood Aristotle better than do our scholars, as one can see simply by perusing their commentaries. Plato and Kant claim that they speak to all men everywhere and forever, and I see no reason to reject those claims *a priori.* But that is precisely what is done when they are taken to be parts of Western Civ. To the extent they are merely that, the appeals against them are justified, for Western Civ is clearly partial, demanding the supplement of all the other Civs. The strength of these appeals is thus in their demand for wholeness or completeness of understanding.

Hence, the real, underlying quarrel is *not* about Western and non-Western but about the possibility of philosophy. Nobody, or practically nobody, argues that natural science is essentially Western. Some efforts have been made in that direction, just as some feminists have tried to show that science is essentially male, but these efforts, aside from their admirable sense of the need for theoretical consistency, have not proved persuasive. There is that big rock of transcultural knowledge or truth, natural science, standing in our midst while we chatter on about the cultural basis of all knowledge. A serious non-Western *Putsch* would require that students learn 50 percent non-Western math, 50 percent non-Western physics, 50 percent non-Western biology, and so forth for medicine and engineering. The reformers stop there because they know they would smack up against a brick wall and discredit their whole movement. But philosophy, they say, is not like that. Perhaps, but I have yet to see a serious discussion about wherein it differs. Differ it does today. But qualitatively? That question ought to keep us busy for a long time. Science is surely somehow transcultural. Religion seems pretty much limited to cultures, even to define them. Is philosophy like science, or is it like religion? What we are witnessing is an attempt to drag it away definitively to the camp of religion.

The universities have dealt with this problem by ceding the despised historicized humanities to the political activists and extremists, leaving undisturbed their nonhistoricized scientific disciplines, which is where the meat and the money are. It is a windfall for administrators to be able to turn all the affirmative action complaints over to the humanities, which act as a lightning rod while their ship continues its stately progress over undisturbed waters. Stanford shows its "concerned," "humane," radical face to its inner community, and its serious technical face to the outside community, particularly to its donors. The humanities radicals will settle for this on the calculation that if they can control the minds of the young, they will ultimately gain political control over the power of science.

The serious scholars in non-Western thought should bring us the powerful *texts* they know of to help us. For the true canon aggregates around the most urgent questions we face. That is the only ground for the study of books. Nietzsche did not seek out Socrates because he was part of the classical canon German boys learned in school. He did so in spite of that fact. Socrates was necessary to him as the profoundest statement of what philosophy is and as the worthiest of rivals. Machiavelli was impelled by real need, not by conformism, when he sought out Xenophon. Male, female, black, white, Greek, barbarian—that was all a matter of indifference, as it should be. Nietzsche reflected on Buddha when he wanted to test the principle of contradiction. That is a model of the way things should be. The last thing we need is a sort of philosophic UN run by bureaucrats for the sake of representation for all peoples.

Each must ultimately judge for himself about the important books, but a good beginning would be to see what other thinkers the thinkers who attract him turn to. That will quickly lead to the top. There are very few who remain there, and they recognize each other. There is no conspiracy; only the desire to know. If we allow ourselves to be seduced by the plausible theses of our day, and turn our backs on the great dialogue, our loss will be irreparable.

In my book I connected this radical historicism with fascism and asserted that the thinking of the European Right had wandered over to the Left in America. This earned me severe and unthinking criticism (with the honorable exception of Richard Rorty). It seems to such critics that I am one of those persons who trivialize unique and terrible phenomena by calling anyone whom I dislike a fascist or a Nazi. But I did not call persons active in the sixties those names. I said that the language of the New Left was no longer truly Marxist and had become imbued with the language of fascism. And anyone with an ear for the speech of intellectuals in Weimar Germany will hear echoes all around us of the dangerous ideas to which they became accustomed.

Since the publication of *The Closing of the American Mind,* fortuitously there has been fresh attention paid to the Nazism of Martin Heidegger, more and more widely recognized as the most intelligent figure contributing to the postmodernist movement. At the same time the late Paul de Man, who as a professor at Yale introduced deconstructionism into the U.S., was revealed to have written, as a young man in his native Belgium, pro-Nazi articles for a collaborationist newspaper. In reading these articles I was struck by the fact that if one suppresses the references to Hitler and Hitlerism, much of it sounds like what one reads in advanced literary reviews today.

The lively debate around these issues has not been very helpful, for it focuses more on questions of personal guilt than on the possible relation of Heidegger's or de Man's thought to the foulest political extremism. The fact that de Man had become a leftist after settling in America proves not a thing. He never seems to have passed through a state where he was attracted by reason or liberal democracy. Those who chose culture over civilization, the real opposition, which we have forgotten, were forced to a position beyond good and evil, for to them good and evil were products of cultures.

This, then, is how the contemporary American intellectual scene looks. Much greater events occurring outside the United States, however, demonstrate the urgency of our task. Those events are epitomized by the Statue of Liberty erected by the Chinese students in Tiananmen Square. Apparently, after some discussion about whether it should be altered to have Chinese rather than *Eurocentric* features, there was a consensus that it did not make any difference.

The terror in China continues, and we cannot yet know what will become of those courageous young persons. But we do know the justice of their cause; and although there is no assurance that it will ultimately triumph, their oppressors have won the universal execration of mankind.

With Marxist ideology a wretched shambles everywhere, nobody believes any longer in Communist legitimacy. Everywhere in the Communist world what is wanted is rational liberal democracy that recognizes men's natural freedom and equality and the rights dependent on them. The people of that world need and want education in democracy and the institutions that actualize it. Such education is one of the greatest services the democracies can offer to the people who still live or recently have lived under Communist tyrannies and long for liberty. The example of the United States is what has impressed them most, and their rulers have been unable to stem the infection.

Our example, though, requires explanations, the kind the Founders gave to the world. And this is where we are failing: the dominant schools in American universities can tell the Chinese students only that they should avoid Eurocentrism, that rationalism has failed, that they should study non-Western cultures, and that bourgeois liberalism is the most despicable of regimes. Stanford has replaced John Locke, *the* philosopher of liberalism, with Frantz Fanon, an ephemeral writer once promoted by Jean-Paul Sartre because of his murderous hatred of Europeans and his espousal of terrorism. However, this is not what the Chinese need. They have Deng Xiaoping to deconstruct their Statue of Liberty. We owe them something much better.

Part Four

Multiculturalism
and
Public Education

10

Multiculturalism: E Pluribus Plures

Diane Ravitch

Questions of race, ethnicity, and religion have been a perennial source of conflict in American education. The schools have often attracted the zealous attention of those who wish to influence the future, as well as those who wish to change the way we view the past. In our history, the schools have been not only an institution in which to teach young people skills and knowledge, but an arena where interest groups fight to preserve their values, or to revise the judgments of history, or to bring about fundamental social change. In the nineteenth century, Protestants and Catholics battled over which version of the Bible should be used in school, or whether the Bible should be used at all. In recent decades, bitter racial disputes—provoked by policies of racial segregation and discrimination —have generated turmoil in the streets and in the schools. The secularization of the schools during the past century has prompted attacks on the curricula and textbooks and library books by fundamentalist Christians, who object to whatever challenges their faith-based views of history, literature, and science.

Given the diversity of American society, it has been impossible to insulate the schools from pressures that result from differences and tensions among groups. When people differ about basic values, sooner or later those disagreements turn up in battles about how schools are organized

Reprinted from *The American Scholar* 59, No. 3 (Summer 1990). Copyright © 1990 by Diane Ravitch. By permission of the publisher.

or what the schools should teach. Sometimes these battles remove a terrible injustice, like racial segregation. Sometimes, however, interest groups politicize the curriculum and attempt to impose their views on teachers, school officials, and textbook publishers. Across the country, even now, interest groups are pressuring local school boards to remove myths and fables and other imaginative literature from children's readers and to inject the teaching of creationism in biology. When groups cross the line into extremism, advancing their own agenda without regard to reason or to others, they threaten public education itself, making it difficult to teach any issues honestly and making the entire curriculum vulnerable to political campaigns.

For many years, the public schools attempted to neutralize controversies over race, religion, and ethnicity by ignoring them. Educators believed, or hoped, that the schools could remain outside politics; this was, of course, a vain hope since the schools were pursuing policies based on race, religion, and ethnicity. Nonetheless, such divisive questions were usually excluded from the curriculum. The textbooks minimized problems among groups and taught a sanitized version of history. Race, religion, and ethnicity were presented as minor elements in the American saga; slavery was treated as an episode, immigration as a sidebar, and women were largely absent. The textbooks concentrated on presidents, wars, national politics, and issues of state. An occasional "great black" or "great woman" received mention, but the main narrative paid little attention to minority groups and women.

With the ethnic revival of the 1960s, this approach to the teaching of history came under fire, because the history of national leaders—virtually all of whom were white, Anglo-Saxon, and male—ignored the place in American history of those who were none of the above. The traditional history of elites had been complemented by an assimilationist view of American society, which presumed that everyone in the American melting pot would eventually lose or abandon those ethnic characteristics that distinguished them from mainstream Americans. The ethnic revival demonstrated that many groups did not want to be assimilated or melted. Ethnic studies programs popped up on campuses to teach not only that "black is beautiful," but also that every other variety of ethnicity is "beautiful" as well; everyone who had "roots" began to look for them so that they too could recover that ancestral past of themselves that had not been homogenized.

As ethnicity became an accepted subject for study in the late 1960s, textbooks were assailed for their failure to portray blacks accurately; within a few years, the textbooks in wide use were carefully screened to eliminate bias against minority groups and women. At the same time, new scholarship about the history of women, blacks, and various ethnic minorities found its way into the textbooks. At first, the multicultural content was awkwardly incorporated as little boxes on the side of the main narrative. Then some of the new social historians (like Stephan Thernstrom, Mary Beth Norton, Gary Nash, Winthrop Jordan, and Leon Litwack) themselves wrote textbooks, and the main narrative itself began to reflect a broadened historical understanding of race, ethnicity, and class in the American past. Consequently, today's history textbooks routinely incorporate the experiences of women, blacks, American Indians, and various immigrant groups.

Although most high school textbooks are deeply unsatisfactory (they still largely neglect religion, they are too long, too encyclopedic, too superficial, and lacking in narrative flow), they are far more sensitive to pluralism than their predecessors. For example, the latest edition of Todd and Curti's *Triumph of the American Nation,* the most popular high school history text, has significantly increased its coverage of blacks in America, including profiles of Phillis Wheatley, the poet; James Armistead, a revolutionary war spy for Lafayette; Benjamin Banneker, a self-taught scientist and mathematician; Hiram Revels, the first black to serve in the Congress; and Ida B. Wells-Barnett, a tireless crusader against lynching and racism. Even better as a textbook treatment is Jordan and Litwack's *The United States,* which skillfully synthesizes the historical experiences of blacks, Indians, immigrants, women, and other groups into the mainstream of American social and political history. The latest generation of textbooks bluntly acknowledges the racism of the past, describing the struggle for equality by racial minorities while identifying individuals who achieved success as political leaders, doctors, lawyers, scholars, entrepreneurs, teachers, and scientists.

As a result of the political and social changes of recent decades, cultural pluralism is now generally recognized as an organizing principle of this society. In contrast to the idea of the melting pot, which promised to erase ethnic and group differences, children now learn that variety is the spice of life. They learn that America has provided a haven for many different groups and has allowed them to maintain their cultural heritage or to assimilate, or—as is often the case—to do both; the choice is theirs, not the state's. They learn that cultural pluralism is one of the norms of a free society; that differences among groups are a national resource rather than a problem to be solved. Indeed, the unique feature of the United States is that its common culture has been formed by the interaction of its subsidiary cultures. It is a culture that has been influenced over time by immigrants, American Indians, Africans (slave and free) and by their descendants. American music, art, literature, language, food, clothing, sports, holidays, and customs all show the effects of the commingling of diverse cultures in one nation. Paradoxical though it may seem, the United States has a common culture that is multicultural.

Our schools and our institutions of higher learning have in recent years begun to embrace what Catherine R. Stimpson of Rutgers University has called "cultural democracy," a recognition that we must listen to a "diversity of voices" in order to understand our culture, past and present. This understanding of the pluralistic nature of American culture has taken a long time to forge. It is based on sound scholarship and has led to major revisions in what children are taught and what they read in school. The new history is—indeed, must be—a warts-and-all history; it demands an unflinching examination of racism and discrimination in our history. Making these changes is difficult, raises tempers, and ignites controversies, but gives a more interesting and accurate account of American history. Accomplishing these changes is valuable, because there is also a useful lesson for the rest of the world in America's relatively successful experience as a pluralistic society. Throughout human history, the clash of different cultures, races, ethnic groups, and religions has often been the cause of bitter hatred, civil conflict, and international war. The ethnic tensions that now are tearing apart Lebanon, Sri Lanka, Kashmir, and various republics of the Soviet Union remind us of the costs of unfettered group rivalry. Thus, it is a matter of more than domestic importance that we closely examine and try to understand that part of our national history in which different groups competed, fought, suffered, but ultimately learned to live together in relative peace and even achieved a sense of common nationhood.

Alas, these painstaking efforts to expand the understanding of American culture into a richer and more varied tapestry have taken a new turn, and not for the better. Almost any idea, carried to its extreme, can be made pernicious, and this is what is happening now to multiculturalism. Today, pluralistic multiculturalism must contend with a new, particularistic multiculturalism. The pluralists seek a richer common culture, the particularists insist that no common culture is possible or desirable. The new particularism is entering the curriculum in a number of school systems across the country. Advocates of particularism propose an ethnocentric curriculum to raise the self-esteem and academic achievements of children from racial and ethnic minority backgrounds. Without any evidence, they claim that children from minority backgrounds will do well in school *only* if they are immersed in a positive, prideful version of their ancestral culture.

If children are of, for example, Fredonian ancestry, they must hear that Fredonians were important in mathematics, science, history, and literature. If they learn about great Fredonians and if their studies use Fredonian examples and Fredonian concepts, they will do well in school. If they do not, they will have low self-esteem and will do badly.

At first glance, this appears akin to the celebratory activities associated with Black History Month or Women's History Month, when schoolchildren learn about the achievements of blacks and women. But the point of those celebrations is to demonstrate that neither race nor gender is an obstacle to high achievement. They teach all children that everyone, regardless of their race, religion, gender, ethnicity, or family origin, can achieve self-fulfillment, honor, and dignity in society if they aim high and work hard.

By contrast, the particularistic version of multiculturalism is unabashedly filiopietistic and deterministic. It teaches children that their identity is determined by their "cultural genes." That something in their blood or their race memory or their cultural DNA defines who they are and what they may achieve. That the culture in which they live is not their own culture, even though they were born here. That American culture is "Eurocentric," and therefore hostile to anyone whose ancestors are not European. Perhaps the most invidious implication of particularism is that racial and ethnic minorities are not and should not try to be part of American cultutre; it implies that American culture belongs only to those who are white and European; it implies that those who are neither white nor European are alienated from American culture by virtue of their race or ethnicity; it implies that the only culture they do belong to or can ever belong to is the culture of their ancestors, even if their families have lived in this country for generations.

The war on so-called Eurocentrism is intended to foster self-esteem among those who are not of European descent. But how, in fact, is self-esteem developed? How is the sense of one's own possibilities, one's potential choices, developed? Certainly, the school curriculum plays a relatively small role as compared to the influence of family, community, mass media, and society. But to the extent that curriculum influences what children think of themselves, it should encourage children of all racial and ethnic groups to believe that they are part of this society and that they should develop their talents and minds to the fullest. It is enormously inspiring, for example, to learn about men and women from diverse backgrounds who overcame poverty, discrimination, physical handicaps, and other obstacles to achieve success in a variety of fields. Behind every such biography of accomplishments is a story of heroism, perseverance, and self-discipline. Learning these stories will encourage a healthy spirit of pluralism, of mutual respect, and of self-respect among children of different backgrounds. The children of American society today will live their lives in a racially and cuturally diverse nation, and their education should prepare them to do so.

The pluralistic approach to multiculturalism promotes a broader interpretation of the common American culture and seeks due recognition for the ways that the nation's many racial, ethnic, and cultural groups have transformed the national culture. The pluralists say, in effect, "American culture belongs to us, all of us; the U.S. is us, and we remake it in every generation." But particularists have no interest in extending or revising American culture; indeed, they deny that a common culture exists. Particularists reject any accommodation among groups, any interactions that blur the distinctions between them. The brand of history that they espouse is one in which everyone is a descendant of either victims or oppressors. By doing so, ancient hatreds are fanned and recreated in each new generation. Particularism has its intellectual roots in the ideology of ethnic separatism and in the black nationalist movement. In the particularist analysis, the nation has five cultures: African American, Asian American, European American, Latin/Hispanic, and Native American. The huge cultural, historical, religious, and linguistic differences within these categories are ignored, as is the considerable intermarriage among these groups, as are the linkages (like gender, class, sexual orientation, and religion) that cut across these five groups. No serious scholar would claim that all Europeans and white Americans are part of the same culture or that all Asians are part of the same culture, or that people of Latin-American descent are of the same culture, or that all people of African descent are of the same culture. Any categorization this broad is essentially meaningless and useless.

Several districts—including Detroit, Atlanta, and Washington, D.C. —are developing an Afrocentric curriculum. *Afrocentricity* has been described in a book of the same name by Moleh Kete Asante of Temple University. The Afrocentric curriculum puts Africa at the center of the students' universe. African Americans must "move away from an [sic] Eurocentric framework" because "it is difficult to create freely when you use someone else's motifs, styles, images, and perspectives." Because they are not Africans, "white teachers cannot inspire in our children the visions necessary for them to overcome limitations." Asante recommends that African Americans choose an African name (as he did), reject European dress, embrace African religion (not Islam or Christianity) and love "their own" culture. He scorns the ideas of universality as a form of Eurocentric arrogance. The Eurocentrist, he says, thinks of Beethoven or Bach as classical, but the Afrocentrist thinks of Ellington or Coltrane as classical; the Eurocentrist lauds Shakespeare or Twain, while the Afrocentrist prefers Baraka, Shange, or Abiola. Asante is critical of black artists like Arthur Mitchell and Alvin Ailey who ignore Afrocentricity. Likewise, he speaks contemptuously of a group of black university students who spurned the Afrocentrism of the local Black Student Union and formed an organization called Inter-race: "Such madness is the direct consequence of self-hatred, obligatory attitudes, false assumptions about society, and stupidity."

The conflict between pluralism and particularism turns on the issue of universalism. Professor Asante warns his readers against the lure of universalism: "Do not be captured by a sense of universality given to you by the Eurocentric viewpoint; such a viewpoint is contradictory to your own ultimate reality." He insists that there is no alternative to Eurocentrism, Afrocentrism, and other ethnocentrisms. In contrast, the pluralist says, with the Roman playwright Terrence, "I am a man: nothing human is alien to me." A contemporary Terrence would say "I am a person" or might be a woman, but the point remains the same: You don't have to be black to love Zora Neale Hurston's fiction or Langston Hughes's poetry or Duke Ellington's music. In a pluralist curriculum, we expect children to learn a broad and humane culture, to learn about the ideas and art and animating spirit of many cultures. We expect that children, whatever their color, will be inspired by the courage of people like Helen Keller, Vaclav Havel, Harriet Tubman, and Feng Lizhe. We expect that their response to literature will be determined by the ideas and images it evokes, not only by the skin color of the writer. But particularists insist that children can learn only from the experiences of people from the same race.

Particularism is a bad idea whose time has come. It is also a fashion spreading like wildfire through the education system, actively promoted by organizations and individuals with a political and professional interest in strengthening ethnic power bases in the university, in the education profession, and in society itself. One can scarcely pick up an educational journal without learning about a school district that is converting to an ethnocentric curriculum in an attempt to give "self-esteem" to children from racial minorities. A state-funded project in a Sacramento high school is teaching young black males to think like Africans and develop the "African Mind Model Technique," in order to free themselves of the racism of American culture. A popular black rap singer, KRS-One, complained in an op-ed article in the *New York Times* that the schools should be teaching blacks about their cultural heritage, instead of trying to make everyone Americans. "It's like trying to teach a dog to be a cat," he wrote. KRS-One railed about having to learn about Thomas Jefferson and the Civil War, which had nothing to do (he said) with black history.

Pluralism can easily be transformed into particularism, as may be seen in the potential uses in the classroom of the Mayan contribution to mathematics. The Mayan example was popularized in a movie called *Stand and Deliver,* about a charismatic Bolivian-born mathematics teacher in Los Angeles who inspired his students (who are Hispanic) to learn calculus. He told them that their ancestors invented the concept of zero; but that wasn't all he did. He used imagination to put across mathematical concepts. He required them to do homework and to go to school on Saturdays and during the Christmas holidays, so that they might pass the Advanced Placement mathematics examination for college entry. The teacher's reference to the Mayans' mathematical genius was a valid instructional device: It was an attention-getter and would have interested even students who were not Hispanic. But the Mayan example would have had little effect without the teacher's insistence that the class study hard for a difficult examination.

Ethnic educators have seized upon the Mayan contribution to mathematics as the key to simultaneously boosting the ethnic pride of Hispanic children and attacking Eurocentrism. One proposal claims that Mexican-American children will be attracted to science and mathematics if they study Mayan mathematics, the Mayan calendar, and Mayan astronomy. Children in primary grades are to be taught that the Mayans were first to discover the zero and that Europeans learned it long afterwards from the Arabs, who had learned it in India. This will help them see that Europeans were latecomers in the discovery of great ideas. Botany is to be learned by study of the agricultural techniques of the Aztecs, a subject of somewhat limited relevance to children in urban areas. Furthermore, "ethnobotanical" classifications of plants are to be substituted for the Eurocentric Linnaean system. At first glance, it may seem curious that Hispanic children are deemed to have no cultural affinity with Spain; but to acknowledge the cultural tie would confuse the ideological assault on Eurocentrism.

This proposal suggests some questions: Is there any evidence that the teaching of "culturally relevant" science and mathematics will draw Mexican-American children to the study of these subjects? Will Mexican-American children lose interest or self-esteem if they discover that their ancestors were Aztecs or Spaniards, rather than Mayans? Are children who learn in this way prepared to study the science and mathematics that are taught in American colleges and universities and that are needed for advanced study in these fields? Are they even prepared to study the science and mathematics taught in *Mexican* universities? If the class is half Mexican-American and half something else, will only the Mexican-American children study in a Mayan and Aztec mode or will all the children? But shouldn't all children study what is culturally relevant for them? How will we train teachers who have command of so many different systems of mathematics and science?

The efficacy of particularist proposals seems to be less important to their sponsors than their value as ideological weapons with which to criticize existing disciplines for their alleged Eurocentric bias. In a recent article entitled "The Ethnocentric Basis of Social Science Knowledge Production" in the *Review of Research in Education*, John Stanfield of Yale University argues that neither social science nor science are objective studies, that both instead are "Euro-American" knowledge systems which reproduce "hegemonic racial domination." The claim that science and reason are somehow superior to magic and witchcraft, he writes, is the product of Euro-American ethnocentrism. According to Stanfield, current fears about the misuse of science (for instance, "the nuclear arms race, global pollution") and the "power-plays of Third World nations (the Arab oil boycott and the American-Iranian hostage crisis) have made Western people more aware of nonscientific cognitive styles. These last events are beginning to demonstrate politically that which has begun to be understood in intellectual circles: namely, that modes of social knowledge such as theology, science, and magic are different, not inferior or superior. They represent different ways of perceiving, defining, and organizing knowledge of life experiences." One wonders: If Professor Stanfield broke his leg, would he go to a theologian, a doctor, or a magician?

Every field of study, it seems, has been tainted by Eurocentrism, which was defined by a professor at Manchester University, George Ghevarughese Joseph, in *Race and Class* in 1987, as "intellectual racism." Professor Joseph argues that the history of science and technology—and in particular, of mathematics—in non-European societies was distorted by racist Europeans who wanted to establish the dominance of European forms of knowledge. The racists, he writes, traditionally traced mathematics to the Greeks, then claimed that it reached its full development in Europe. These are simply Eurocentric myths to sustain an "imperialist/ racist theology," says Professor Joseph, since mathematics was found in Egypt, Babylonia, Mesopotamia, and India long before the Greeks were supposed to have developed it. Professor Joseph points out too that Arab scientists should be credited with major discoveries traditionally attributed to William Harvey, Isaac Newton, Charles Darwin, and Sir Francis Bacon. But he is not concerned only to argue historical issues; his purpose is to bring all of these different mathematical traditions into the school classrooms so that children might study, for example, "traditional African designs, Indian *rangoli* patterns and Islamic art" and "the language and counting systems found across the world."

This interesting proposal to teach ethnomathematics comes at a time when American mathematical educators are trying to overhaul present practices, because of the poor performance of American children on national and international assessments. Mathematics educators are attempting to change the teaching of their subject so that children can see its uses in everyday life. There would seem to be an incipient conflict between those who want to introduce real-life applications of mathematics and those who want to teach the mathematical systems used by ancient cultures. I suspect that most mathematics teachers would enjoy doing a bit of both, if there were time or student interest. But any widespread movement to replace modern mathematics with ancient ethnic mathematics runs the risk of disaster in a field that is struggling to update coexisting curricula. If, as seems likely, ancient mathematics is taught mainly to minority children, the gap between them and middle-class white children is apt to grow. It is worth noting that children in Korea, who score highest in mathematics on international assessments, do not study ancient Korean mathematics.

Particularism is akin to cultural Lysenkoism, for it takes as its premise the spurious notion that cultural traits are inherited. It implies a dubious, dangerous form of cultural predestination. Children are taught that if their ancestors could do it, so could they. But what happens if a child is from a cultural group that made no significant contribution to science or mathematics? Does this mean that children from that background must find a culturally appropriate field in which to survive? How does a teacher find the right cultural buttons for children of mixed heritage? And how in the world will teachers use this technique when the children in their classes are drawn from many different cultures, as is usually the case? By the time that every culture gets its due, there may be no time left to teach the subject itself. This explosion of filiopietism (which, we should remember, comes from adults, not from students) is reminiscent of the period some years ago when the Russians claimed that they had invented everything first; as we now know, this nationalist braggadocio did little for their self-esteem and nothing for their economic development. We might reflect, too, on how little social prestige has been accorded in this country to immigrants from Greece and Italy, even though the achievements of their ancestors were at the heart of the classical curriculum.

Filiopietism and ethnic boosterism lead to all sorts of odd practices. In New York State, for example, the curriculum guide for eleventh grade

American history lists three "foundations" for the United States Constitution, as follows:

A. Foundations
  1. Seventeenth- and eighteenth-century Enlightenment thought
  2. Haudenosaunee political system
      a. Influence upon colonial leadership and European intellectuals (Locke, Montesquieu, Voltaire, Rousseau)
      b. Impact on Albany Plan of Union, Articles of Confederation, and U.S. Constitution
  3. Colonial experience

Those who are unfamiliar with the Haudenosaunee political system might wonder what it is, particularly since educational authorities in New York State rank it as equal in importance to the European Enlightenment and suggest that it strongly influenced not only colonial leaders but the leading intellectuals of Europe. The Haudenosaunee political system was the Iroquois confederation of five (later six) Indian tribes in upper New York State, which conducted war and civil affairs through a council of chiefs, each with one vote. In 1754, Benjamin Franklin proposed a colonial union at a conference in Albany; his plan, said to be inspired by the Iroquois Confederation, was rejected by the other colonies. Today, Indian activists believe that the Iroquois Confederation was the model for the American Constitution, and the New York State Department of Education has decided that they are right. That no other state sees fit to give the American Indians equal billing with the European Enlightenment may be owing to the fact that the Indians in New York State (numbering less than forty thousand) have been more politically effective than elsewhere or that other states have not yet learned about this method of reducing "Eurocentrism" in their American history classes.

Particularism can easily be carried to extremes. Students of Fredonian descent must hear that their ancestors were seminal in the development of all human civilization and that without the Fredonian contribution, we would all be living in caves or trees, bereft of art, technology, and culture. To explain why Fredonians today are in modest circumstances, given their historic eminence, children are taught that somewhere, long ago, another culture stole the Fredonians' achievements, palmed them off as their own, and then oppressed the Fredonians.

I first encountered this argument almost twenty years ago, when I was a graduate student. I shared a small office with a young professor, and I listened as she patiently explained to a student why she had given him a D on a term paper. In his paper, he argued that the Arabs had stolen mathematics from the Nubians in the desert long ago (I forget in which century this theft allegedly occurred). She tried to explain to him about the necessity of historical evidence. He was unconvinced, since he believed that he had uncovered a great truth that was beyond proof. The part I couldn't understand was how anyone could lose knowledge by sharing it. After all, cultures are constantly influencing one another, exchanging ideas and art and technology, and the exchange usually is enriching, not depleting.

Today, there are a number of books and articles advancing controversial theories about the origins of civilization. An important work, *The African Origin of Civilization: Myth or Reality,* by Senegalese scholar Cheikh Anta Diop, argues that ancient Eygpt was a black civilization, that all races are descended from the black race, and that the achievements of "western" civilization originated in Egypt. The views of Diop and other Africanists have been condensed into an everyman's paperback titled *What They Never Told You in History Class* by Indus Khamit Kush. This latter book claims that Moses, Jesus, Buddha, Mohammed, and Vishnu were Africans; that the first Indians, Chinese, Hebrews, Greeks, Romans, Britains, and Americans were Africans; and that the first mathematicians, scientists, astronomers, and physicians were Africans. A debate currently raging among some classicists is whether the Greeks "stole" the philosophy, art, and religion of the ancient Egyptians and whether the ancient Egyptians were black Africans. George G. M. James's *Stolen Legacy* insists that the Greeks "stole the Legacy of the African Continent and called it their own." James argues that the civilization of Greece, the vaunted foundation of European culture, owed everything it knew and did to its African predecessors. Thus, the roots of Western civilization lie not in Greece and Rome, but in Egypt, and, ultimately, in black Africa.

Similar speculation was fueled by the publication in 1987 of Martin Bernal's *Black Athena: The Afroasiatic Roots of Classical Civilization,* Volume 1, *The Fabrication of Ancient Greece, 1785–1985,* although the controversy predates Bernal's book. In a fascinating foray into the politics of knowledge, Bernal attributes the preference of Western European scholars for Greece over Egypt as the fount of knowledge to nearly two centuries of racism and "Europocentrism," but he is uncertain about the color of the ancient Egyptians. However, a review of Bernal's book last year in the *Village Voice* began, "What color were the ancient Egyptians? Blacker than Mubarak, baby." The same article claimed that white racist archeologists chiseled the noses off ancient Egyptian statues so that future generations would not see the typically African facial characteristics. The debate reached the pages of the *Biblical Archeology Review* last year in an article titled "Were the Ancient Egyptians Black or White?" The author, classicist Frank J. Yurco, argues that some Egyptian rulers were black, others were not, and that "the ancient Egyptians did not think in these terms." The issue, wrote Yurco, "is a chimera, cultural baggage from our own society that can only be imposed artificially on ancient Egyptian society."

Most educationists are not even aware of the debate about whether the ancient Egyptians were black or white, but they are very sensitive to charges that the schools' curricula are Eurocentric, and they are eager to rid the schools of the taint of Eurocentrism. It is hardly surprising that America's schools would recognize strong cultural ties with Europe since our nation's political, religious, educational, and economic institutions were created chiefly by people of European descent, our government was shaped by European ideas, and nearly 80 percent of the people who live here are of European descent. The particularists treat all this history as a racist bias toward Europe, rather than as the matter-of-fact consequences of European immigration. Even so, American education is not centered on Europe. American education, if it is centered on anything, is centered on itself. It is "Americentric." Most American students today have never studied any world history; they know very little about Europe, and even less about the rest of the world. Their minds are rooted solidly in the here and now. When the Berlin Wall was opened in the fall of 1989, journalists discovered that most American teen-agers had no idea what it was, nor why its opening was such a big deal. Nonetheless, Eurocentrism provides a better target than Americentrism.

In school districts where most children are black and Hispanic, there has been a growing tendency to embrace particularism, rather than pluralism. Many of the children in these districts perform poorly in academic classes and leave school without graduating. They would fare better in school if they had well-educated and well-paid teachers, small classes, good materials, encouragement at home and school, summer academic programs, protection from the drugs and crime that ravage their neighborhoods, and higher expectations of satisfying careers upon graduation. These are expensive and time-consuming remedies that must also engage the larger society beyond the school. The lure of particularism is that it offers a less complicated anodyne, one in which the children's academic deficiencies may be addressed—or set aside—by inflating their racial pride. The danger of this remedy is that it will detract attention from the real needs of schools and the real interests of children, while simultaneously arousing distorted race pride in children of all races, increasing racial antagonism and producing fresh recruits for white and black racist groups.

The particularist critique gained a major forum in New York in 1989, with the release of a report called "A Curriculum of Inclusion," produced by a task force created by the State Commissioner of Education, Thomas Sobol. In 1987, soon after his appointment, Sobol appointed a Task Force on Minorities to review the state's curriculum for instances of bias. He did this not because there had been complaints about bias in the curriculum, but because—as a newly appointed state commissioner whose previous job had been to superintend the public schools of a wealthy suburb, Scarsdale—he wanted to demonstrate his sensitivity to minority concerns. The Sobol task force was composed of representatives of African American, Hispanic, Asian American, and American Indian groups.

The task force engaged four consultants, one from each of the aforementioned racial or ethnic minorities, to review nearly one hundred teachers' guides prepared by the state. These guides define the state's curriculum, usually as a list of facts and concepts to be taught, along with model activities. The primary focus of the consultants, not surprisingly, was the history and social studies curriculum. As it happened, the history curriculum had been extensively revised in 1987 to make it multicultural, in both American and world history. In the 1987 revision the time given to Western Europe was reduced to one-quarter of the year, as part of a two-year global studies sequence in which equal time was allotted to seven major world regions, including Africa and Latin America.

As a result of the 1987 revision in American and world history, New York State had one of the most advanced multicultural history–social studies curricula in the country. Dozens of social studies teachers and consultants had participated, and the final draft was reviewed by such historians as Eric Foner of Columbia University, the late Hazel Hertzberg of Teachers College, Columbia University, and Christopher Lasch of the University of Rochester. The curriculum was overloaded with facts, almost to the point of numbing students with details and trivia, but it was not insensitive to ethnicity in American history or unduly devoted to European history.

But the Sobol task force decided that this curriculum was biased and Eurocentric. The first sentence of the task force report summarizes its major thesis: "African Americans, Asian Americans, Puerto Ricans/Latinos, and Native Americans have all been the victims of an intellectual and educational oppression that has characterized the culture and institutions of the United States and the European American world for centuries."

The task force report was remarkable in that it vigorously denounced bias without identifying a single instance of bias in the curricular guides under review. Instead, the consultants employed harsh, sometimes inflammatory, rhetoric to treat every difference of opinion or interpretation as an example of racial bias. The African-American consultant, for example, exorciates the curriculum for its "White Anglo-Saxon (WASP) value system and norms," its "deep-seated pathologies of racial hatred" and its "white nationalism"; he decries as bias the fact that children study Egypt as part of the Middle East instead of as part of Africa. Perhaps Egypt should be studied as part of the African unit (geographically, it is located on the African continent); but placing it in one region rather than the other is not what most people think of as racism or bias. The "Latino" consultant criticizes the use of the term "Spanish-American War" instead of "Spanish-Cuban-American War." The Native American consultant complains that tribal languages are classified as "foreign languages."

The report is consistently Europhobic. It repeatedly expresses negative judgments on "European Americans" and on everything Western and European. All people with a white skin are referred to as "Anglo-Saxons" and "WASPs." Europe, says the report, is uniquely responsible for producing aggressive individuals who "were ready to 'discover, invade and conquer' foreign land because of greed, racism and national egoism." All white people are held collectively guilty for the historical crimes of slavery and racism. There is no mention of the "Anglo-Saxons" who opposed slavery and racism. Nor does the report acknowledge that some whites have been victims of discrimination and oppression. The African-American consultant writes of the Constitution, "There is something vulgar and revolting in glorifying a process that heaped undeserved rewards on a segment of the population while oppressing the majority."

The New York task force proposal is not merely about the reconstruction of what is taught. It goes a step further to suggest that the history curriculum may be used to ensure that "children from Native American, Puerto Rican/Latino, Asian American, and African American cultures will have higher self-esteem and self-respect, while children from European cultures will have a less arrogant perspective of being part of the group that has 'done it all.' "

In February of 1990, Commissioner Sobol asked the New York Board of Regents to endorse a sweeping revision of the history curriculum to make it more multicultural. His recommendations were couched in measured tones, not in the angry rhetoric of his task force. The board supported his request unanimously. It remains to be seen whether New York pursues the particularist path marked out by the Commissioner's advisory group or finds its way to the concept of pluralism within a democratic tradition.

The rising tide of particularism encourages the politicization of all curricula in the schools. If education bureaucrats bend to the political and ideological winds, as is their wont, we can anticipate a generation of struggle over the content of the curriculum in mathematics, science, literature, and history. Demands for "culturally relevant" studies, for ethnostudies of all kinds, will open the classroom to unending battles over whose version is taught, who gets credit for what, and which ethno-interpretation is appropriate. Only recently have districts begun to resist the demands of fundamentalist groups to censor textbooks and library books (and some have not yet begun to do so).

The spread of particularism throws into question the very idea of American public education. Public schools exist to teach children the general skills and knowledge that they need to succeed in American society, and the specific skills and knowledge that they need in order to function as American citizens. They receive public support because they have a public function. Historically, the public schools were known as "common schools" because they were schools for all, even if the children of all the people did not attend them. Over the years, the courts have found that it was unconstitutional to teach religion in the common schools, or to separate children on the basis of their race in the common schools. In their curriculum, their hiring practices, and their general philosophy, the public schools must not discriminate against or give preference to any racial or ethnic group. Yet they are permitted to accommodate cultural diversity by, for example, serving food that is culturally appropriate or providing library collections that emphasize the interests of the local community. However, they should not be expected to teach children to view the world through an ethnocentric perspective that rejects or ignores the common culture. For generations, those groups that wanted to inculcate their religion or their ethnic heritage have instituted private schools—after school, on weekends, or on a full-time basis. There, children learn with others of the same group—Greeks, Poles, Germans, Japanese, Chinese, Jews, Lutherans, Catholics, and so on—and are taught by people from the same group. Valuable as this exclusive experience has been for those who choose it, this has not been the role of public education. One of the primary purposes of public education has been to create a national community, a definition of citizenship and culture that is both expansive and *inclusive*.

This curriculum in public schools must be based on whatever knowledge and practices have been determined to be best by professionals—

experienced teachers and scholars—who are competent to make these judgments. Professional societies must be prepared to defend the integrity of their disciplines. When called upon, they should establish review committees to examine disputes over curriculum and to render judgment, in order to help school officials fend off improper political pressure. Where genuine controversies exist, they should be taught and debated in the classroom. Was Egypt a black civilization? Why not raise the question, read the arguments of the different sides in the debate, show slides of Egyptian pharaohs and queens, read books about life in ancient Egypt, invite guest scholars from the local university, and visit museums with Egyptian collections? If scholars disagree, students should know it. One great advantage of this approach is that students will see that history is a lively study, that textbooks are fallible, that historians disagree, that the writing of history is influenced by the historian's politics and ideology, that history is written by people who make choices among alternative facts and interpretations, and that history changes as new facts are uncovered and new interpretations win adherents. They will also learn that cultures and civilizations constantly interact, exchange ideas, and influence one another, and that the idea of racial or ethnic purity is a myth. Another advantage is that students might once again study ancient history, which has all but disappeared from the curricula of American schools. (California recently introduced a required sixth grade course in ancient civilizations, but ancient history is otherwise *terra incognita* in American education.)

The multicultural controversy may do wonders for the study of history, which has been neglected for years in American schools. At this time, only half of our high school graduates ever study any world history. Any serious attempt to broaden students' knowledge of Africa, Europe, Asia, and Latin America will require at least two, and possibly three years of world history (a requirement thus far only in California). American history, too, will need more time than the one-year high-school survey course. Those of us who have insisted for years on the importance of history in the curriculum may not be ready to assent to its redemptive power, but hope that our new allies will ultimately join a constructive dialogue that strengthens the place of history in the schools.

As cultural controversies arise, educators must adhere to the principle of "E Pluribus Unum." That is, they must maintain a balance between the demands of the one—the nation of which we are common citizens— and the many—the varied histories of the American people. It is not necessary to denigrate either the one or the many. Pluralism is a positive value, but it is also important that we preserve a sense of an American community—a society and a culture to which we all belong. If there is no overall community with an agreed-upon vision of liberty and justice, if we all have a collection of racial and ethnic cultures, lacking any common bonds, then we have no means to mobilize public opinion on behalf of people who are not members of our particular group. We have, for example, no reason to support public education. If there is no larger community, then each group will want to teach its own children in its own way, and public education ceases to exist.

History should not be confused with filiopietism. History gives no grounds for race pride. No race has a monopoly on virtue. If anything, a study of history should inspire humility, rather than pride. People of every racial group have committed terrible crimes, often against others of the same group. Whether one looks at the history of Europe or Africa or Latin America or Asia, every continent offers examples of inhumanity. Slavery has existed in civilizations around the world for centuries. Examples of genocide can be found around the world, throughout history, from ancient times right through to our own day. Governments and cultures, sometimes by edict, sometimes simply following tradition, have practiced not only slavery, but human sacrifice, infanticide, cliterodectomy, and mass murder. If we teach children this, they might recognize how absurd both racial hatred and racial chauvinism are.

What must be preserved in the study of history is the spirit of inquiry, the readiness to open new questions and to pursue new understandings. History, at its best, is a search for truth. The best way to portray this search is through debate and controversy, rather than through points of fixed beliefs and multiple facts. Perhaps the most dangerous aspect of school history is its tendency to become Official History, a sanctified version of the Truth taught by the state to captive audiences and embedded in beautiful mass-market textbooks as holy writ. When Official History is written by committees responding to political pressures, rather than by scholars synthesizing the best available research, then the errors of the past are replaced by the politically fashionable errors of the present. It may be difficult to teach children that history is both important and uncertain, and that even the best historians never have all the pieces of the jigsaw puzzle, but it is necessary to do so. If state education departments permit the revision of their history courses and textbooks to become an exercise in power politics, then the entire process of state-level curriculum-making becomes suspect, as does public education itself.

The question of self-esteem is extraordinarily complex, and it goes well beyond the content of the curriculum. Most of what we call self-esteem is formed in the home and in a variety of life experiences, not only in school. Nonetheless, it has been important for blacks—and for other racial groups—to learn about the history of slavery and of the civil rights movement; it has been important for blacks to know that their ancestors actively resisted enslavement and actively pursued equality; and it has been important for blacks and others to learn about black men and women who fought courageously against racism and who provide models of courage, persistence, and intellect. These are instances where the content of the curriculum reflects sound scholarship, and at the same time probably lessens racial prejudice and provides inspiration for those who are descendants of slaves. But knowing about the travails and triumphs of one's forebears does not necessarily translate into either self-esteem or personal accomplishment. For most children, self-esteem—the self-confidence that grows out of having reached a goal—comes not from learning about the monuments of their ancestors but as a consequence of what they are able to do and accomplish through their own efforts.

As I reflected on these issues, I recalled reading an interview a few years ago with a talented black runner. She said that her model is Mikhail Baryshnikov. She admires him because he is a magnificent athlete. He is not black; he is not female; he is not American-born; he is not even a runner. But he inspires her because of the way he trained and used his body. When I read this, I thought how narrow-minded it is to believe that people can be inspired *only* by those who are exactly like them in race and ethnicity.

11

Multiculturalism without Hierarchy: An Afrocentric Reply to Diane Ravitch

Molefi Kete Asante

We are all implicated in the positions we hold about society, culture, and education. Although the implications may take quite different forms in some fields and with some scholars, such as the consequences and our methods and inquiry on our systems of values, we are nevertheless captives of the positions we take, that is, if we take those positions honestly.

In a recent article in the *American Scholar* (Summer 1990), Diane Ravitch reveals the tensions between scholarship and ideological perspectives in an exceedingly clear manner. The positions taken in her article "Multiculturalism: E Pluribus Plures" accurately demonstrates the thesis that those of us who write are implicated in what we choose to write. This is not a profound announcement since most fields of inquiry recognize that a researcher's presence must be accounted for in research or a historian's relationship to data must be examined in seeking to establish the validity of conclusions. This is not to say that the judgment will be invalid because of the intimacy of the scholar with the information but rather that in accounting for the scholar's or researcher's presence we are likely to know better how to assess the information presented. Just as a researcher may

Reprinted from *The American Scholar* 60, No. 25 (Spring 1991). Copyright © 1991 by Molefi Kefe Asante. By permission of the publisher. Molefi Kefe Asante is professor and chair of the African American Studies Department, Temple University, and the founder of the Afrocentric School of Thought.

be considered an intrusive presence in an experiment, the biases of a scholar may be just as intrusive in interpreting data or making analysis. The fact that a writer seeks to establish a persona of a noninterested observer means that such a writer wants the reader to assume that an unbiased position is being taken on a subject. However, we know that as soon as a writer states a proposition, the writer is implicated and such implication holds minor or extreme consequences.

The remarkable advantage of stating aims and objectives prior to delivering an argument is that the reader knows precisely to what the author is driving. Unfortunately, too many writers on education either do not know the point they are making or lose sight of their point in the making. Such regrettably is the case with Diane Ravitch's article on multicultural education.

Among writers who have written on educational matters in the last few years, Professor Ravitch of Columbia University's Teacher's College is considered highly quotable and therefore, in the context of American educational policy, influential. This is precisely why her views on multiculturalism must not remain unchallenged. Many of the positions taken by Professor Ravitch are similar to the positions taken against the Freedmen's Bureau's establishment of black schools in the South during the 1860s. Then, the white conservative education policymakers felt that it was necessary to control the content of education so that the recently freed Africans would not become self-assured. An analysis of Ravitch's arguments will reveal what Martin Bernal calls in *Black Athena* "the neo-Aryan" model of history. Her version of multiculturalism is not multiculturalism at all, but rather a new form of Eurocentric hegemonism.

People tend to do the best they can with the information at their disposal. The problem in most cases where intellectual distortions arise is ignorance rather than malice. Unlike in the political arena where oratory goes a long way, in education, sooner or later the truth must come out. The proof of the theory is in the practice. What we have seen in the past twenty-five years is the gradual dismantling of the educational kingdom built to accompany the era of white supremacy. What is being contested is the speed of its dismantling. In many ways, the South African regime is a good parallel to what is going on in American education. No longer can the structure of knowledge which supported white hegemony be defended; whites must take their place, not above or below, but alongside the rest of humanity. This is a significantly different reality than we have experienced in American education and there are several reasons for this turn of events.

The first reason is the accelerating explosion in the world of knowledge about cultures, histories, and events seldom mentioned in American education. Names of individuals and their achievements, views of historiography and alternatives to European perspectives have proliferated due to international interaction, trade, and computer technology. People from other cultures, particularly non-Western people, have added new elements into the educational equation. A second reason is the rather recent intellectual liberation of large numbers of African-descended scholars. While there have always been African scholars in every era, the European hegemony, since the 1480s, in knowledge about the world, including Africa, was fairly complete. The domination of information, the naming of things, the propagation of concepts, and the dissemination of interpretations were, and still are in most cases in the West, a Eurocentric hegemony. During the twentieth century, African scholars led by W. E. B. Du Bois began to break from the intellectual shackles of Europe and make independent inquiries into history, science, origins, and Europe itself. For the first time in five hundred years, a cadre of scholars, trained in the West, but largely liberated from the hegemonic European thinking began to expose numerous distortions, often elevated to "truth" in the works of Eurocentric authors. A third reason for the current assault on the misinformation spread by white hegemonic thinkers is the conceptual inadequacy of simply valorizing Europe. Few whites have ever examined their culture critically. Those who have done so have often been severely criticized by their peers: the cases of Sidney Willhelm, Joe Feagin, Michael Bradley, and Basil Davidson are well known.

As part of the Eurocentric tradition, there seems to be silence on questions of hegemony, that is, the inability to admit the mutual conspiracy between race doctrine and educational doctrine in America. Professor Ravitch and others would maintain the facade of reasonableness even in the face of arguments demonstrating the irrationality of both white supremacist ideas on race and white hegemonic ideas in education. They are corollary and both are untenable on genetic and intellectual grounds.

EUROCENTRIC HEGEMONISM

Let us examine the argument of the defenders of the Eurocentric hegemony in education more closely. The status quo always finds its best defense in territoriality. Thus, it is one of the first weapons used by the defenders of the white hegemonic education. Soon after my book *The Afrocentric Idea* was published, I was interviewed on "The Today Show" along with Herb London, the New York University professor/politician who is one of the founders of the National Association of Professors. When I suggested the possibility of schools weaving information about other cultures into the fabric of the teaching-learning process, Professor London interrupted that "there is not enough *time* in the school year for what Asante wants." Of course there is, if there is enough for the Eurocentric information, there is enough time for cultural information from other groups. Professor Ravitch uses the same argument. Her strategy is to cast serious examinations of the curriculum as pressure groups, much like creationists in biology. Of course, the issue is neither irrational nor sensational; it is pre-eminently a question of racial dominance, the maintenance of which, in any form, I oppose. On the contrary, the status quo defenders, like the South African Boers, believe that it is possible to defend what is fundamentally anti-intellectual and immoral: the dominance and hegemony of the Eurocentric view of reality on a multicultural society. There is space for Eurocentrism in a multicultural enterprise so long as it does not parade as universal. No one wants to banish the Eurocentric view. It is a valid view of reality where it does not force its way. Afrocentricity does not seek to replace Eurocentricity in its arrogant disregard for other cultures.

THE PRINCIPAL CONTRADICTIONS

A considerable number of white educators and some blacks have paraded in single file and sometimes in concert to take aim at multiculturalism. In her article Professor Ravitch attempts to defend the indefensible. Believing, I suspect, that the best defense of the status quo is to attack, she attacks diversity, and those that support it, with gusto, painting straw fellows along the way. Her claim to support multiculturalism is revealed to be nothing more than an attempt to apologize for white cultural supremacy in the curriculum by using the same logic as white racial supremacists used in trying to defend white racism in previous years. She assumes falsely that there is little to say about the rest of the world, particularly about Africa and African Americans. Indeed, she is willing to assert, as Herbert London has claimed, that the school systems do not have enough time to teach all that Afrocentrists believe ought to be taught. Nevertheless, she assumes that all that is not taught about the European experience is valid and necessary. There are some serious flaws in her line of reasoning. I shall attempt to locate the major flaws and ferret them out.

Lip service is paid to the evolution of American education from the days of racial segregation to the present when "new social historians" routinely incorporate the experiences of other than white males. Nowhere does Professor Ravitch demonstrate an appreciation for the role played by the African American community in overcoming the harshest elements of racial segregation in the educational system. Consequently, she is unable to understand that more fundamental than eliminating racial segregation has to be the removal of racist thinking, assumptions, symbols, and materials in the curriculum.

However, there is no indication that Professor Ravitch is willing to grant an audience to this reasoning because she plods deeper into the same quagmire by attempting to conceptualize multiculturalism, a simple concept in educational jargon. She posits a *pluralist* multiculturalism—a redundancy—then suggests a *particularistic* multiculturalism—an oxymoron—in order to beat a dead horse. The ideas are nonstarters because they have no reality in fact. I wrote the first book in this country on transracial communication and edited the first handbook on intercultural communication, and I am unaware of the categories Professor Ravitch seeks to forge. She claims that the pluralist multiculturalist believes in pluralism and the particularistic multiculturalist believes in particularism. Well, multiculturalism in education is almost self-defining. It is simply the idea that the educational experience should reflect the diverse cultural heritage of our system of knowledge. I have contended that such is not the case and cannot be the case until teachers know more about the African American, Native American, Latino, and Asian experiences. This position obviously excites Professor Ravitch to the point that she feels obliged to make a case for "mainstream Americans."

THE MYTH OF MAINSTREAM

The idea of "mainstream American" is nothing more than an additional myth meant to maintain Eurocentric hegemony. When Professor Ravitch speaks of mainstream, she does not have Spike Lee, Aretha Franklin, or John Coltrane in mind. Bluntly put, "mainstream" is a code word for "white." When a dean of a college says to a faculty member, as one recently said, "You ought to publish in mainstream journals," the dean is not meaning *Journal of Black Studies* or *Black Scholar*. As a participant in the racist system of education, the dean is merely carrying out the traditional function of enlarging the white hegemony over scholarship. Thus, when the status quo defenders use terms like "mainstream," they normally mean "white." In fact, one merely has to substitute the words "white controlled" to get at the real meaning behind the code.

MISUNDERSTANDING MULTICULTURALISM

Misunderstanding the African American struggle for education in the United States, Professor Ravitch thinks that the call to multiculturalism is a matter of anecdotal references to outstanding individuals or descriptions of civil rights. But neither acknowledgement of achievements per se, nor descriptive accounts of the African experience adequately conveys the aims of the Afrocentric restructuring, as we shall see. From the establishment of widespread public education to the current emphasis on massaging the curriculum toward an organic and systemic recognition of cultural pluralism, the African American concept of nationhood has been always central. In terms of Afrocentricity, it is the same. We do not seek segments of modules in the classroom but rather the infusion of African American studies in every segment and in every module. The difference is between "incorporating the experiences" and "infusing the curriculum with an entirely new life." The real unity of the curriculum comes from infusion, not from including African Americans in what Ravitch would like to remain a white contextual hegemony she calls mainstream. No true mainstream can ever exist until there is knowledge, understanding, and acceptance of the role Africans have played in American history. One reason the issue is debated by white scholars such as Ravitch is because they do not believe there is substantial or significant African information to infuse. If she knew or believed that it was possible to have missed something, she would not argue against it. What is at issue is her own educational backgroud. Does she know classical Africa? Did she take courses in African American studies from qualified professors? Those who know do not question the importance of Afrocentric or Latino infusion into the educational process.

THE MISUSE OF SELF-ESTEEM

Professor Ravitch's main critique of the Afrocentric, Latinocentric, or Americentric (Native American) project is that it seeks to raise "self-esteem and self-respect" among Africans, Latinos, and Native Americans. It is important to understand that this is not only a self-serving argument, but a false argument. In the first place, I know of no Afrocentric curriculum planner—Asa Hilliard, Wade Nobles, Leonard Jeffries, Don McNeely being the principal ones—who insist that the primary aim is to raise self-esteem. The argument is a false lead to nowhere because the curriculum planners I am familiar with insist that the fundamental objective is to provide *accu-*

rate information. A secondary effect of accuracy and truth might be the adjustment of attitudes by both black and white students. In several surveys of college students, research has demonstrated that new information changes attitudes in both African American and white students. Whites are not so apt to take a superior attitude when they are aware of the achievements of other cultures. They do not lose their self-esteem, they adjust their views. On the other hand, African Americans who are often as ignorant as whites about African achievements adjust their attitudes about themselves once they are exposed to new information. There is no great secret in this type of transformation. Ravitch, writing from the point of view of those whose cultural knowledge is reinforced every hour, not just in the curriculum, but in every media, smugly contends that she cannot see the value of self-esteem. Since truth and accuracy will yield by-products of attitude adjustments, the Afrocentrists have always argued for the accurate representation of information.

Afrocentricity does not seek an ethnocentric curriculum. Unfortunately, Diane Ravitch chose to ignore two books that explain my views on this subject, *The Afrocentric Idea* (1987) and *Kemet, Afrocentricity and Knowledge* (1990) and instead quotes from *Afrocentricity* (1980), which was not about education but about personal and social transformation. Had she read the later works she would have understood that Afrocentricity is not an ethnocentric view in two senses. In the first place, it does not valorize the African view while downgrading others. In this sense, it is unlike the Eurocentric view, which is an ethnocentric view because it valozies itself and parades as universal. It becomes racist when the rules, customs, and/or authority of law or force dictate it as the proper view. This is what often happens in school curricula. In the second place, as to method, Afrocentricity is not a naive racial theory. It is a systematic approach to presenting the African as subject rather than object. Even Ravitch might be taught the Afrocentric Method!

AMERICAN CULTURE

There is no common American culture as is claimed by the defenders of the status quo. There is a hegemonic culture to be sure, pushed as if it were a common culture. Perhaps Ravitch is confusing concepts here. There is a common American *society* which is quite different from a common American culture. Certain cultural characteristics are shared by those within the society but the meaning of *multicultural* is "many cultures." To believe in multicultural education is to assume that there are many cultures. The reason Ravitch finds confusion is because the only way she can reconcile the "many cultures" is to insist on many "little" cultures under the hegemony of the "big" white culture. Thus, what she means by multiculturalism is precisely what I criticized in *The Afrocentric Idea,* the acceptance of other cultures within a Eurocentric framework.

In the end, the neat separation of pluralist multiculturalists and particularistic multiculturalists breaks down because it is a false, straw separation developed primarily for the sake of argument and not for clarity. The real division on the question of multiculturalism is between those who truly seek to maintain a Eurocentric hegemony over the curriculum and those who truly believe in cultural pluralism without hierarchy. Ravitch defends the former position.

Professor Ravitch's ideological position is implicated in her misreading of several scholars' works. When Professor John Stanfield writes that modes of social knowledge such as theology, science, and magic are different, not inferior or superior, Ravitch asks, "If Professor Stanfield broke his leg, would he go to a theologian, a doctor, or a magician?" Clearly she does not understand the simple statement Stanfield is making. He is not writing about *uses* of knowledge, but about *ranking* of knowledge. To confuse the point by providing an answer for a question never raised is the key rhetorical strategy in Ravitch's case. Thus, she implies that because Professor George Ghevarughese Joseph argues that mathematics was developed in Egypt, Babylonia, Mesopotamia, and India long before it came to Europe, he seeks to replace modern math with "ancient ethnic mathematics." This is a deliberate misunderstanding of the professor's point: mathematics in its modern form owes debts to Africans and Asians.

Another attempt to befuddle issues is Ravitch's gratuitous comment that Koreans "do not study ancient mathematics" and yet they have high scores. There are probably several variables for the Koreans making the highest scores "in mathematics on international assessments." Surely one element would have to be the linkage of Korean traditions in mathematics to present mathematical problems. Koreans do not study European theorists prior to their own; indeed they are taught to honor and respect the ancestral mathematicians. This is true for Indians, Chinese, and Japanese. In African traditions, the *European* slave trade broke the linkage, and the work of scholars such as Ahmed Baba and Hypathia remains unknown to the African American and thus does not take its place in the family of world mathematics.

Before Professor Ravitch ends her assualt on ethnic cultures, she fires a volley against the Haudenosaunee political system of Native Americans. As a New Yorker, she does not like the fact that the state's curriculum guide lists the Haudenosaunee Confederation as an inspiration to the United States Constitution alongside the Enlightenment. She says readers "might wonder what it is." Bluntly put, a proper education would acquaint students with the Haudenosaunee Confederation, and in that case Professor Ravitch's readers would know the Haudenosaunee as a part of the conceptual discussion that went into the development of the American political systems. Only a commitment to white hegemony would lead a writer to assume that whites could not obtain political ideas from others.

Finally, she raises a "controversy" that is no longer a controversy among reputable scholars: Who were the Egyptians? Most scholars accept a simple answer: They were Africans. The question of whether or not they were black was initially raised by Eurocentric scholars in the nineteenth century seeking to explain the testimony of the ancient Greeks, particularly Herodotus and Diodorus Siculus, who said that Egyptians were "Black with woolly hair." White hegemonic studies that sought to maintain the false notion of white racial supremacy during the nineteenth century fabricated the idea of a European or an Asian Egyptian to deny Africa its classical past and to continue the Aryan myth. It is shocking to see Professor Ravitch raise this issue in the 1990s. It is neither a controversial issue nor should it be to those familiar with the evidence.

The debate over the curriculum is really over a vision of the future of the United States. Keepers of the status quo, such as Professor Ravitch, want to maintain a "white framework" for multiculturalism because they have no faith in cultural pluralism without hierarchy. A common culture does not exist, but this nation is on the path toward it. Granting all the difficulties we face in attaining this common culture, we are more likely to reach it when we allow the full participation of all ethnic groups in a quest for a usable curriculum. In the end, we will find that such a curriculum, like inspiration, will not come from this or that individual model but from integrity and accuracy.

12

Reply to Asante

Diane Ravitch

In responding to Professor Asante's critique of my article, "Multiculturalism: E Pluribus Plures," I had continually to reread what I had written,
because I did not recognize my article from his description. His repeated
allegations of racism and "neo-Aryanism" are not supported by quotations from the text, because nothing in my article validates his outrageous
charges either directly or by inference. His statements associating my views
with those who opposed the education of black children after the Civil
War and with white South Africans are simply mud-slinging. He acknowledges in passing that my view of multiculturalism is shared by some black
educators, but this anomaly does not cause him to pause in his scurrilous
allegations of racism.

In the article, I described the major changes that have occurred in
the school curriculum over the past generation. I stated that the teaching
of American history had long ignored the historical experiences of minority groups and women, and that recent scholarship had made it possible,
indeed necessary, to forge historical narratives that accurately represent
the diverse nature of our society. The resulting effort to weave together
the different strands of our historical experience, I argued, provides a more
accurate portrait of the American people than the flawed historical account that it replaced. Children in school now learn, I wrote, "that cultural

Reprinted from *The American Scholar* 60, No. 2 (Spring 1991). Copyright © 1991 by
Diane Ravitch. By permission of the publisher.

pluralism is one of the norms of a free society; that differences among groups are a national resource rather than a problem to be solved. Indeed, the unique feature of the United States is that its common culture has been formed by the interaction of its subsidiary cultures. It is a culture that has been influenced over time by immigrants, American Indians, Africans (slave and free) and by their descendants. American music, art, literature, language, food, clothing, sports, holidays, and customs all show the effects of the commingling of diverse cultures in one nation. Paradoxical though it may seem, the United States has a common culture that is multicultural."

I then went on to argue that demands for diversification of the curriculum had in some instances been pressed to the extremes of ethnocentrism; that some educators want not a portrait of the nation that shows how different groups have shaped our history, but immersion of children in the ancestral exploits of their own race or ethnic group. In trying to explain the bifurcation of the multicultural movement, I struggled to find the right nomenclature for the two competing strains of thought, and I used the terms *pluralistic* and *particularistic*. Professor Asante is right that I should not have called one of them "pluralistic multiculturalism" and the other "particularistic multiculturalism." While pluralism *is* multicultural, particularism is not. Pluralism and particularism are opposite in spirit and methods. The demands for ethnocentrism associated with the Afrocentric movement should not be seen as an extreme form of multiculturalism, but as a *rejection* of multiculturalism. Afrocentrism and other kinds of ethnocentrism might better be described as racial fundamentalism. What has confused the matter is the fact that Afrocentrists present their program in public forums as "multicultural," in order to shield from public view their assertions of racial superiority and racial purity, which promote not the racial understanding that our society so desperately needs, but racial antagonism.

Professor Asante and others in the Afrocentric movement like Leonard Jeffries, Jr., Wade Nobles, and Asa Hilliard are inconsistent about whether Afrocentrism is for descendants of Africans only, or for everyone. Their literature sometimes claims that everyone—not only blacks—must learn that all the achievements of civilization originated in Africa; but at other times, Afrocentrists appear to endorse the idea that each racial group should study its own peculiar history (which I call "multiple-centrisms"). The former version of Afrocentrism veers toward racism, with its specious claims about the superiority of those whose skin is darkened by melanin and its attacks on whites as the "ice people." The latter, the "multiple-centrisms" approach, is in its way even more dangerous, because it is insidious. The "multiple-centrisms" position is superficially appealing, because on the surface it gives something to everyone: African Americans may be Afrocentric, Asian Americans may be Asiacentric, Native Americans may be Native Americentric, and Latinos may be Latinocentric, while those who are of European descent may be taught to feel guilt and shame for the alleged misdeeds of their ancestors. This "multiple-centrisms" model is now a hot educational trend, emanating from Portland, Oregon, where the local office of multicultural education has prepared Afrocentric curricular materials and plans to develop similar materials for Asian Americans, Latino Americans, Native Americans, and Pacific Islanders. This was also the organizing principle of Commissioner Thomas Sobol's "task force on minorities" in New York State, whose misnamed "Curriculum of Inclusion" called not for inclusion of minority cultures into a pluralistic mainstream but for "multiple-centrisms."

The "multiple-centrisms" approach is deeply flawed. It confuses race with culture, as though everyone with the same skin color has the same culture and history. It ignores the fact that within every major racial group, there are many different cultural groups, and within each major racial group, there exist serious ethnic and cultural tensions. Furthermore, the "multiple-centrisms" approach denies the *synchretistic* nature of all cultures and civilizations that mingle, and the multiple ways in which they change one another. Neither world history nor American history is the story of five racial groups; such a concept leads to false history and to racial stereotyping. This gross oversimplification of history and culture could be taken seriously only in a society where educators are themselves either intimidated or uneducated.

Professor Asante relentlessly argues against positions that I did not take and attributes to me things that I did not write. For example, Professor Asante quotes Herbert London of New York University to the effect that there is "not enough time in the school year" to teach black history and proceeds to say that I "use the same argument." He does not quote me because he cannot find support for his statement in my article. In fact, I do believe in the importance of teaching black history, drawing on the work of such respected scholars of African American history as John Hope Franklin, Eric Foner, Eugene Genovese, Gary Nash, Leon Litwack, Winthrop Jordan, and Nathan Huggins. It is not possible to teach the history of the United States accurately without teaching black history.

Professor Asante willfully misconstrues a reference that I made to "mainstream Americans." The context was as follows: I wrote about how American history textbooks had for generations ignored race, ethnicity, and religion, and how "the main narrative paid little attention to minority groups and women. With the ethnic revival of the 1960s, this approach to the teaching of history came under fire, because the history of national leaders—virtually all of whom were white, Anglo-Saxon, and male—ignored the place in American history of those who were none of the above. The traditional history of elites had been complemented by the assimilationist view of American society, which presumed that everyone in the American melting pot would eventually lose or abandon those ethnic characteristics that distinguished them from mainstream Americans. The ethnic revival demonstrated that many groups did not want to be assimilated or melted." Professor Asante distorts this to claim that I felt "obliged to make a case for 'mainstream Americans.' " I nowhere made a case for the mainstream, nor did I describe who was included or excluded in this putative "mainstream." I wrote: "The pluralistic approach to multiculturalism promotes a broader interpretation of the common American culture and seeks due recognition for the ways that the nation's many racial, ethnic, and cultural groups have transformed the national culture. The pluralists say, in effect, 'American culture belongs to us, all of us; the U.S. is us, and we make it in every generation.' " By this description, Spike Lee and Aretha Franklin are very much part of the common culture; and the American mainstream. So are Duke Ellington, Count Basie, Bill Cosby, Eddie Murphy, Oprah Winfrey, William Raspberry, Carl Lewis, Marion Barry, Malcolm X, Jackie Robinson, Leontyne Price, Langston Hughes, James Weldon Johnson, Countee Cullen, Alice Walker, Martin Luther King, Jr., Frederick Douglass, Jesse Jackson, Henry Gates, Derrick Bell, Jr., and Kenneth B. Clark. As for publishing in "mainstream" journals, Professor Asante misunderstands the dean. She (or he) does not mean that one must publish in a *white* journal; she means that one gains credibility in the academic world by publishing in a journal that has clear standards of scholarship, where false charges of racism, character assassination, and out-of-context quotations are not permissible.

Professor Asante asserts that the ethnocentric curriculum does not claim to raise the self-esteem of students of the same racial or ethnic group. This is not correct. Professor Wade Nobles, whom he cites, runs a state-funded program in California called the HAWK Federation Youth Development and Training Program which aims to immerse young black males in African and African American culture; its purpose, according to the program's brochure, is to address "simultaneously the problems of substance abuse prevention [sic], gang violence, academic failure and low aspirations and poor self-esteem." The New York State task force report, "A Curriculum of Inclusion," whose chief consultant was Professor Leonard Jeffries, Jr., repeatedly asserts the relationship between the curriculum and the self-esteem of students. The report claims that a rewriting of the curriculum will promote "higher self-esteem and self-respect" among children from racial minorities "while children from European cultures will have a less arrogant perspective of being part of the group that has 'done it all.' "

After stating that the leaders of the Afrocentric movement do not rest their case on building self-esteem, but rather on truth, Professor Asante then claims that Korean students do well in mathematics because "they are taught to honor and respect the ancestral mathematicians. This is true for Indians, Chinese, and Japanese." Here is the full-blown ethnocentric promise: You can do well if you are taught that your ancestors did it before you. Professor Asante offers no evidence for his statements about Asian children, because none exists. According to Professor Harold Stevenson of the University of Michigan, who has conducted extensive cross-cultural studies of mathematics education in the United States, Japan, and China, children in Japan and China do not study "the ancestral mathematics." They study mathematics; they learn to solve problems.

Of course, everyone needs to know that they, and people like them, are respected as equals in the society they live in. But to assume that self-esteem is built on reverence for one's ancestors is highly questionable. If this were true, the highest academic achievement in the Western world would be recorded by children of Greek and Italian ancestry, since they are the descendants of ancient Greece and Rome; but this is not the case either in the United States or in international assessments. In fact, according to a recent article in the *New York Times,* Italian-American students —the lineal descendants of Cicero and Julius Caesar—have the lowest achievement and the highest dropout rate of any white ethnic group in New York City schools.

Nor is it clear that self-esteem (in the sense of feeling good about yourself) is a reliable indicator of academic achievement. In the most recent international assessment of mathematics, Korean children had the highest achievement and American children had the lowest achievement. When the students were asked whether they were good in mathematics, the Koreans had the lowest score, and the Americans had the highest score. In other words, the Americans had the highest self-esteem and the lowest achievement; the Koreans had the lowest self-esteem and the highest achievement. Why did the Korean students fare so well? Consider the research report that accompanied the assessment results: "Korea's success can be partially attributed to the nation's and parents' strong interest in education, reflected in a 220-day school year. While there is virtually no adult illiteracy in the country, only 13 percent of Korea's parents have completed some post-secondary education. They nonetheless see education as the hope for their children and grandchildren. Everyone recognizes that Korea's job market is very demanding and the scientific and technological areas carry high prestige." Another contributing factor to Korean success is a national curriculum that is two-to-three years more advanced than the mathematics that American children study. Presumably, what Korean children learn is not that they are the greatest, but that those who care about them expect them to work hard and to study, and that if they do, they will succeed.

Professor Asante's appeal to the instructional power of ethnocentrism ignores the fact that Asian children in the United States out-perform children of all other racial and ethnic groups in mathematics; the SAT mathematics scores of Asian students are far above those of other groups. Asian American children study mathematics in the same classrooms, using the same textbooks as their classmates; they do not study their "ancestral mathematicians." But, according to numerous studies, Asian children do more homework, take school more seriously, and study harder than children of other groups. The enormous success of Asian American students in American schools and universities suggests that their hard work pays off in academic achievement.

One of Professor Asante's most remarkable statements is: "Few whites have ever examined their culture critically." As I survey my own bookshelf, I see the works of scores of critics of American culture, of European culture, and of white racism. I see books by John Dewey, Gunnar Myrdal, and Karl Marx, among many others; I see the works of feminists, liberals, conservatives, radicals, Marxists, and other critics. Professor Asante is under the misapprehension that everything written about Europe or the United States by white scholars is celebratory, perhaps because he believes that every writer is irredeemably ethnocentric.

The purpose of historical study is not to glorify one's ancestors, nor anyone else's ancestors, but to understand what happened in the past and to see events in all their complexity. The fascination of historical study is that what we know about the past changes as scholars present new interpretations supported by evidence. The problem with the ethnocentric approach is that it proposes to teach children the greatness of their ancestors, based on claims that have not been validated by reputable scholars. So, in the Afrocentric curriculum, children are taught that the ancient Egyptians were responsible for the origins of mathematics, science, philosophy, religion, art, architecture, and medicine. No other civilization made any noteworthy contribution to any field, though all learned at the feet of the ancient Egyptians. The ancient Egyptians are shown as the most perfect civilization in all history. They did not enslave the Hebrews; indeed, unlike other ancient civilizations, they held no slaves at all. They were unrelated to today's Arab population, which allegedly did not arrive in Egypt until the seventh or eighth century. Such assertions ought to be reviewed by qualified, reputable scholars before they are taught in compulsory public schools. Nor is the relationship of African American children to the ancient Egyptians altogether clear, since the Africans who were brought in chains to the Western hemisphere were not from Egypt, but from West Africa.

The issue here is not the color of the ancient Egyptians; nor is it a matter of debate that Egypt is on the African continent or that it was a great civilization. What does matter is the claim that a single ancient civilization was responsible for every significant advance in the history of humankind. No civilization can claim credit for every idea, discovery, and forward movement in the history of humanity. Every great civilization grows by exchanging ideas, art, and technology with other civilizations.

Professor Asante is generously willing to permit "Eurocentrism" to survive "so long as it does not parade as universal." But there are elements in every civilization that have universal resonance, and every serious study of world history demonstrates the movement of ideas, art, and technology across the national boundaries and across oceans and continents. Those ideas, those artistic achievements, and those technological advances that are most successful do become truly universal. Aspects of American popular culture, some amalgam of jeans, Coca-Cola, jazz and rock, has become part of the universal culture, as mediated by television and Hollywood. It is not only the West that has produced ideas, art, and technology that are universal; the educated person learns about universal features in all great civilizations. Picasso and other great modern artists freely acknowledged their debt to African art. Whether one is in Tokyo, Paris, Buenos Aires, New York, or any other great cosmopolitan center, the multiple influences of Europe, Asia, Africa, the United States, and Latin America are everywhere apparent.

This is why, for example, in California, the recently adopted history curriculum for the state requires all children to study three years of world history. All children will learn about the art, ideas, religions, and culture of the world's great civilizations. For the first time in American history, American public school children will study not only ancient Greece and Rome, but also the African kingdoms of Mali and Ghana, the Aztecs, Mayans, and Incas, and the ancient civilizations of China and India.

But they also study those elements of the Western democratic ideology that have become universal over time and that provide a standard for human rights activists on every continent today. This is not just a political system based on the consent of the governed (a revolutionary concept in world history), but a philosophy that promotes the ideas of individualism, choice, personal responsibility, the pursuit of happiness, and belief in progress. In the spring of 1989, Chinese students in Tiananmen Square carried signs that quoted Patrick Henry and Thomas Jefferson. In the fall of 1989, Czechoslovakian students sang "We shall overcome" and quoted Martin Luther King, Jr. In the fall of 1990, Gibson Kamau Kuria, a Kenyan human rights lawyer and dissident, went into exile in the United States. Kamau Kuria resisted the undemocratic actions of the Kenyan government and appealed to the democratic standards contained in the Universal Declaration of Human Rights.

Some of Professor Asante's complaints about Eurocentrism in the United States are built upon legitimate grievances against the racism that excluded knowledge of black history and achievements from the curriculum of schools and universities for most of our nation's history. I, too, would banish the Eurocentrism found in the textbooks of earlier generations, because their monocultural perspective led to wild inaccuracies and pervasive bias. If, however, Asante's scorn for Eurocentrism is a reflexive aversion to everything European or white, then his own view leads to wild inaccuracies and pervasive bias. Europe has a unique place in the history of the United States for a variety of reasons. Europe is significant for Americans because our governmental institutions were created by men of British descent who had been educated in the ideas of the European Enlightenment; they argued their ideas extensively in print, so the sources of their beliefs are not a secret. Europe is important, too, because the language that most Americans speak is English, and throughout American history, there have been close cultural, commercial, and political ties with European nations. And, not least, Europe is important to America as the source of seminal political ideas, including democracy, socialism, capitalism, and Marxism.

Europe, of course, is not the whole story, not of the United States and not of the world. We Americans—coming as we do from every part of the globe—have been significantly influenced, and continue to be influenced, by people who do not trace their origins to Europe. Our openness to ideas and people from all over the world makes our society dynamic. What is most exciting about American culture is that it is a blending of elements of Europe, Africa, Latin America, and Asia. Whether or not we have a melting pot, we do have a cultural mosaic or at the very least a multitextured tapestry of cultures. Whatever our differences, we are all Americans.

Behind this exchange between Professor Asante and me is a disagreement about the meaning of truth and how it is ascertained. The Afrocentrists alternately say that they want to teach the Truth, the lost, stolen, or hidden truths about the origins of all things; or they say that "truth" is defined by who is in power. Take your choice: either there is absolute Truth or all "truth" is a function of power. I make a different choice. I reject the absolute truths of fundamentalists, and I reject the relativistic idea that truth depends on power alone. I claim that what we know must be constantly tested, challenged, and reexamined, and that decisions about knowledge must be based on evidence and subject to revision. Reason and intelligence, not skin color and emotion, must be the ultimate arbiters of disputes over fact.

Professor Asante suggests that we disagree about our vision of the future of the United States. He is right. I fear that Afrocentrism intends to replace the discredited white supremacy of the past with an equally disreputable theory of African supremacy. The theory of white supremacy was wrong and socially disastrous; so is the theory of black supremacy. I fear that the theory of "multiple-centrisms" will promote social fragmentation and ethnocentrism, rather than social understanding and amity. I think we will all lose if we jettison the notion of the common good and learn to identify only with those people who look just like ourselves. The ethnocentrists believe that children should learn to "think with their blood," as the saying goes. This is the way to unending racial antagonism, as well as disintegration of the sense of mutuality on which social progress depends.

13

Education and the Racist Road to Barbarism

George Reisman

Major changes are taking place in the philosophy of American education, changes which are potentially capable of having an enormous impact on all aspects of American life. The changes are inspired by what the *New York Times* refers to as the "Eurocentrism critique." According to the *Times*, "Eurocentrism" is a pejorative term supposed to describe "a provincial outlook that focuses overwhelmingly on European and Western culture while giving short shrift to Asia, Africa, and Latin America."

A typical manifestation of "Eurocentrism," according to its critics, is the statement that Columbus discovered America. This statement, which most children in America may have learned as their very first fact of history, is now regarded as controversial. Indeed, it is held to be positively offensive because it implies that "there had been no other people on the continent" before Columbus arrived. Traditional American education in general is denounced for seeing non-Western civilization and the rest of the world "only through a Western lens." Only through that "lens," it is held, can, for example, African art be regarded as primitive.

In an effort to eliminate such alleged Western and European "bias," schools are altering the way in which history, literature, and the arts are being taught. Recent changes at Stanford University, where a course on Western civilization was replaced by one in which non-Western ideas had to be included, are only one case in point. The revisions in the history curriculum in California's public school system, to emphasize Indian and African cultures, are another. Curricula and textbooks are being widely rewritten, and, as evidence of the depth of the changes, the *Times* reports that efforts are underway "to reconstruct the history of African tribes, going beyond relying on accounts of Western travelers to examining indigenous sources, often oral, and adapting anthropological approaches."

The implications of these changes are enormous. The acceptance of the "Eurocentrism" critique and its denial of such propositions as Columbus discovered America speaks volumes about the state of the educational establishment in general.

In order to understand the implications, it is first necessary to remind oneself what Western civilization is. From a historical perspective, Western civilization embraces two main periods: the era of Greco-Roman civilization and the era of modern Western civilization, which latter encompasses the rediscovery of Greco-Roman civilization in the late Middle Ages, and the periods of the Renaissance, the Enlightenment, and the Industrial Revolution. Modern Western civilization continues down to the present moment, of course, as the dominant force in the culture of the countries of Western Europe and the United States and the other countries settled by the descendants of West Europeans. It is an increasingly powerful force in the rapidly progressing countries of the Far East, such as Japan, Taiwan, and South Korea, whose economies rest on "Western" foundations in every essential respect.

From the perspective of intellectual and cultural content, Western civilization represents an understanding and acceptance of the following: the laws of logic; the concept of causality and, consequently, of a universe ruled by natural laws intelligible to man; on these foundations, the whole known corpus of the laws of mathematics and science; the individual's self-responsibility based on his free will to choose between good and evil; the value of man above all other species on the basis of his unique possession of the power of reason; the value and competence of the individual human being and his corollary possession of individual rights, among them the right to life, liberty, property, and the pursuit of happiness; the need for limited government and for the individual's freedom from the state; on this entire preceding foundation, the validity of capitalism, with its unprecedented and continuing economic development in terms of division of labor, technological capital accumulation, and rising living standards; in addition, the importance of visual arts and literature depicting man as capable of facing the world with confidence in his power to succeed, and music featuring harmony and melody.

WESTERN CIVILIZATION IS OPEN TO EVERYONE

Once one recalls what Western civilization is, the most important thing to realize about it is that *it is open to everyone.* Indeed, important elements of "Western" civilization did not even originate in the West. The civilization of the Greeks and Romans incorporated significant aspects of science that were handed down from Egypt and Babylon. Modern "Western" civilization includes contributions from people living in the Middle East and China during the Dark Ages, when Western Europe had reverted to virtual barbarism. Indeed, during the Dark Ages, "Western" civilization resided much more in the Middle East than in Western Europe. (It is conceivable that if present trends continue, in another century it might reside more in the Far East than in the West.)

The truth is that just as one does not have to be from France to like French-fried potatoes or from New York to like a New York steak, one does not have to be born in Western Europe or be of West European descent to admire Western civilization, or, indeed, even to help build it. Western civilization is not a product of geography. *It is a body of knowledge and values.* Any individual, any society, is potentially capable of adopting it and thereby becoming "Westernized." The rapidly progressing economies of the Far East are all "Western" insofar as they rest on a foundation of logic, mathematics, science, technology, and capitalism—exactly the same logic, mathematics, science, technology, and capitalism that are essential features of "Western" civilization.

For the case of a Westernized individual, I must think of myself. I am not of West European descent. All four of my grandparents came to the United States from Russia, about a century ago. Modern Western civilization did not originate in Russia and hardly touched it. The only connection my more remote ancestors had with the civilization of Greece and Rome was probably to help in looting and plundering it. Nevertheless, I am thoroughly a Westerner. I am a Westerner because of the *ideas and values* I hold. I have thoroughly internalized all of the leading features of Western civilization. They are now *my* ideas and *my* values. Holding these ideas and values as I do, I would be a Westerner wherever I lived and whenever I was born. I identify with Greece and Rome, and not with my ancestors of that time, because I share the ideas and values of Greece and Rome, not those of my ancestors. To put it bluntly, my ancestors were savages—certainly up to about a thousand years ago, and, for all practical purposes, probably as recently as four or five generations ago.

I know nothing for certain about my great-grandparents, but if they lived in rural Russia in the middle of the nineteenth century, they were almost certainly totally illiterate, highly superstitious, and primitive in every way. On winter nights, they probably slept with farm animals in their hut to keep warm, as was once a common practice in Northern Europe, and were personally filthy and lice-infested. I see absolutely nothing of value in their "way of life," if it can be called a way of life, and I am immeasurably grateful that my grandparents had the good sense to abandon it and come to America, so that I could have the opportunity of becoming a "Westerner" and, better still, an American "Westerner," because, in most respects, since colonial times, the United States has always been, intellectually and culturally, the *most* Western of the Western countries.

Thus, I am a descendant of savages who dwelt in Eastern Europe—and before that probably the steppes of Asia—who has been Westernized and now sees the world entirely through a Western "lens," to use the term of the critics of "Eurocentrism." Of course, it is not really a lens through which I see the world. It is much more fundamental than that. I have developed a Western *mind,* a mind enlightened and thoroughly transformed by the enormous body of knowledge that represents the substance of Western civilization, and I now see the world entirely on the basis of that knowledge.

For example, I see the world on the foundation of the laws of logic, mathematics, and science that I have learned. And whenever something new or unexpected happens, which I do not understand, I know that it must nevertheless have a cause which I am capable of discovering. In these respects, I differ profoundly from my savage ancestors, who lacked the knowledge to see the world from a scientific perspective and who probably felt helpless and terrified in the face of anything new or unknown because, lacking the principle of causality and knowledge of the laws of logic, they simply had no basis for expecting to be able to come to an understanding of it.

It is on the basis of the same foundation of knowledge that I regard the discoverer of the Western hemisphere to be Columbus, rather than the very first human beings to arrive on the North American continent (probably across a landbridge from Asia), and rather than the Norwegian Leif Ericson. I consider Columbus to be the discoverer not because of any such absurd reason as a preference for Europeans over Asiatics (Leif Ericson was as much a European as Columbus), but because it was

Columbus who opened the Western hemisphere to the civilization I have made my own. Columbus was the man who made it possible to bring to these shores *my ideas and values*. It is not from the perspective of the residence of my ancestors, who were certainly not Italian or Spanish or even West European, that I regard Columbus as the discoverer of America, but from the perspective of the residence of my ideas and values. Just as at an earlier time, they resided in Greece and Rome rather than in the Russia of my ancestors, so in the fifteenth and sixteenth centuries, the home of my ideas and values was in Western Europe. I hold Columbus to have been the discoverer of America from *that perspective*. This is the perspective that *any* educated person would hold.

There is no need for me to dwell any further on my own savage ancestors. The plain truth is that *everyone's* ancestors were savages—indeed, at least 99.5 percent of everyone's ancestors were savages, even in the case of descendants of the founders of the world's oldest civilizations. For mankind has existed on earth for a million years, yet the very oldest of civilizations—as judged by the criterion of having possessed a written language—did not appear until less than 5,000 years ago. The ancestors of those who today live in Britain or France or most of Spain were savages as recently as the time of Julius Caesar, slightly more than 2,000 years ago. Thus, on the scale of mankind's total presence on earth, today's Englishmen, Frenchmen, and Spaniards earn an ancestral savagery rating of 99.8 percent. The ancestors of present-day Germans and Scandinavians were savages even more recently, and thus today's Germans and Scandinavians probably deserve an ancestral savagery rating of at least 99.9 percent.

It is important to stress these facts to be aware how little significance is to be attached to the members of any race or linguistic group achieving civilization sooner rather than later. Between the descendants of the world's oldest civilizations and those who might first aspire to civilization at the present moment, there is a difference of at most one-half of one percent on the time scale of man's existence on earth.

These observations should confirm the fact that there is no reason for believing that civilization is in any way a property of any particular race or ethnic group. It is strictly an *intellectual matter*—ultimately, a matter of the presence or absence of certain fundamental ideas underlying the acquisition of further knowledge.

Those peoples who possess a written language may be called civilized, inasmuch as writing is an indispensable means for the transmission of substantial knowledge, and thus for the accumulation of knowledge from generation to generation. Those who possess not only a written language but also knowledge of the laws of logic and the principle of causality are in a position to accumulate and transmit incomparably more knowledge than people who possess merely the art of writing alone. On this basis, Greco-Roman civilization is on a higher plane than any that had preceded it.

Finally, a civilization which possesses still further fundamental applications of human reason, such as the far more extensive development and elaboration of the principles of mathematics and science, the existence of the freedoms of speech and press, and the development of a division of labor economy, is a higher civilization than even that of Greece and Rome. (The freedoms of speech and press are an essential guarantee of the individual's right to disseminate knowledge without being stopped by the fears or superstitions of any group backed by the coercive power of the state. A division of labor economy makes possible a corresponding multiplication of the amount of knowledge applied to production and to meeting the needs of human life, for such knowledge exists essentially in proportion to the number of separate occupations being practiced, each with its own specialized body of knowledge. Equally or even more important, a division of labor economy means that geniuses can devote their talents full time to such fields as science, education, invention, and business, with a corresponding progressive increase in knowledge and improvements in human life.)

Such a civilization, of course, is our very own, modern Western civilization—incomparably the greatest civilization which has ever existed, and which, until fairly recently, had repeatedly been carried to its very highest points in most respects right here in the United States.

(Reference to an objective superiority of one civilization or culture over another, encounters the opposition of a profound, self-righteous hatred of the very idea. Thus, cultures may practice ritual sacrifice, cannibalism, mass expropriation, slavery, torture, and wholesale slaughter—all of this is accepted as somehow legitimate within the context of the culture concerned. The only alleged sin, the only alleged act of immorality in the world is to display contempt for such cultures, and to uphold as superior the values of Western culture. Then one is denounced as an imperialist, racist, and virtual Nazi.

It should be realized that those who take this view do not regard as the essential evil of Nazism its avowed irrationalism, its love of force and violence, and its acts of destruction and slaughter. All this they could accept, and do accept in the case of other cultures, such as that of primitive tribes, ancient Eygpt, the civilization of the Aztecs and Incas, the Middle Ages, and Soviet Russia. What they hold to be the evil of Nazism was its assertion that Nazi culture was superior to other cultures. The claim of superiority of one culture over another is the one evil in their eyes. Needless to say, of course, it is only on the basis of the recognition of objective values that one can seriously condemn Nazism—not for its absurd claims of superiority, but as a primitive, barbaric culture of the type one would expect to find among savages.)

The fact that civilization is an intellectual matter is not known to the critics of "Eurocentrism." In their view, Western civilization is a matter not even so much of geography as it is of *racial membership*. It is, as they see it, the civilization of the *white man*. In reporting the changes in California's world history curriculum, the *Times* notes, significantly, that Hispanic, Asian, and black students now make up a majority of the 4.4 million pupils in the state. It quotes the co-author of the new curriculum as saying many educators believe that "people who have non-European backgrounds don't feel their antecedents lie in Europe." Another critic of "Eurocentrism," who is described as "heading an overhauling of the public school curriculum of Camden, N.J., to stress . . . a more 'Afrocentric and Latinocentric' approach," is quoted as saying, "We are not living in a Western country. The American project is not yet completed. It is only in the eyes of the Eurocentrists who see it as a Western project, which means to hell with the rest of the people who have yet to create the project."

In these statements, Western civilization is clearly identified with people of a certain type, namely, the West Europeans and their descendants, who are white. Students descended from Asiatics or Africans, it is assumed, can feel at home only to the extent that the curriculum is revised to give greater stress to "the ancient civilizations of China, India and Africa, the growth of Islam and the development of sub-Saharan Africa." The critics of "Eurocentrism" proclaim themselves to be opponents of racism. In fact, they accept exactly the same false premise they claim to oppose— namely, that civilization, or the lack of it, is racially determined.

In earlier centuries, men of European descent observed the marked cultural inferiority of the native populations of Africa, Asia, and the Western hemisphere, and assumed that the explanation lay in a racial inferiority of these peoples. In passing this judgment, they forgot the cultural state of their own ancestors, which was as much below their own as was that of any of these peoples. They also overlooked the very primitive cultural state of many Europeans then living in the eastern part of the continent, and of Caucasians living in the Middle East. Even more important, they failed to see how in accepting racism, they contradicted the essential "Western" doctrine of individual free will and individual responsibility for choices made. For in condemning people as inferior on the basis of their race, they were holding individuals morally responsible for circumstances over which they had absolutely no control. At the same time, they credited themselves with accomplishments which were hardly their creations, but those of a comparative handful of other individuals, most of whom had happened to be of the same race and who, ironically enough, had had to struggle against the indifference or even outright hostility of the great majority of the members of their own race in order to create civilization.

Today, the critics of "Eurocentrism" rightly refuse to accept any form of condemnation for their racial membership. They claim to hold that race is irrelevant to morality and that therefore people of every race are as good as people of every other race. But then they assume that if people of all races are equally good, *all civilizations and cultures must be equally good.* They derive civilization and culture from race, just as the European racists did. And this is why they too must be called racists. They differ from the European racists only in that while the latter started with the judgment of an inferior civilization or culture and proceeded backwards to the conclusion of an inferior race, the former begin with the judgment of an equally good race and proceed forward to the conclusion of an equally good civilization or culture. The error of both sets of racists is the same: the belief that civilization and culture are racially determined.

The racism of these newer racists, which is now being imposed on the educational system, implies a radical devaluation of civilization, knowledge, and education. The new racists do not want students to study non-Western civilizations and the conditions of primitive peoples from the perspective of seeing how they lag behind Western civilization and what they might do to catch up. Study from that perspective would be denounced as seeing the world through a "Western lens." It would be considered offensive to people of non-West European origin.

No, what they want is to conduct the study of the various civilizations and even the state of outright savagery itself in a way that makes all appear *equal.* It is assumed, for example, that black students can feel the equal of white students only if their sub-Saharan ancestors are presented as, in a fundamental sense, culturally *equivalent* to modern West Europeans or Americans.

Now such a program means the explicit obliteration of distinctions between levels of civilization, and between civilization and savagery. It presents ignorance as the equivalent of knowledge, and superstition as the equivalent of science. Everything—logic, philosophy, science, law, technology—is to be ignored, and a culture limited to the level of making dugout canoes is to be presented as the equivalent of one capable of launching space ships. And all this is for the alleged sake of not offending anyone who supposedly must feel inferior if such a monumental fraud is not committed.

I believe, contrary to the expectations of the new racists, that their program must be grossly offensive to the very students it is designed to reassure. I know that I would be personally outraged if I were told that my intellectual capacities and personal values had been irrevocably defined for me by my ancestors and that now I was to think of myself in terms of the folkways of Russian peasants. I believe that if my ancestors had been Africans and, for example, I wanted to be an artist, I could readily accept the fact that art produced on the basis of a knowledge of perspective, geometry, human anatomy, and the refraction of light was a higher form of art than that produced in ignorance of such considerations. I would readily accept the fact that the latter type of art was, indeed, primitive. I would not feel that I was unable to learn these disciplines merely because my ancestors or other contemporary members of my race had not. I would feel the utmost contempt for the deliberate, chosen primitiveness of those "artists" (almost all white) who had reverted to the level of art of my (and their) primitive ancestors.

Race is not the determinant of culture. Not only is Western civilization open to the members of every race, but its present possessors are also potentially capable of losing it, just as the people of the Western Roman Empire once lost the high degree of civilization they had achieved. What makes the acceptance of the "Eurocentrism" critique so significant is that it so clearly reveals just how tenuous our ability to maintain Western civilization has become.

The preservation of Western civilization is not automatic. In the span of less than a century, virtually the entire population at the end consists of people who were not alive at the beginning. Western civilization, or any civilization, can continue only insofar as its intellectual substance lives on in the minds of new generations.

And it can do so only if it is imparted to young minds through education. *Education is the formal process of transmitting the intellectual substance of civilization from one generation to the next and thereby developing the uncultivated minds of children into those of civilized adults.* Western civilization is imparted to young minds in the teaching of Euclidean geometry and Newtonian physics, no less than in the teaching of the philosophy of Plato and Aristotle or the plays of Shakespeare. It is imparted in the teaching of every significant subject, from arithmetic to nuclear physics, from reading and writing to the causes of the rise and fall of civilizations. Wherever the intellectual substance of Western civilization is known, its transmission to the minds of students is virtually *coextensive with the process of education.* For the intellectual substance of Western civilization is nothing other than the highest level of knowledge attained anywhere on earth, in virtually every aspect of every field, and if the purpose of education is to impart knowledge, then its purpose is to impart Western civilization.

Thus, to the extent that the process of education is undermined, the whole of civilization must also be undermined, starting a generation later. These results will appear more and more striking as time goes on and as more and more defectively educated people take the place of those whose education was better. The worsening effects will likely be further intensified as those whose own education was defective become educators themselves and thus cause succeeding generations to be still more poorly educated.

Education in the United States has been in obvious decline for decades, and, in some ways that are critical but not obvious, perhaps for generations. The decline has become visible in such phenomena as the rewriting of college textbooks to conform with the more limited vocabularies of present-day students. It is visible in the functional illiteracy of large numbers of high school and even college graduates, in their inability to articulate their thoughts or to solve relatively simple problems in mathematics or even plain arithmetic, and in their profound lack of elementary knowledge of science and history.

I believe that the decline in education is probably responsible for the widespread use of drugs. To live in the midst of a civilized society with a level of knowledge closer perhaps to that of primitive man than to what a civilized adult requires (which, regrettably, is the intellectual state of many of today's students and graduates) must be a terrifying experience, urgently calling for some kind of relief, and drugs may appear to many to be the solution.

I believe that this also accounts for the relatively recent phenomenon of the public's fear of science and technology. Science and technology are increasingly viewed in reality as they used to be humorously depicted in Boris Karloff or Bela Lugosi movies, namely, as frightening "experiments" going on in Frankenstein's castle, with large numbers of present-day American citizens casting themselves in a real-life role of terrified and angry Transylvanian peasants seeking to smash whatever emerges from such laboratories. This attitude is the result not only of lack of education in science, but more fundamentally, loss of the ability to think critically— an ability which contemporary education provides little or no basis for developing. Because of their growing lack of knowledge and ability to think, people are becoming increasingly credulous and quick to panic.

Thus the critique of "Eurocentrism"—and any changes in curricula that may result from it—can hardly be blamed for inaugurating the decline in American education. On the contrary, it is a product of that decline. The fact that it is being accepted almost without opposition is evidence of how far the decline has already gone.

The equivalence of all cultures, the equivalence of civilization and savagery, is the avowed claim of the doctrine of cultural relativism, which has long been accepted by practically the whole of the educational establishment. It in turn is a consequence of the still older, more fundamental doctrine that there is no objective foundation for values—that all value-judgments are arbitrary and subjective. The new racists are now merely cashing in on this view and attempting to apply it on the largest possible scale, in the process substantially altering the manner in which subjects are taught. Today's educational establishment has fewer compunctions about putting absurd ideas into practice probably because of the deteriorated state of its own education. (Many of its members were educated in the 1960s, in the environment of the "student rebellion.")

The fact that the educational and intellectual establishments are fully in agreement with the fundamental premises of the new racists helps to explain why even when their members are opposed to the "Eurocentrism" critique, they have nothing of substance to say against it. As reported by the *Times,* the objections raised amounted to nothing more than complaints about the difficulty of finding non-European writers, philosophers, and artists to replace the European ones dropped from the curricula, and grumblings about the lack of Americans able to teach authoritatively about non-European cultures.

In capitulating to the "Eurocentrism" critique, the educational establishment has reached the point of reducing education to a level below that of ordinary ward politics: education is now to be a matter of pressure-group politics based on the totally false assumptions of racism. If there are now more black, Hispanic, or Asian students than white students in an area, then that fact is to be allowed to determine the substance of education, in the belief that these groups somehow "'secrete," as it were, a different kind of civilization and culture than do whites and require a correspondingly different kind of education.

Colleges in the United States have demonstrated such utter philosophical corruption in connection with this subject that if there were a group of students willing to assert with pride their descent from the Vandals or Huns and to demand courses on the cultural contributions of their ancestors, the schools would provide such courses. All that the students would have to do to get their way is to threaten to burn down the campus.

But what best sums up everything involved is this: from now on, in the state of California, a student is to go through twelve years of public school, and the explicit goal of his education is that at the end of it, if he envisions Columbus being greeted by spear-carrying savages, and he happens not to be white, he should identify with the savages—and if he does happen to be white, and therefore is allowed to identify with Columbus, he should not have any idea of why it is any better to identify with Columbus that with the savages.

This is no longer an educational system. Its character has been completely transformed and it now clearly reveals itself to be what for many decades it has been in the process of becoming: namely, an agency working for the *barbarization* of youth.

The value of education is derived from the value of civilization, whose guardian and perpetuator education is supposed to be. An educational system dedicated to the barbarization of youth is a self-contradictory monstrosity that must be cast out and replaced with a true educational system. But this can be done only by those who genuinely understand, and are able to defend, the *objective* value of Western civilization.

This article is available in pamphlet form from Jefferson School of Philosophy, Economics, and Psychology, P.O. Box 2934 Laguna Hills, CA 92654. Single copy price $3.25, quantity rates (for distribution only, not for resale, except to bookstores and other retailers): 2–10 copies $2.50 each, 50 or more copies $1.00 each. California residents please add sales tax.

Part Five

Quotas and Campus Diversity

14

Accrediting Bodies Must Require a Commitment to Diversity

Stephen S. Weiner

American colleges and universities are undergoing massive changes in the racial and ethnic composition of their student bodies. What is the relation between those changes and issues of educational quality? What role should accrediting agencies play in shaping campus actions concerning diversity and quality?

In 1988, after extensive discussion among our 152 accredited and candidate institutions, the Accrediting Commission for Senior Colleges and Universities of the Western Association of Schools and Colleges decided that every accredited institution, as part of its commitment to educational quality, should be expected to make continuing progress toward becoming a multiracial, multicultural institution. The Accrediting Commission for Community and Junior Colleges in our region and the Middle States Association of Colleges and Schools have taken similar stands.

Our commission recognizes that today's college students will come to maturity as parents, workers, voters, and professionals in a world that has no majority. Colleges and universities must keep that world very much in mind as they shape the educational experiences they offer. As the Asso-

from *The Chronicle of Higher Education* (October 10, 1990). Copyright © 1990 by Stephen S. Weiner. Reprinted by permission of the author. The author's views are not necessarily those of the Accrediting Commission for Senior Colleges and Universities of the Western Association of Schools and Colleges.

ciation of American Colleges declared in its 1985 report "Integrity in the College Curriculum":

All study is intended to break down the narrow certainties and provincial vision with which we are born. In a sense, we are all from the provinces, including New Yorkers and Bostonians, whose view of the world can be as circumscribed as that of native Alaskans who have never left their village. . . . At this point in history colleges are not being asked to produce village squires but citizens of a shrinking world and a changing America.

Diversity is already a fact of life both in our region and on our campuses. The proportion of Caucasians in California's population is predicted to drop below 50 percent within the next fifteen years. In 1988 white, non-Hispanic students accounted for 65 percent of the state's college enrollment, compared with close to 80 percent for the nation as a whole. In Hawaii, white, non-Hispanic students make up 30 percent of campus enrollments. While changes in the composition of the population have affected our region earlier than most others, there is a steady shift to a more diverse population throughout the United States. Thus, the issue now is less whether racial and ethnic diversity is coming than it is how to harness that diversity to the cause of educational improvement.

The commission's expectations regarding diversity affect virtually every aspect of campus life, and, therefore, each of our accrediting standards. For example, the commission's standard on institutional integrity now includes this statement: "The institution demonstrates its commitment to the increasingly significant educational role played by diversity of ethnic, social, and economic backgrounds among its members by making positive efforts to foster such diversity." This standard requires institutions to have equal-opportunity and affirmative action policies.

"Appreciation of cultural diversity" has been added to the commission's expectations concerning the outcomes of undergraduate education, along with competence in written and oral communication, quantitative skills, and the habit of critical analysis of data and argument. With respect to the learning environment, the commission expects that each institution will have "an academic community that significantly involves its various populations."

What do we expect from institutions and our visiting teams?

First, we ask both institutions and our teams not to define the challenge of diversity—or its attainment—solely in terms of numbers of minority group students or faculty, staff, or governing-board members. Contrary to the fear expressed by some, we are not pressing for the adoption of quotas. Having members of minority groups in each constituency of an institution, especially in leadership positions, is essential and a prerequisite for meaningful dialogue about diversity. But our concerns go well beyond such counting exercises to the culture of the campus, the value placed upon diversity in different aspects of campus life, and the ability of the campus to bridge the contrasting perception of reality held by members of different ethnic and racial groups. Interviews, focus-group discussions, and the analysis of institutional data (such as student-retention rates) often reveal a gulf in perception. Whites perceive minority group members as being treated well, while people of color often recount experiences that convince them that they are still "outsiders" and that their status on campus is both marginal and vulnerable. The first step toward addressing the tensions that arise from such diametrically opposed views is to know that they exist.

Second we look for presidential and faculty leadership in affirming that "diversity" does not mean a narrow effort to benefit only members of minority groups, but a commitment of talent and resources to widen everyone's intellectual grasp and personal understanding. Diversity is not a "problem" to be solved so that colleges and universities can get on with "real business." A permanent part of the "real business" of higher education is examining how diversity and educational quality should be pursued both inside and outside the classroom. Presidents and faculty leaders need to attend to the requisites of affirmative action in employment and admissions policies, support candid assessment of the existing campus climate concerning diversity, and take the lead in articulating a vision of how a diverse and educationally challenging campus community can develop.

Third, campuses should have written plans on how to achieve diversity that have been subjected to broad and searching discussion. The plans should address curricula, recruiting and retention strategies for students and faculty and staff members, student-life programs, and academic support for students. The plans should have goals and some way of assessing whether the goals are being achieved. We have found that writing such plans forces disciplined thought and commitment. The purpose of the plans is not for campus leaders to become caught in the slavish grip of a document, but rather to prompt them to come back to these issues on a continuing basis.

Finally, we expect each of our visiting teams to address diversity issues in their report evaluating the institution. Our teams' reports do not impose solutions on a campus. Rather, in a collegial spirit, they analyze the institution's self-study; ask questions; report perceptions, problems and opportunities that become evident during the visits; and praise worthwhile efforts that are under way.

To help visiting teams achieve these objectives, the commission's staff has undertaken new efforts to recruit, select, and train team members. Last year, more than 20 percent of our team members were people of color, and more than 30 percent were women. Almost 50 percent of our team members last year were new to the accreditation process, including many white males who strongly support the commission's new standards. We found that the quality of teams' reports last year, in addressing all of the commission's standards, was higher than ever.

After conducting fifty comprehensive visits under the new standards, we have learned this most important leson: that to achieve an academic community that embraces diversity, we first have to learn how to talk about it. Issues involving race and ethnicity have emotional and political overtones, and many people feel uncomfortable discussing their perceptions, feelings, and aspirations.

Two steps seem to help in getting the discussion started. The first is to remind ourselves that "diversity" should not be a code word for granting preferences to one group over another. Rather, we are seeking to build a campus community where all people, regardless of professional role, ethnicity, or gender, will be respected, will have the maximum possible opportunity for professional development, and will be productive. In particular, we are seeking to create campus cultures where individuals and groups are deeply committed to teaching one another and learning from one another. When people begin to understand that diversity is about bringing people together, rather than driving them apart, they become far more willing to contribute their thoughts and their energy.

Second, even after assurances that the goal of diversity is community building, people need to be given "protected space" in which to talk. By that I mean the guarantee that people may speak freely and candidly, in a diverse group, without fear that they will be punished or ostracized for expressing controversial opinions. At times, discussions about diversity are emotional. But the discussion must go beyond emotion. We have to be willing to think hard and anew and to explore uncomfortable questions.

We have learned other things as well.

Conflict and disagreement often accompany progress on diversity. The campus where students are demonstrating in the president's office may be just the one that has most seriously and thoughtfully engaged the issues. And, it is also true that there are times when an ugly racial incident galvanizes a campus to take constructive steps that are long overdue.

With only rare exceptions, college leaders in our region agree that diversity and educational quality are intertwined and, therefore, both are the proper concern of the regional accrediting commission. But we also find that institutions fall along a wide spectrum in their initial capacity to respond to the commission's expectations.

Institutional wealth is a poor predictor of achievement with respect to diversity. Some colleges have made enormous strides within the constraints of very limited budgets. Some wealthy and prestigious institutions are just beginning to make progress.

Campuses are changing and so is the nature of accreditation. Accrediting bodies stand at the boundary between higher education and the public. We seek to inform the public about proper standards of higher education to affirm that certain institutions meet those standards. In turn, we must also serve as a medium to insure that public concerns are reflected in the dialogue about quality in higher education.

Accreditation should be about more than the setting of minimum standards. Our role, which must be carried out with great care and deliberation, is also to challenge even the best colleges and universities to rethink their contribution to society as a whole. As accrediting bodies play that role, we do not, and will not, please everyone. But as we ask tougher and better questions about the meaning of quality, we join the campuses in taking risks that are well worth taking.

15

Accreditation by Quota:
The Case of Baruch College

William R. Beer

On April 5, 1990, the *New York Times* reported that Dr. Joel Segall, president of Baruch College of the City University of New York, was resigning from his job, following a critical review by the Middle States Association of Schools and Colleges. There was no allegation that Baruch was anything less that an excellent college. In fact, it is widely regarded as one of the four top business colleges in the country and trains almost one out of every three of the certified public accountants working in New York. Rather, the complaint was that there were not enough "minorities" in the faculty and administration and that not enough "minorities" graduated. Disturbing though this is, even more unsettling is the fact that the criticism was concocted by the central offices of the accrediting agency, acting independently of its own guidelines and evaluation team.

The attack on Segall and the Baruch faculty represents an ominous direction taken by accreditation. For the first time, an accrediting agency is criticizing the ethnic composition of a college's graduating class, as well as making specific complaints about the racial makeup of its faculty and staff. According to a source on the Department of Education's National Advisory Committee on Accreditation and Institutional Eligibility, such

From *Academic Questions* (Fall 1990). Copyright © 1990 by William R. Beer. Reprinted by permission of Transaction.

a step is entirely unprecedented. No other accrediting agency has ever undertaken an aggressive role in attempting to impose racial quotas on faculty, administrators, and graduates.

In itself, the attempt to control the ethnicity of university personnel is nothing new. In the last twenty years, the concept of affirmative action has evolved into a quota system in which white males are routinely excluded, as John Bunzel has documented in a recent article in the *American Scholar*. Although deeply threatening to the integrity of the university because they undermine the concept of professional peer review, quotas imposed on personnel committees have been a long time aborning, and it does not appear that they will be easily abolished. Until recently, however, the federal government was the principal agency in this coercion. Now, it appears, the effort has shifted from government to private agencies such as Middle States, accompanied by the notion that henceforth a college may have its accreditation withheld if it does not graduate the right percentage of certain ethnic groups.

A RACIAL GRADUATION QUOTA?

When asked if a college could be found delinquent for failing to graduate sufficient numbers of "minority" students, Dr. Howard I. Simmons, executive director of the Middle States Association, agreed that Middle States does use an "outcomes-based approach" for granting or withholding its approval. He denied that Middle States has any "hard and fast rules" regarding minority retention rates, indicating there is "never a single standard" in assessing a school's performance in this regard.

Simmons has claimed that his approach comes from *Characteristics of Excellence in Higher Education: Standards for Accreditation,* the handbook used by Middle States. In fact, there is no statement whatsoever in that manual concerning minority retention rates. When this was pointed out Simmons changed his mind and said that accreditation is granted or withheld on a case-by-case basis. "I know that sounds hard to understand," he admitted, "but that's how they do it. The team decides differently for each school." There are "so many factors involved" that there can be "no quantitative standards" for evaluating a college. So much for the objective criteria of accreditation.

The use of an unstated but *de facto* racial graduation quota puts university administrators in a vulnerable position, since there is no way to tell whether Middle States will charge them with not having satisfied the goal of graduating sufficient numbers of designated minority groups.

The lack of precision permits Middle States to deny that they are seeking any exact outcome, thereby avoiding legal action. At the same time, when it suits them they can use the "outcomes-based approach" as a potential threat to colleges seeking accreditation. Knowing that they will be held to an inexact but real racial graduation quota, residents and deans will be inclined to design programs to increase graduation prospects for protected groups.

Middle States can thus obtain the desired outcome without ever having to invoke the threat explicitly, and all the while remain protected from public scrutiny. Simmons admits having adopted the same tactic with many other institutions, but because of the secrecy involved in the accreditation process, he has not had to be held publicly accountable.

The other criticism leveled against Baruch is that it does not employ enough "minorities." In reality, this argument is absurd since many Baruch professors are Jewish and non-white Asians. But in education-speak, such individuals are not defined as "minorities." Middle States is actually arguing that Baruch's faculty has too many non-Hispanic whites and not enough blacks for a student body that includes many blacks and Hispanics. Thus, the broader question at issue is whether or not white instructors can adequately teach "minority" students. The "diversity" of a student body, according to Middle States, must be matched by a corresponding "diversity" of faculty and administrators. This belief is so widespread amongst academic administrative congnoscenti that few question it. When the logic of such a concept is challenged, the usual response is that a white professor cannot be as good a "role model" for a black student as a black professor.

While one may suggest that professors can serve as inspirational mentors to college students, no evidence exists that such individuals must be of the same sex, race, or cultural background. The idea of "role model," in short, is fraudulently applied in the field of higher education.

Indeed, if such a concept did make sense, it would have exactly the opposite results of what Middle States ostensibly desires. It would mean not only that black students should be counseled to take courses only from black professors. If black students need black professors as role models to spur them to greater levels of achievement, white students require and deserve the same kind of encouragement. Taken to its logical conclusion, the "role model" argument is actually a strong justification for racial segregation in higher education. If black students respond best to black professors, they ought to maximize their chances by enrolling at all-black colleges. The same would apply *mutatis mutandis,* to white students.

In the classic accreditation process, institutions are evaluated on the basis of the stringency or laxity of their education standards. In the past, if a college was found to be too lax, accreditation was withheld, or perhaps conditionally granted pending correction of certain deficiencies. But now, for the first time, a college's accrediation has been "deferred," not because its standards are too low, but because they are too high. An institution of higher learning is being directed to arrange its faculty, administration, and curriculum so that a *de facto* racial graduation quota can be filled. Aside from some serious issues of law, this initiative represents the latest step in the abolition of institutional autonomy and faculty control over the hiring process.

It is no coincidence that this new and arbitrary direction has been taken by a private accrediting agency. In 1989 the Supreme Court issued a series of decisions that seriously undermined the ability of government to require institutions to use racial and sexual quotas in hiring and promotions. Though this was a serious setback for those who would like to see a political system governed by racial and sexual entitlement, they have evidently regrouped.

For example, under the sponsorship of Senators Kennedy and Hawkins, the Civil Rights bill of 1990 currently being argued in Congress would reimpose on employers the burden of proving that they did not discriminate against minorities in hiring. Since it is virtually impossible to prove that something has not occured, the result will be that employers (including colleges and universities) will be obliged to adopt quotas in hiring in order to forstall potential lawsuits. This is particularly likely because the same legislation will require employers to pay the cost of employees' litigation, thus encouraging plaintiffs to make complaints of discrimination free of charge.

On the level of academic rhetoric, the tactic has been to substitute "diversity" for the now-tainted "affirmative action," since it is widely recognized that the latter has produced discriminatory preferential hiring. Surveys show that most blacks, as well as most whites, are opposed to preferential treatment for blacks. Using "diversity" sounds better because the term is vague and it is hard to say one is against it. But the Baruch case shows what "diversity" truly means; it is simply old wine in new bottles.

That there is no logical or empirical justification for racial quotas in hiring or graduation should not need saying. But Simmons and his allies are not governed by logic or facts; they are driven by a sense of moral righteousness that is impervious to any argument. Rather than conforming to consistent and objective standards of excellence, Simmons makes up the rule as he goes along. Rather than appealing to the intellects, Simmons tugs at peoples' basic emotions in order to impose his political agenda on higher education.

Conclusion

16

Final Thoughts on Political Correctness: Some Proposals

Dinesh D'Souza

Each fall some thirteen million students, 2.5 million of them minorities, enroll in American colleges.[1] Most of these students are living away from home for the first time. Yet their apprehension is mixed with excitement and anticipation. At the university, they hope to shape themselves as whole human beings, both intellectually and morally. Brimming with idealism, they wish to prepare themselves for full and independent lives in the workplace, at home, and as citizens who are shared rulers of a democratic society. In short, what they seek is liberal education.

By the time these students graduate, very few colleges have met their need for all-around development. Instead, by precept and example, universities have taught them that "all rules are unjust" and "all preferences are principled"; that justice is simply the will of the stronger party; that standards and values are arbitrary, and the ideal of the educated person is largely a figment of bourgeois white male ideology, which should be cast aside; that individual rights are a red flag signaling social privilege, and should be subordinated to the claims of group interest; that all knowledge can be reduced to politics and should be pursued not for its

Reprinted with the permission of The Free Press, a Division of Macmillan, Inc., from *Illiberal Education: The Politics of Race and Sex on Campus* by Dinesh D'Souza. Copyright © 1991 by Dinesh D'Souza.

own sake but for the political end of power; that convenient myths and benign lies can substitute for truth; that double standards are acceptable as long as they are enforced to the benefit of minority victims; that debates are best conducted not by rational and civil exchange of ideas, but by accusation, intimidation, and official prosecution; that the university stands for nothing in particular and has no claim to be exempt from outside pressures; and that the multiracial society cannot be based on fair rules that apply to every person, but must rather be constructed through a forced rationing of power among separatist racial groups. In short, instead of liberal education, what American students are getting is its diametrical opposite, an education in closed-mindedness and intolerance, which is to say, illiberal education.

Ironically the young blacks, Hispanics, and other certified minorities in whose name the victim's revolution is conducted are the ones least served by the American university's abandonment of liberal ideals. Instead of treating them as individuals, colleges typically consider minorities as members of a group, important only insofar as their collective numbers satisfy the formulas of diversity. Since many of these students depend on a college degree to enhance their career opportunities, their high dropout rate brings tremendous suffering and a sense of betrayal. Even more than others, minority students arrive on campus searching for principles of personal identity and social justice; thus they are particularly disillusioned when they leave empty-handed. Moreover, most minority graduates will admit, when pressed, that if their experience in college is any indication, the prospects for race relations in the country at large are gloomy. If the university model is replicated in society at large, far from bringing ethnic harmony, it will reproduce and magnify the lurid bigotry, intolerance, and balkanization of campus life in the broader culture.

WHAT'S WRONG WITH DIVERSITY

Although university leaders speak of the self-evident virtues of diversity, it is not at all obvious why it is necessary to first-rate education. Universities such as Brandeis, Notre Dame, and Mount Holyoke, which were founded on principles of religious and gender homogeneity, still manage to provide an excellent education. Similarly, foreign institutions such as Oxford, Cambridge, Bologna, Salamanca, Paris, and Tokyo display considerable cultural singularity, yet they are regarded as among the best in the world.

The question is not whether universities should seek diversity, but what kind of diversity. It seems that the primary form of diversity which universities should try to foster is diversity of mind. Such diversity would enrich academic discourse, widen its parameters, multiply its objects of inquiry, and increase the probability of obscure and unlikely terrain being investigated. Abroad one typically encounters such diversity of opinion even on basic questions such as how society should be organized. In my high school in Bombay, for example, I could identify students who considered themselves monarchists, Fabian socialists, Christian democrats, Hindu advocates of a caste-based society, agrarians, centralized planners, theocrats, liberals, and Communists. In European universities, one finds a similar smorgasbord of philosophical convictions.

By contrast, most American students seem to display striking agreement on all the basic questions of life. Indeed, they appear to regard a true difference of opinion, based upon convictions that are firmly and intensely held, as dangerously dogmatic and an offense against the social etiquette of tolerance. Far from challenging these conventional prejudices, college leaders tend to encourage their uncritical continuation. "Universities show no interest whatsoever in fostering intellectual diversity," John Bunzel, former president of San Jose State University, says bluntly. Evidence suggests that the philosophical composition of the American faculty is remarkably homogenous,[2] yet Bunzel says that universities are not concerned. "When I raise the problem with leaders in academe, their usual response is that [the imbalance] is irrelevant, or that there cannot be litmus tests for recruitment."

But universities do take very seriously the issue of *racial* underrepresentation. Here they are quite willing to consider goals, quotas, litmus tests, whatever will rectify the tablulated disproportion. "What we're hoping," said Malcolm Gillis, a senior official at Duke, "is that racial diversity will ultimately lead to intellectual diversity."

The problem begins with a deep sense of embarrassment over the small number of minorities—blacks in particular—on campuses. University officials speak of themselves as more enlightened and progressive than the general population, so they feel guilty if the proportion of minorities at their institutions is smaller than in surrounding society. Moreover, they are often pressured by politicians who control appropriations at state schools, and by student and faculty activists on campus. As a consequence, universities agree to make herculean efforts to attract as many blacks, Hispanics, and other certified minorities as possible to their institution.

[T]he number of minority applicants who would normally qualify for acceptance at selective universities is very small; therefore, in order to meet ambitious recruitment targets, affirmative action must entail fairly drastic compromises in admissions requirements. University leaders are willing to use unjust means to achieve their goal of equal representation. In one of the more radical steps in this direction, the California legislature is considering measures to *require* all state colleges to accept black, Hispanic, white, and Asian students in proportion with their level in the population, regardless of the disparity in academic preparation or qualifications among such groups.[3]

The first consequence of such misguided policies is a general misplacement of minority students throughout higher education. Thus a student whose grades and qualifications are good enough to get him into Rutgers or Penn State finds himself at Williams or Bowdoin, and the student who meets Williams' and Bowdoin's more demanding requirements finds himself at Yale or Berkeley. Many selective universities are so famished for minority students that they will accept virtually anyone of the right color who applies. In order to fulfill affirmative action objectives, university admissions officers cannot afford to pay too much attention to the probability of a student succeeding at the university.

For many black, Hispanic, and American Indian students who may have struggled hard to get through high school, the courtship of selective universities comes as a welcome surprise. As we have seen, they receive expenses-paid trips to various colleges, where they are chaperoned around campus, introduced to deans and senior faculty, and most of all assured that their presence is avidly desired, indeed that the university would be a poorer place if they chose to go somewhere else. These blandishments naturally enhance the expectations of minority students. These expectations are reinforced by such focused events as the minority freshmen orientation, where black, Hispanic, American Indian, and foreign students are given to understand that they are walking embodiments of the university's commitment to multiculturalism and diversity. Universities emphasize that they are making no accommodations or compromises to enroll affirmative action students; on the contrary, they insist that these students will make a special contribution that the university could not obtain elsewhere.

Their lofty hopes, however, are not realized for most affirmative action students. During the first few weeks of class, many recognize the degree to which they are academically unprepared, relative to other students. At Berkeley, for instance, admissions office data show that the average black freshman's GPA and test scores fall in the 6th percentile of scores for whites and Asians; anthropology professor Vincent Sarich remarks, "As we get more and more selective among Asians and whites, the competitive gap necessarily increases."[4] Yet once these students get to class, professors at demanding schools such as Berkeley take for granted that they know who wrote *Paradise Lost,* that they are capable of understanding Shakespearean English, that they have heard of Max Weber and the Protestant ethic, that they can solve algebraic equations, that they know something about the cell and the amoeba. Students are expected to read several hundred pages of literature, history, biology, and other subjects every week, and produce analytical papers, appropriately footnoted, on short notice.

Unfortunately the basic ingredients of what E. D. Hirsch terms "cultural literacy" are by no means uniformly transmitted in American high schools, nor are regular intellectual habits of concentration and discipline. Thus in the first part of freshman year, affirmative action students with relatively weak preparation often encounter a bewildering array of unfamiliar terms and works. Coping with them, says William Banks, professor of Afro-American Studies at Berkeley, "can be very confusing and frustrating." While they wrestle with the work load, affirmative action students also notice that their peers seem much more comfortable in this academic environment, quicker in absorbing the reading, more confident and fluent in their speech and writing. Even if affirmative action students work that much harder, they discover that it is not easy to keep pace, since the better prepared students also work very hard.

For many minority students, especially those from disadvantaged backgrounds, these problems are often complicated by a difficult personal adjustment to a new environment. It is not easy going from an inner-city high school to a college town with entirely new social routines, or settling into a dormitory where roommates have a great deal more money to spend, or cultivating the general university lifestyle that is familiar to prep schoolers and sons and daughters of alumni but alien to many minority and foreign students.

University leaders have discovered how displaced and unsettled minority freshmen can be, and typically respond by setting up counseling services and remedial education programs intended to assure blacks and Hispanics that they do belong, and that they can "catch up" with other students. Neither of these university resources is well used, however. Students who are struggling to keep up with course work hardly have time to attend additional classes in reading comprehension and alegebra. If they do enroll in these programs, they run the risk of falling further behind in class. Relatively few minority students attend counseling because they correctly reject the idea that there is something wrong with them. Nor would the therapeutic assurances of freshman counselors do much to solve their academic difficulties. For many minority undergraduates, therefore, the university's quest for racial equality produces a conspicuous academic inequality.

SEPARATE AND UNEQUAL

As at Berkeley, Michigan, and elsewhere, many minority students seek comfort and security among their peers who are in a similar situation. Thus they may sign up for their campus Afro-American Society or Hispanic Association or ethnic theme house or fraternity, where they can share their hopes and frustrations in a relaxed and candid atmosphere, and get guidance from older students who have traveled these strange paths. The impulse to retreat into exclusive enclaves is a familiar one for minority groups who have suffered a history of persecution; they feel there is strength and safety in numbers, and tend to develop group consciousness and collective orientation partly as a protective strategy.[5]

But when minority students demand that the college recognize and subsidize separatist institutions, the administration is placed in a dilemma.[6] The deans know that to accede to these demands is problematic, given their public commitment to integration of students from different backgrounds—indeed the promise of such interaction is one of the main justifications for the goal of diversity sought through affirmative action. At the same time, university leaders realize how dislocated many minority students feel, and how little the university itself can do to help them. Further, the administration does not know how it could possibly say no to these students, and harbors vague and horrific fears of the consequences.

[V]irtually every administration ends by putting aside its qualms and permitting minority institutions to flourish. The logical extreme may be witnessed at California State University at Sacramento, which has announced a new plan to establish an entirely separate "college within a college" for blacks.[7] To justify this separatist subsidy, university leaders have developed a model of "pluralism," which they insist is not the same thing as integration. Since integration implies the merging of various ethnic groups into a common whole, it does not really contribute to diversity. By contrast, pluralism implies the enhancement of distinct ethnic subcultures—a black culture, Hispanic culture, American Indian culture, and a (residual) white culture—which it is hoped will interact in a harmonious and mutually enriching manner.

There is a good deal of camaraderie and social activity at the distinctive minority organizations. Most of them, especially ethnic residence halls and fraternities, help to give newly arrived minority students a sense of belonging. They do not, however, offer any solution to the dilemma facing those students who are inadequately prepared for the challenges of the curriculum. Virtually none of the minority organizations offers study programs or tutorials for affirmative action students. Indeed, some separatist institutions encourage anti-intellectualism, viewing it as an authentic black cultural trait. As researchers Signithia Fordham of Rutgers and John Ogbu of Berkeley describe it, "What appears to have emerged in some segments of the black community is a kind of cultural orientation which defines academic learning as 'acting white,' and academic success as the prerogative of white Americans."[8] Thus many minority freshmen who are struggling academically find no practical remedy in the separate culture of minority institutions.

What they do often find is a novel explanation for their difficulties. Older students tell the newcomers that they should be aware of the pervasive atmosphere of bigotry on campus. Although such racism may not be obvious at first, minority freshmen should not be deceived by appearances. Racism is vastly more subtle than in the past, and operates in various guises, some of them as elusive as baleful looks, uncorrected mental stereotypes, and the various forms of deceptively "polite" behavior.[9] In addition to looking out for such nuances, minority freshmen and sophomores are further warned not to expect much support from the university, where "overt racism" has given way to "institutional racism," evident in the disproportionately small numbers of minorities reflected on the faculty and among the deans and trustees.[10] Everywhere, forces of bigotry are said to conspire against permitting minority students the "racism-free environment" they need to succeed.

Typically, minority beneficiaries are strong supporters of preferential treatment, although their natural pride requires that its nature be disguised. They may speak more freely about it among themselves, but among white students and in the mainstream campus discussion, they understandably refrain from admitting that academic standards were adjusted to make their enrollment possible. Instead, these students assert, often under the banner of their minority organization, that the view that blacks, Hispanics, and American Indians benefit at the expense of overrepresented students is itself evidence of pervasive bigotry. Consequently, in the minds of minority students, affirmative action is not a cause of their academic difficulties, but an excuse for white racism which is the real source of their problems.

Once racism is held accountable for minority unrest, it is now up to students to find, expose, and extirpate it. Here the university leadership steps in with offers of assistance. Eager to deflect frustration and anger from the president's office, the administration seeks to convince minority activists that the real enemy is latent bigotry among their fellow students and professors, and that their energies are best invested in combating white prejudice.

Meanwhile, feminists and homosexual activists typically seek to exploit the moral momentum of the race issue. Just as blacks and Hispanics are victimized by arbitrary race discrimination, they assert, women are subjugated by gender bigotry and homosexuals are tyrannized by similar prejudice in the area of sexual orientation. Feminists, for instance, associate themselves with the black cause by insisting that marriage has always been a form of "domestic slavery." These groups promote the idea that they suffer the oppression of a common enemy. Many administrators believe in their cause and agree to link it with the campaign against white racism. Thus while women comprise between 40 and 60 percent of most university populations, they are routinely classified as vulnerable "minorities." Seeking to eradicate the various species of bigotry, the university's reeducation effort narrows to target the white, male, heterosexual element. As at Penn State, Wisconsin, and Michigan, universities set up committees and task forces to investigate the problem of latent and subtle bigotry. Minority students and faculty typically dominate these committees. Surveys are drawn up. Hearings are scheduled. In a Kafkaesque turn of events, the academic inequality of minority students is blamed on the social prejudices of their white male peers.

THE NEW RACISM

Most white students do not take gender and homosexuality very seriously as political issues. Even the most sympathetic find it hard to believe that the female condition has historically been the moral equivalent of Negro slavery, nor do they equate ethnicity, which is an arbitrary characteristic, with homosexuality, which is a sexual preference. The race question, however, places white students in a very uncomfortable situation. Many of them arrive on campus with tolerant, but generally uninformed views. They may not have known many blacks or Hispanics in the past, yet they are generally committed to equal rights regardless of race or background, and they seem open to building friendships and associations with people who they know have been wronged through history.

Since the time they applied to college, many students know that certain minorities have benefited from preferential treatment in admission. It is possible that some minority classmates did not need affirmative action to get in, but it is not possible to know which ones, and the question seems somewhat superfluous anyway. Even students who support the concept of affirmative action in theory are discomfited when they see that it is now more difficult for them to get into the universities for which they have studied hard to prepare. Moreover, even if they win admission, many have friends who they believe were denied admission to places like Berkeley in order to make room for minority students with weaker scores and grades.

This seems unfair to many white and Asian students, and it is little solace to tell them that they must subordinate their individual rights to the greater good of group equality via proportional representation. Asian American students, unembarrassed by any traditional group advantages in American society, vehemently reject the idea that they should suffer in order to create space for underrepresented black and Hispanic groups who suffered no maltreatment or disadvantage at the hands of Asians. . . .

White and Asian students are reminded of these concerns when they see the obvious difference in preparation and performance among various groups in the classroom. Black and Hispanic academic difficulties confirm the suspicion that universities are admitting students based on different sets of standards—a sort of multiple-track acceptance process. Yet this may not be stated in public, partly because most universities continue to deny that they lower admissions requirements for select minorities, and partly because favored minorities would take offense at such "insensitivity." Consequently, white and Asian students talk about affirmative action only in private. But since students live and study in close quarters, it is impossible to conceal these sentiments for long, and soon affirmative action students begin to suspect that people are talking behind closed doors about the issue that is most sensitive to them. White and Asian students frequently attempt to prevent confrontation with blacks and Hispanics by making passionate public proclamations of their fidelity to the causes of civil rights, feminism, and gay rights. But for many, a gap opens up between their personal and public views.

When minority students develop separatist cultures on the campus, white students tend to have a mixed response. For those who are actually prejudiced, minority self-segregation comes as a relief, because it removes blacks and Hispanics from the mainstream of campus life, and because it reinforces bigoted attitudes of racial inferiority. Many whites, however, are merely puzzled at minority separatism, because it goes so sharply against what they have heard from the university about integration and cultural interaction. As students at Berkeley, Michigan, and Harvard asked earlier, where is the "diversity" that is supposed to result from the interaction of racial and gender "perspectives"? What affirmative action seems to produce instead is group isolation. Eleanor Holmes Norton, former head of the Equal Employment Opportunity Commission under President Carter and now a professor at Georgetown Law School, complains that the new separatism is "exactly what we were fighting against—it is antithetical to what the civil rights movement was all about. It sets groups apart, and it prevents blacks from partaking of the larger culture." Historian Arthur Schlesinger adds that "the melting pot has yielded to the Tower of Babel," and with the loss of a common multiracial identity, "We invite the fragmentation of our culture into a quarrelsome spatter of enclaves, ghettos and tribes."[11] Somehow the intended symphony has become a cacophony.

White students generally have no desire to set up their own racially exclusive unions, clubs, or residence halls. But, as we have repeatedly heard, they cannot help feeling that the university is practicing a double standard by supporting minority institutions to which whites may not belong, and many agree with *Washington Post* columnist William Raspberry that "you cannot claim both full equality and special dispensation."[12] Separatist institutions irritate many whites on campus not because they are separate, but because in most cases they become institutional grievance factories. Many of these groups are quick to make accusations of bigotry, to the point where any disagreement with the agenda of the Afro-American Society or the Third World Alliance is automatic evidence of racism. Antiwhite rhetoric goes unchecked on campus, evoking at best an eerie silence. Thus, while it is possible to ignore minority self-segregation in principle, such indifference becomes harder when the groups serve as base camps for mounting ideological assaults against everyone else. "Pluralism" becomes a framework for racial browbeating and intimidation.

When they discover resentment among students over preferential treatment and minority separatism, university administrators conclude that they have discovered the latent bigotry for which they have been searching. Consequently, many universities institute "sensitivity" training programs, such as Harvard's notorious AWARE week, to cure white students of their prejudice. As at Michigan, the University of Connecticut, Stanford, and Emory, some schools go so far as to outlaw racially or sexually "stigmatizing" remarks—even "misdirected laughter" and "exclusion from conversation"—which are said to make learning for minorities impossible. On virtually every campus, there is a de facto taboo against a free discussion of affirmative action or minority self-segregation, and efforts to open such a discussion are considered presumptively racist. Thus measures taken to enhance diversity have instead created a new regime of intellectual conformity.[13]

S. Frederick Starr, president of Oberlin College, remarks that "diversity should not be the prerogative of any particular ideological agenda. But now it means subscribing to a set of political views." Donald Kagan, dean of arts and sciences at Yale, concurs. "It is common in universities today to hear talk of politically correct opinions, or PC for short. These are questions that are not really open to argument. It takes real courage to oppose the campus orthodoxy. To tell you the truth, I was a student during the days of McCarthy, and there is less freedom now than there was then."

One of the saddest effects of the divisiveness of campus life—remarked on by professors and students across the spectrum—is that few true friendships are formed between white and black students. Perhaps the main reason is that, as Aristotle said, friendship presumes equality between people who share common interests and goals. Many white and black students find that, socially and intellectually, they have little in common with each other. As Berkeley professor [Troy] Duster's research shows, these differences are not reduced, but heightened, over time. Indeed they are converted into group differences, and these groups view each other across chasms that are virtually impossible to cross. Relations between white and minority groups are usually hostile since they are defined by allegations of white oppression and minority victimization: consequently, whites are forced into a defensive posture against political irredentism from highly self-conscious minority groups.

Campus browbeating and balkanization come to public attention by way of the outcomes they produce—the racial joke and the racial incident. Both represent white exasperation with perceived unfairness, double standards, and suppression of independent thought on the American campus. Jokes are ways for malcontents to express feelings which lack a respectable outlet. As with David Makled and Andrew Milot at Michigan, and the editors of the *Harvard Salient,* many whites whose prejudices should have been challenged and diminished through their human interaction with minorities find their stereotypes partially confirmed. Yet they know the risk of speaking their mind, so their views burrow underground, and sometimes resurface in the form of crude pranks and humor.

In one of his speeches, Malcolm X implied the omnipresence of white racism by asking: What do you call a black man with a Ph.D? Answer: Nigger. What was intended with passionate seriousness by Malcolm X, I was surprised to discover, is now part of the culture of racial humor on campus. Something that was a cause of soul-searching, two decades ago, is today the occasion for laughter. The reason for the amusement is preferential treatment: who knows what the black man with the Ph.D is capable of doing? The Ph.D has been placed, by affirmative action, into invisible quotation marks. The humor comes from the recognition of this fact, combined with the necessity not only of denying it in public, but of appearing appropriately shocked when such a suggestion is raised.

Similarly, racial incidents represent the uncorking of a very tightly sealed bottle. A careful examination of these incidents, at Michigan and Stanford and Temple and elsewhere, reveals that most of them are connected to preferential treatment and minority double standards. At Bryn Mawr, for example, a freshman found an anonymous note slipped under her door. "Hey, Spic," it read, "If you and your kind can't handle the work here, don't blame it on the racial thing. Why don't you just get out? We'd all be a lot happier."[14] At George Washington University in 1987, students countered Black History Month by announcing a "White History Week Party."[15] And, for the first time the American campus now has university-sponsored white student unions. It is impossible to separate this "new racism" on campus from the old racism, because the bigotry which results from preferential treatment strengthens and reinforces the old bigotry which preferential policies were instituted to fight.

In one sense, the new racism is different, however. The old racism was based on prejudice, whereas the new racism is based on conclusions. Prejudice, of course, means prejudgment, judgment in the absence of information. This was an accurate way to describe many of the old racists of the earlier part of this century: they knew little about blacks, encountered few in the course of life, and disliked them based on the fear that stems from ignorance. The solutions for the old racism were education, enlightenment, and consciousness-raising. American society began an experiment in integration. By meeting blacks, living alongside them, eating with them, befriending them, the expectation was that whites would recognize common human interests which surpassed group differences, and that they would quickly lose their stereotypes. And to a considerable extent, this project has worked. The old racism is not dead, by any means, but it is truly powerful only in small pockets of society, and it is discredited morally and politically in all sectors of public life.

The new bigotry is not derived from ignorance, but from experience. It is harbored not by ignoramuses, but by students who have direct and first-hand experience with minorities in the close proximity of university settings. The "new racists" do not believe they have anything to learn about minorities; quite the contrary, they believe they are the only ones who are willing to face the truth about them. Consequently, they are not uncomfortable about their views, believing them to be based on evidence. They feel they occupy the high ground, while everyone else is performing pirouettes and somersaults to avoid the obvious.

Both university leaders and minority activists sense the durability of the new racism, and its resistance to correction by means of liberal reeducation. Even sensitivity sessions and other awareness requirements, backed by censorship codes, do not seem able to penetrate the inner reaches of human conviction; at best, they only regulate its outward expression.

But in fact, many administrators are privately ambivalent about combating these private suspicions about minorities, because they share them. Most of them, too, are among the new racists on the American campus. Their attitude towards minority students, however optimistic it might once have been, has turned to resigned condescension. They do not believe that they can afford to apply mainstream standards to minority students, because they are certain that minorities would fare badly, causing the institution to suffer serious embarrassment. Nor do they feel able to resist minority demands, however unreasonable they appear, lest these students react in some terrible and irrational way. Therefore, like presidents Donald Kennedy of Stanford, Lattie Coor of the University of Vermont, and Joseph Duffey of the University of Massachusetts at Amherst, they consistently acquiesce in these demands, abdicating their responsibility to both the students and the institution itself.[16]

The university leadership generally holds not that minorities are inferior, but that they might be treated *as though* they are inferior. The old racists sought to prove inferiority through ridiculous methods such as craniology; the new racists in the dean's office take inferiority for granted. The new racism among university leaders differs from its counterpart among undergraduates only in the sense that imprudent undergradutes, sometimes inadvertently, say what they think; by contrast, university leaders only act on those presumptions, confining their personal communication to meaningful glances, rolling eyes, and the rest of the insignia of administrative tact and prudence. In this sense, minority students are entirely correct in their frustrated belief that there exists in the establishment a subtle racism that is virtually impossible to document.

Whenever racial incidents occur, as we saw at Michigan and elsewhere, university leaders solemnly proclaim that these demonstrate how bad the problems of racism, sexism, and homophobia continue to be, and how "more needs to be done" in the form of redoubled preferential treatment programs, minority cultural centers, sensitivity training, and so on.[17] But the new racism cannot be fought with the more vehement application of preferential treatment, teach-ins, reeducation seminars, and censorship; indeed these tactics, which are tailored to address the old racism, only add to the new problem. In fact, to a considerable extent they are the problem because they legitimize a regime of double standards that divides and balkanizes the campus. However well-intended, university policies generally supply the oxygen with which the new racism breathes and thrives. This is why incidents of bigotry are confined predominantly to northern progressive campuses.

VICTIM STATUS

Neither the hostility of white students nor the condescension of the administration goes unnoticed by minority students. Their awareness only intensifies their insecurity, because now they find it impossible to distinguish their friends from their enemies. Being intelligent people, they sense that some of their harshest critics might be uttering truths which they must face, while some of their most obsequious flatterers are not really friends with their best interests at heart. For many, therefore, it is hard to trust anyone outside the separatist enclave.

With the encouragement of the university administration and activist faculty, many minority students begin to think of themselves as victims. Indeed, they aspire to victim status. They do not yearn to be oppressed, of course; rather, they seek the moral capital of victimhood.[18] Like Rigoberta Menchu, they tend to see their lives collectively as a historical melodrama involving the forces of good and evil, in which they are cast as secular saints and martyrs. These roles allow them to recover the sense of meaning, and of place, which otherwise seems so elusive.

Many campuses have witnessed the somewhat strange phenomenon of various minority groups—blacks, Hispanics, American Indians, foreign students, feminists, homosexuals, and so on—climbing aboard the victim bandwagon. Even as they work in concert on some issues, these groups compete to establish themselves as the most oppressed of all. Everybody races to seize the lowest rung of the ladder. By converting victimhood into a certificate of virtue, minorities acquire a powerful moral claim that renders their opponents defensive and apologetic, and immunizes themselves from criticism and sanction. Ultimately, victimhood becomes a truncheon with which minority activists may intimidate nonminorities —thus the victim becomes a victimizer while continuing to enjoy superior moral credentials.[19]

Victimhood may provoke sympathy, but it does not, by itself, produce admiration. Being historically oppressed is nothing to be ashamed of, but neither is it an intrinsic measure of social status or moral worth. What evokes admiration is the spectacle of oppressed victims struggling against their circumstances, heroically, despite the odds. In this way victimhood can pave the way for greatness.[20] Yet the current victim psychology makes it impossible for them to be relieved of their oppression. Most university administrators understand this and cynically play along. A few, however, genuinely hope that in meeting minority demands, eventually the old wounds will heal, and they will settle down and become part of the academic culture. This philanthropic enterprise seems bound to fail, because it misses the central irony: even as they rail against their oppressors, minority activists cannot afford to lose their victim status.

When resistance to sometimes outrageous minority demands sufaces among students, these activists often express indignation and outrage. Sometimes they are entirely justified in so responding to gross racial incidents, which are calculated to inflame black and Hispanic sentiments and advertise white resentment. But minority sensibilities have become so touchy that any criticism of the activist agenda is automatically termed racist. . . . [E]ven narrative descriptions of controversial policies such as preferential treatment are regarded as improper. Through protest, many minority activists rediscover the power and prestige that they felt denied in the classroom, since accusations and takeovers typically put white students on the defensive and bring immediate concessions and accommodations from the administration.

Minority group sensibility and group activism are very strong on most campuses, and it is difficult for black students who are not part of the affirmative action crowd, and who wish to integrate with white students and focus on their studies, to do so without abuse and ostracism. Politically uncooperative students are sometimes called "Oreos" or "Incognegroes"— black on the outside and white on the inside. Most intelligent black students who succeed in college maintain a shrewd tactical alliance with the local Afro-American Society or ethnic club, but give themselves enough flexibility to pursue independent intellectual and social activities as well.

DOWN WITH ARISTOTLE

Although minority activists dominate race relations on campus, their original trouble began in the classroom, and it is to the classroom that their political energy ultimately returns. This phase of the struggle begins with a new recognition. Usually within the atmosphere of their separate enclaves, and often under the tutelage of an activist professor, minority students learn that extensive though their experience has been with campus bigotry, the subtlest and yet most pervasive form of racism thrives undiscovered, right in front of their eyes. The curriculum, they are told at Stanford and Duke and other colleges, reflects a "white perspective." Specifically, as Stanford Professor Clayborne Carson [has] said, it reflects a predominant white, male, European, and heterosexual mentality which, by its very nature, is inescapably racist, indisputably sexist, and manifestly homophobic.

This realization comes as something of an epiphany. Many minority students can now explain why they had such a hard time with Milton and Publius and Heisenberg. Those men reflected white aesthetics, white philosophy, white science. Obviously minority students would fare much better if the university assigned black or Latino or Third World thought. Then the roles woud be reversed: they would perform well, and other students would have trouble. Thus the current curriculum reveals itself as the hidden core of academic bigotry.

At first minority students may find such allegations hard to credit, since it is unclear how differential equations or the measurement of electron orbits embody racial and gender prejudices. Nevertheless, in humanities and social science disciplines, younger scholar-advocates of the *au courant* stripe are on hand to explain that the cultural framework for literature or history or sociology inevitably reflects a bias in the selection or application of scholarly material. Restive with the traditional curriculum, progressive academics such as Edward Said at Columbia and Stanley Fish and Henry Gates at Duke seek a program which integrates scholarship and political commitment, and they form a tacit partnership with minority activists in order to achieve this goal. Since all knowledge is political, these scholar-advocates assert, minorities have a right to demand that their distinct perspective be "represented" in the course readings. Ethnic Studies professor Ronald Takaki of Berkeley unabashedly calls this "intellectual affirmative action."[21]

Tempted by these arguments, many minority leaders make actual head-counts of the authors and authorities in the curriculum, and they find accusations of white male predominance to be proven right. Why are Plato and Locke and Madison assigned in philosophy class but no black thinkers? How come so few Hispanics are credited with great inventions or dis-coveries? Feminists ask: Why is only a small percentage of the literature readings by women? These protests sometimes extend beyond the humanities and social sciences; at a recent symposium, mathematics professor Marilyn Frankenstein of the University of Massachusetts at Boston accused her field of harboring "Eurocentric bias" and called for "ethno-mathematics" which would analyze numerical models in terms of workforce inequalities and discrimination quotients.[22]

Few minority students believe that democratic principles of "equal representation" should be rigorously applied to curricular content. Femi-nists make this argument because they want to replace alleged sexists like Aquinas and Milton with Simone de Beauvoir and Gloria Steinem. Blacks, Hispanics, and American Indians generally assent to this proposition be-cause it provides an immediate explanation for the awkward gaps in academic performance. Not only are these differences evident in classroom discussion, grades, and prizes, but also in suspension and dropout statistics. Minority students must face the disquieting fact that many of their peers at places like Berkeley fail to graduate, if indeed they even stay through freshman year. It seems irresistible to adopt the view that if only the curriculum were broadened or revised to reflect black (or female, or Third World) perspectives, these academic gaps would close or possibly reverse themselves.

But it seems insufficient merely to agitate for a more "diverse" reading list, since the other apparatus of institutional racism would still be in place. In particular, it has not escaped the attention of minority activists that on all the indices of academic merit, from SAT scores to grades to law review seats and annual prizes, their groups do disproportionately poorly. Since democratic principle presumes that equality is the natural condition of mankind, what possible reason can there be for this inequality, other than discrimination of some sort? Consequently, as . . . in the case of Berkeley, the tests are said to be racially and perhaps sexually biased. Prima facie evidence of such bias is that all groups do not score evenly. Thus, minority student groups demand that the tests be abandoned or revised to allow "equal opportunity," which is defined as an outcome in which all groups perform equally well. Yet this does not eliminate group differences; it merely renders them invisible.[23]

PROFILES IN COWARDICE

Many university presidents are not intellectual leaders but bureaucrats and managers; their interest therefore is not in meeting the activist argument but in deflecting it, by making the appropriate adjustments in the interest of stability. When a debate over the canon erupts, university heads typically take refuge in silence or incomprehensibility; thus one Ivy League president responded to Allan Bloom's book by saying that the purpose of liberal education was to "address the need for students to develop both a private self and a public self, and to find a way to have those selves converse with each other."[24] Earlier incidents reveal the posture of presidents Heyman of Berkeley, Kennedy of Stanford, Cheek of Howard, Duderstadt of Michigan, Brodie of Duke, and Bok of Harvard to be a curious mixture of pusillanimity, ideology, and opportunism.

. . . [A]t Stanford, Duke, and Harvard, when minority groups, assisted by activist professors, urge the transformation of the curriculum toward a "race and gender" agenda, they face potential opposition from a large segment of faculty who may be sympathetic to minority causes but at the same time believe that the curriculum should not be ideologically apportioned. These dissenters are branded as bigots, sexists, and homophobes, regardless of their previous political bona fides. If minority faculty and student activists are not a numerical majority, they inevitably are a kind of Moral Majority, and they wield the formidable power to affix a scarlet letter to their enemies. Few dare to frontally oppose the alliance between minority groups and faculty activists; like Stanford's Linda Paulson, most wrestle with their conscience and win and even professors with qualms end up supporting curricular transformation with the view that change is inevitable.

The reason that most people in authority at the university have such a difficult time with the canon lobby is that, while championing the principle of "representation" in admission, they have acknowledged the indeterminacy of merit standards, the unreliability of standardized tests, the need to reform tests so that different groups fare equally, the inevitability of political considerations entering into the assignment of merit, and so on. It seems a bit late in the day for college presidents, deans, and professors to assert that the curriculum should be exempt from this egalitarian critique.

Moreover, most university leaders have no answer to the charge that the curriculum reflects a white male culture, and consequently embodies all the hateful prejudices that whites have leveled against other peoples throughout history. Nor can they explain why, if not for discrimination, minority students aren't doing as well as other students. As . . . with Harvard's "Myths and Realities" letter, universities have insisted from the outset that standards have not been lowered, so why do black and Hispanic students fall behind if not for curricular racism? And won't the rationing of books among different ethnic "perspectives" make an indispensable contribution to "diversity"?

Thus begins the process, already far advanced, of downplaying or expelling the core curriculum of Western classics in favor of a non-Western and minority-oriented agenda. Universities like Stanford, Berkeley, and Harvard establish ethnic studies requirements, multicultural offerings, Afro-American Studies and Women's Studies departments. The typical rationale is that white professors cannot effectively communicate with, or provide role models for, minority students. This argument is somewhat transparent, since it relies on the premise that interracial identification is impossible, and no one has ever alleged that minority professors are racially or culturally disabled from teaching white students. College administrators will privately admit that "minority perspectives" is a pretext for meeting affirmative action goals. The so-called "studies" programs also serve the purpose of attracting minority students who are having a difficult time with the "white" curriculum, but who . . . feel psychologically at home in a department like Afro-American Studies.

What transpires in the "race and gender" curriculum is anything but "diverse." As we saw at Harvard, typically these programs promulgate rigid political views about civil rights, feminism, homosexual rights, and other issues pressed by the activists who got these departments set up in the first place. Thomas Short, a professor of philosophy at Kenyon College, observes that "ideological dogmatism is the norm, not the exception, in the 'studies' programs, especially Women's Studies. Intimidation of nonfeminists in the classroom is routine." Short adds that, curiously, ideologues in these programs practice the very exclusion that they claim to have suffered in the past.

Even if some faculty in the "race and gender" curriculum seek to promote authentic debate or intellectual diversity, this is difficult in an atmosphere where activist students profess to be deeply offended by views which fall outside the ideological circumference of their victim's revolution. Once a professor finds himself the object of vilification and abuse for tackling a politcal taboo . . . others absorb the message and ensure that their own classes are appropriately deferential.

Eugene Genovese, a Marxist historian and one of the nation's most distinguished scholars on slavery, admits that "there is just too much dogmatism in the field of race and gender scholarship." Whatever diversity obtains, Genovese argues, is frequently "a diversity of radical positions." As a result, "Good scholars [who] are increasingly at risk are starting to run away, and this is how our programs become ghettoized."

The new awareness of racially and sexually biased perspectives is not confined to the "studies" programs, however; minority activists inevitably bring their challenging political consciousness into other courses as well, although this usually does not happen until junior or senior year. At this point, the students begin to function as sensitivity monitors, vigilant in pointing out instances of racism and sexism in the course readings or among student comments. Other students may inwardly resent such political surveillance, but seldom do professors resist it: indeed they often praise it as precisely the sort of "diversity" that minority students can bring to the classroom.

Minority students are often given latitude to do papers on race or gender victimization, even if only tangentially related to course material: thus some write about latent bigotry in Jane Austen, or tabulate black underrepresentation in the university administration. Minority activists can be offended when they do not receive passing grades on such papers, because they believe that their consciousness of oppression is far more advanced than that of any white professor. Further, they know how reluctant most professors are to get involved in an incident with a black or Hispanic student; hence they can extract virtually any price from faculty anxious to avoid "racial incidents."

University administrations and faculty also permit, and sometimes encourage, minority students to develop myths about their own culture and history, such as the "black Egypt" industry evident at Howard and elsewhere. This cultural distortion is routine in multicultural and Third World studies—the case of Stanford in typical. Bernard Lewis, professor of Near Eastern studies at Princeton, describes what he calls "a new culture of deceit on the campus," and adds, "It is very dangerous to give in to these ideas, or more accurately, to these pressures. It makes a mockery of scholarship to say: my nonsense is as good as your science." But even university officials who agree with Lewis say they aren't sure what they can do to counter these distortions, since the ideological forces behind them are so strong.

Although curricular and extracurricular concessions by the university greatly increase the power of minority activists, it is not clear that they help minority students use knowledge and truth as weapons against ignorance and prejudice, nor that they assuage the problems of low morale and low self-esteem which propelled them in this direction to begin with. Nor does an apparently more even "balance of power" between minority and nonminority students produce greater ethnic harmony. In fact . . . many minority students find themselves increasingly embittered and estranged during their college years, so that by the time they graduate they may be virtually isolated in a separatist culture, and espouse openly hostile sentiments against other groups.

At graduation time, it turns out that only a fraction of the minority students enrolled four years earlier are still around, and even among them the academic record is mixed: a good number (most are probably not affirmative action beneficiaries) have performed well, but a majority conspicuously lag behind their colleagues, and a sizable group has only finished by concentrating in congenial fields such as Afro-American or Ethnic Studies, under the direction of tolerant faculty advisers. Relatively few of these students have developed to their full potential over the past four years, or have emerged ready to assume positions of responsibility and leadership in the new multiracial society.

PRINCIPLES OF REFORM

No community can be built on the basis of preferential treatment and double standards, and their existence belies university rhetoric about equality. Conflicting standards of excellence and justice are the root of the bitter and divisive controversies over admissions, curricular content, and race relations on campus. In each case, the university administration is directly responsible for betraying student idealism and replacing it with cynicism and resentment. To remedy the problem, it is necessary to return to fundamental principles; as G. K. Chesterton said, we cannot discuss reform without reference to form.

First, liberal education is education for rulers. In ancient times, princes, aristocrats, and gentry sought liberal education to prepare them for the responsibilities of government. We do not share this elitist conception of liberal education, but this does not imply that we should change the definition. In a democratic society, every citizen is a ruler, who joins in exercising the duties of government. Consequently, instead of abandoning the highest ideals of liberal learning, we should extend them beyond previously confined social enclaves. In this modern view, liberal education is an opportunity for all citizens in a democratic society. Contrary to what some activists allege, liberal education is consistent with democracy; indeed it enables democratic rule to reach its pinnacle.

Second, democracy is not based on the premise of equal endowments, but of equal rights. It does not guarantee success, but it does aspire to equal opportunity. This opportunity is extended not to groups as such, but to individuals, because democracy respects the moral integrity of the human person, whose rights may not be casually subordinated to collective interests. Democracy requires representation, but in no sense does it mandate proportional representation based on race. Consequently it is entirely consistent with democracy for liberal education to treat students equally, as individuals.

Third, there is no conflict between equal opportunity for individuals in education and the pursuit of the highest standards of academic and extracurricular excellence. After all, equal opportunity means opportunity to achieve, and we achieve more when more is expected of us. Test scores and grade point averages are mere measurements of achievement, which are necessary to register how much progress is being made. They provide a common index for all who seek to improve themselves, regardless of race, sex, or background. High standards do not discriminate against anyone except those who fail to meet them. Such discrimination in entirely just and ought not to be blamed for our individual differences.

Fourth, liberal education settles issues in terms of idealism, not interest; in terms of right, not force. There is nothing wrong with universities confronting controversial contemporary issues, especially those involving human difference that are both timely and timeless. Nor is radicalism itself the problem; if radical solutions may not be contemplated in the university, where else would they be considered? Because they are sanctuary institutions universities can be a philosophical testing ground for programs of revolutionary transformation which, if improperly executed, might lead to lawlessness, violence, or anarchy. "The university sponsors moral combat in an atmosphere where ideas can be tested short of mortal combat," in the words of sociologist Manfred Stanley of Syracuse University.[25]

Fifth, liberal education in a multicultural society means global education. Provincialism has always been the enemy of that broad-minded outlook which is the very essence of liberal learning. Today's liberally educated student must be conversant with some of the classic formulations of other cultures, and with the grand political and social currents which bring these cultures into increased interaction with the West. Such education is best pursued when students are taught to search for universal standards of judgment which transcend particularities of race, gender, and culture; this gives them the intellectual and moral criteria to evaluate both their own society and others. There is much in both to affirm and to criticize.

THREE MODEST PROPOSALS

Nonracial Affirmative Action. Universities should retain their policies of preferential treatment, but alter their criteria of application from race to socioeconomic disadvantage. This means that, in admissions decisions, universities would take into account such factors as the applicant's family background, financial condition, and primary and secondary school environment, giving preference to disadvantaged students as long as it is clear that these students can be reasonably expected to meet the academic challenges of the selective college. Race or ethnicity, however, would cease to count either for or against any applicant.

Ordinarily the admissions policy of selective universities should be based on academic and extracurricular merit. Preferential treatment is justified, however, when it is obvious that measurable indices of merit do not accurately reflect a student's learning and growth potential. Every admissions officer knows that a 1,200 SAT score by a student from Harlem or Anacostia, who comes from a broken family and has struggled against peer pressure and a terrible school system, means something entirely different from a 1,200 score from a student from Scarsdale or Georgetown, whose privileges include private tutors and SAT prep courses.

Universities seem entirely justified in giving a break to students who may not have registered the highest scores, but whose record suggests that this failure is not due to lack of ability or application but rather to demonstrated disadvantage. Universities are right to see the academic potential in these students, whose future performance may well outdistance that of better-prepared seventeen-year-olds whose path to success has been relatively smooth.

The greatest virtue of preferences based on socioeconomic factors is that such an approach restores to the admissions process the principle of treating people as individuals and not simply as members of ethnic groups. Each applicant is assessed as a person, whose achievements are measured in the context of individual circumstances. Skin color no longer makes a dubious claim to be an index of merit, or an automatic justification for compensation. No longer will a black or Hispanic doctor's son, who has enjoyed the advantages of comfort and affluence, receive preference over the daughter of an Appalachian coal miner or a Vietnamese street vendor. Regardless of pigment, any student who can make a genuine case that his grades or scores do not reflect his true potential has a chance to substantiate this claim in a tangible and measurable way.

Ordinarily it might seem an extraordinarily complex calculus to weigh such factors as family background, income, and school atmosphere. Fortunately, colleges already have access to, and in many cases use, this data. The application forms give applicants ample opportunity to register this information, and the financial aid office assiduously tabulates family assets and income. By integrating admissions and financial aid information, universities are in a good position to make intelligent determinations about socioeconomic factors that advanced, or impeded, a student's opportunities.

Since minorities are disproportionately represented among the disadvantaged, there is little question that they would benefit disproportionately from such a program. The disadvantages imposed by slavery, segregation, and past discrimination would still count as a plus, if they could be shown to translate into socioeconomic disadvantage currently suffered by the student applicant.

It is true that affirmative action seats must necessarily be limited, and any expansion of the program beyond its current beneficiary groups means that the number of blacks and Hispanics who benefit will necessarily be reduced. But this does not mean that fewer blacks and Hispanics will be enrolled in American universities—only that fewer will gain admission to the most selective colleges. In other words, a black student who cannot demonstrate socioeconomic disadvantage, whose credentials qualify him for Temple University, but who under preferential treatment could be admitted to Columbia, will probably now have to attend Temple. This outcome does not apper to be unjust.

Moreover, black and Hispanic graduation rates are likely to increase, because only students whose potential is hidden due to previous disadvantage would enjoy preferential treatment, in the reasonable expectation that they will be able to realize their capabilities and compete effectively with other students. All other students, whether white or black or Asian, would be admitted to colleges whose criteria correspond to their measured capabilities. Thus they would compete in a free and fair academic environment, and would not be subject to the undue pressures of intellectual mismatch. Placed in an appropriate university setting, these students would have every opportunity for graduation and academic success commensurate with effort.

Additionally, this kind of affirmative action loses the special stigma that is attached to racial preference. No longer would universities be forced to explain the anomaly of enforcing racial discrimination as a means to combat racial discrimination. The euphemism and mendacity currently employed to justify preferential treatment can stop—the new program can be explicitly stated and defended. The rationale for racial grievance among groups dissolves. Nobody gets to feel privileged, or injured, on acccount of race. Nobody may infer that members of other races are collectively inadequate to the standards of the institution. Whether or not they benefit from preferential treatment, all minority students are liberated from the raised eyebrow that currently belittles their achievements.

Choice Without Separatism. Universities should discourage the practice of minority self-segregation on campus by refusing to recognize and fund any group which is racially separatist and excludes students based on skin color. Universities should, however, sanction groups based on a shared intellectual or cultural interest, even if these groups appeal predominantly or exclusively to minority students.

What this means is that universities would not permit a Black Students Association, but they would permit a W. E. B. Du Bois Society based on interest in the writings of the early twentieth-century author. Colleges would refuse to support a Latino Political Club but they would permit a Sandino Club based on interest in the thought of the Nicaraguan revolutionary hero. This principle could extend beyond race, so that universities would decline to fund a homosexual association but would fund a Sappho Society.

In all cases, university-funded groups should be built around intellectual and cultural interests, not skin color or sexual proclivity. This seems congruent with the purpose of a liberal education, which is to foster the development and exchange of ideas. Thought and expression are the currency in which universities trade and specialize. The consolidation of identity based on race or sexuality may be a project that some students ardently seek, but it falls outside the province of universities, which in fact have a declared interest in breaking down barriers based on accidental features.

If this solution is adopted, no longer will universities have to justify double standards in which they profess allegiance to cultural exchange, and then foster minority subcultures on campus; nor will they need to account for encouraging minority-pride groups but not white-pride groups such as the ones at Temple and Florida State. The new approach has the advantage of permitting both honesty and consistency.

Also, the idea of funding groups based on shared interests has the benefits of free association as well as inclusiveness: all students attracted to the principles embodied by the organization may join; nobody may be turned away on grounds of race or sex. There is no reason to think a Malcolm X Society, for instance, would not attract any white or Hispanic or Asian students, but if only blacks happen to join, at least others would have been extended the opportunity. In some cases, perhaps, groups will be formed on the mere pretext of a shared idea, but inevitably this pretense will be challenged by some persistent outsider who insists on signing up and who cannot be refused membership.

Equality and the Classics. Universities can address their curricular problems by devising a required course or sequence for entering freshmen which exposes them to the basic issues of equality and human difference, through a carefully chosen set of classic texts that deal powerfully with those issues. Needless to say, non-Western classics belong in this list when they address questions relevant to the subject matter. Such a solution would retain what Matthew Arnold termed "the best that has been thought and said," but at the same time engage the contemporary questions of ethnocentrism and prejudice in bold and provocative fashion.

It seems that currently both the teaching of Western classics as well as the desire to study other cultures have encountered serious difficulties in the curriculum. As the case of Stanford illustrates, an uncritical examination of non-Western cultures, in order to favorably contrast them with the West, ends up as a new form of cultural imperialism, in which Western intellectuals project their own domestic prejudices onto faraway countries, distorting them beyond recognition to serve political ends.[26] Even where universities make a serious effort to avoid this trap, it remains questionable whether they have the academic expertise in the general undergraduate program to teach students about the history, religion, and literature of Asia, Africa, and the Arab world.

The study of other cultures can never compensate for a lack of thorough familiarity with the founding principles of one's own culture.[27] Just as it would be embarrassing to encounter an educated Chinese who had never heard of Confucius, however well versed he may be in Jefferson, so also it would be a failure of liberal education to teach Americans about the Far East without immersing them in their own philosophical and literary tradition "from Homer to the present." Universal in scope, these works prepare Westerners to experience both their own, as well as other, ideas and civilizations.[28]

The problem is that many of the younger generation of faculty in the universities express lack of interest, if not contempt, for the Western classics. Either they regard the books as flawed for their failure to endorse the full emancipation of approved minorities, or they reject their metaphysical questions as outdated and irrelevant. Naturally, young people will not investigate these texts, which are often complex and sometimes written in archaic language, if they do not believe their efforts will be repaid. Unfortunately, many undergraduates today seem disinclined to read the classics, but not because they oppose or detest them. Their alienation is more radical: they are indifferent to them. For them the classics have retreated into what Lovejoy called "the pathos of time."

Yet a survey of these books immediately suggests that many of them are fully aware of, and treat with great subtlety, the problems of prejudice, ethnocentrism, and human difference. Long before Willie Horton raised, in American minds, the specter of a dark-skinned man sexually assaulting a white woman, Iago raised this possibility with Brabantio. Will he allow his "fair daughter" to fall into "the gross clasps of a lascivious Moor"? If he does not intervene, Iago warned, "You'll have your daughter covered with a Barbary horse." *Othello* and the *Merchant of Venice,* Shakespeare's Venetian plays, are both subtle examinations of nativism and ethnocentrism. Both engage issues of ethnic and sexual difference. They reflect a cosmopolitan society's struggle to accommodate the alien while maintaining its cultural identity. Othello is the tragedy of a foreign warrior who depended on Desdemona's love to legitimate his full citizenship in his new country—when Iago casts that love into doubt, not just his marriage but his identity was fundamentally threatened. By contrast with Othello, Shylock is the outsider who refused to integrate, and pressed his principles into uncompromising conflict with those of Christian civilization.[29] These timeless examples of the tension between community and difference are precisely what young people today should confront, and respond to in terms of their own experience.

The relevance of the classical tradition to questions of beauty and equality and freedom has not gone unrecognized by perceptive black thinkers and writers. Traveling in Vienna, W. E. B. Du Bois wrote, "Here Marcus Aurelius, the Roman Caesar died; here Charlemagne placed the bounds of his empire that ruled the world five centuries. . . . Around Vienna the intrigues and victories of Napoleon centered. . . . And here, after the downfall of the great Tyrant, sat the famous congress which parcelled out the world and declared the African slave a stench in the nostrils of humanity."[30] Du Bois saw the grandeur and degradation in a single unifying thought—slavery was the West's tragic flaw; yet it was tragic precisely because of the greatness of the civilization that encompassed it.

Paul Robeson recalled that his father took him "page by page through Virgil and Homer and other classics."[31] As a result, Robeson says, "a love of learning, a ceaseless quest for truth in all its fullness—this my father taught." Robeson believed that the Latin and Greek classics were just as much the treasure of the American black as of the American white. When Robeson played Othello on Broadway, he created a national sensation. Audiences found *Othello,* in Robeson's words, "painfully immediate in its unfolding of evil, innocence, passion, dignity and nobility, and contemporary in its overtones of a clash of cultures, and of the partial acceptance and consequent effect upon one of a minority group." Othello's jealousy thus "becomes more credible, the blow to his pride more understandable, the final collapse of his individual world more inevitable."[32] In 1943–44 Robeson's *Othello* set a record for a Shakespearean play on Broadway, running for almost three hundred consecutive performances.

*   *   *

For a variety of reasons, university presidents and deans will not implement even the most obvious and sensible reform proposals. First, being for the most part bureaucrats rather than intellectual leaders, they lack the vision and imagination to devise new and innovative policies, preferring to continue familiar programs and echo their accompanying bromides. Second, university officials feel physically and morally intimidated by minority activists; as a result, the activists set the agenda and timorous administrators usually go along. Third, and perhaps most serious, many no longer believe in the emancipation brought about by liberal education, and are quite willing to sacrifice liberal principles to achieve expedient ends.

The liberal university is a distinctive and fragile institution. It is not an all-purpose instrument for social change. Its function is indeed to serve the larger society which supports and sustains it, yet it does not best do this when it makes itself indistinguishable from the helter-skelter of pressure politics, what Professor Susan Shell of Boston College terms "the academic equivalent of Tammany Hall." Nothing in this [essay] should be taken to deny the legitimate claim of minorities who have suffered unfairly, nor should reasonable aid and sympathy be withheld from them. But the current revolution of minority vicitims threatens to destroy the highest ideals of liberal education, and with them that enlightenment and understanding which hold out the only prospects for racial harmony, social justice, and minority advancement.

Many university leaders are supremely confident that nothing can jeopardize their position, and they regard any criticism with disdain.[33] As Professor Alan Kors of the Univeristy of Pennsylvania has remarked, "For the first time in the history of American higher education, the barbarians are running the place." Liberal education is too important to entrust to those self-styled revolutionaries. Reform, if it comes, requires the involvement of intelligent voices from both inside and outside the university—students who are willing to take on reigning orthodoxies, professors and administrators with the courage to resist the activist high tide, and parents, alumni, and civic leaders who are committed to applying genuine principles of liberal learning to the challenges of the emerging multicultural society.

NOTES

1. In 1988, there were 10.3 million whites, 1.1 million blacks, 680,000 Hispanics, 497,000 Asian Americans, 93,000 American Indians, and 361,000 foreign students enrolled in American colleges. See "1988 College Enrollment," U.S. Department of Education, table reprinted in *Chronicle of Higher Education,* April 11, 1990, p. A–1.

2. A recent Carnegie Foundation report shows that the number of philosophically liberal professors is more than double the number of conservative professors. In humanities departments, where presumably ideology is most likely to manifest itself in the classroom, the ratio is almost four to one. For faculty under the age of forty, the ratio is almost three to one, suggesting that the imbalance is likely to become greater in the future. See *The Condition of the Professoriate* (Washington, D.C: Carnegie Foundation, 1989), p. 143.

3. See Assembly Bill 462, introduced by member Tom Hayden (February 2, 1989) and Assembly Bill 3993, introduced by member Willie Brown (March 2, 1990) in the California legislature, 1989–90 session. Copies obtained from office

of Assemblyman Hayden. Although the wording of these bills is somewhat ambiguous, some critics believe that their effect will be to require not only admission, but also passing grades, promotion, and graduation, at the same rate for all racial groups. See John Bunzel, "Inequitable Equality on Campus," *Wall Street Journal*, July 25, 1990; Abigail Thernstrom, "On the Scarcity of Black Professors," *Commentary* (July 1990).

4. See Bunzel, "Inequitable Equality on Campus."

5. The long history of segregation and discrimination has produced a "heightened sense of group consciousness" among blacks, and a "stronger orientation toward collective values and behavior" than exists among whites. See Gerald Jaynes and Robin Williams, eds., *A Common Destiny: Blacks and American Society* (Washington, D.C.: National Academy Press, 1989), p. 13.

6. For example, Cornell president Frank Rhodes remarks, "We face an unresolved conflict between the natural impulse toward proud, separate racial and ethnic identity on the one hand and the genuine desire, on the other, for meaningful integration that transcends differences of background." See Frances Dinkelspiel, "In Rift at Cornell, Racial Issues of the 60s Remain," *New York Times*, May 3, 1989.

7. California State University officials, led by faculty member Otis Scott, are planning to establish Cooper-Woodson College as a special adjunct to the university. "Is it separatist?" Scott asked. "No more than the separation that already exists between [black] students and the institution. We are committed to creating a comprehensive support network for African-American students." Cited by Karen O'Hara, "Sacramento State May Try Black University Structure," *Black Issues in Higher Education*, May 10, 1990, p. 13.

8. Seth Mydans, "Black Identity vs. Success and Seeming White," *New York Times*, April 25, 1990, p. B-9. Although the study by Fordham and Ogbu focused on black high schools, Fordham said in an interview that her findings also apply to black culture on college campuses.

9. This view even claims some scholarly support. One study concluded that "research on nonverbal behavior shows that white college students often sit further away, use a less friendly voice tone, make less eye contact, and more speech errors, and terminate the interview faster when interacting with a black rather than a white." See Thomas Pettigrew, "New Patterns of Racism: The Different Worlds of 1984 and 1964," *Rutgers Law Reivew* 37 (1985): 673, 689.

10. At the University of Virginia, for instance, minority students demanded to know why a larger proportion of blacks than whites were charged with honor code violations, and many called for the abolition of the allegedly bigoted and discriminatory honor system. See Darryl Brown, "Racism and Race Relations in the University," *University of Virginia Law Review* 76 (1989): 295, 334. See also Editorial, "Dishonorable Schoolboys," *Washington Times*, April 9, 1990.

11. Arthur Schlesinger, "When Ethnic Studies Are Un-American," *Wall Street Journal*, April 23, 1990.

12. William Raspberry, "Why the Racial Slogans?" *Washington Post,* September 20, 1989.

13. A vivid recent example of this is the case of Linda Chavez, former staff director of the U.S. Civil Rights Commission, who was invited to be the commencement speaker at the University of Northern Colorado in May 1990. When a campus Hispanic group and several other students and faculty protested, however, President Robert Dickeson rescinded Chavez's invitation. "The intent of the university in inviting Linda Chavez was to be sensitive to cultural diversity and the committee making the decision intended to communicate the importance of cultural pluralism," the university explained in a press release. "It is clear that the decision was both uninformed and gave the appearance of being grossly insensitive." Although Chavez's role as a prominent Hispanic woman apparently accounted for her selection, the problem turned out to be her conservative views, in particular, her opposition to preferential treatment and bilingualism. As Chavez herself observed in the *Chronicle of Higher Education,* "The problem with the cultural pluralist model is that not all blacks, Hispanics or women think alike." Diversity, Chavez charged, was invoked in this instance "to keep out certain ideas and certain people, to foreclose debate, to substitute ideological catechism for the free inquiry usually associated with a university." See "The Importance of Cultural Pluralism," press release by University of Northern Colorado, reprinted in *Wall Street Journal,* May 9, 1990; Linda Chavez, "The Real Aim of the Promoters of Cultural Diversity Is to Exclude Certain People and to Foreclose Debate," *Chronicle of Higher Education,* July 18, 1990, p. B–1; Carol Innerst, "Chavez Encounters Big Chill," *Washington Times,* May 4, 1990, p. 1.

14. Nancy Gibbs, "Bigots in the Ivory Tower," *Time,* May 7, 1990, p. 104.

15. Sari Horwitz, "Black Students Protest GWU Party," *Washington Post,* February 8, 1987, p. A–15.

16. In a somewhat comical recent episode, after instituting a series of multicultural measures on campus, President William Gerberding of the University of Washington at Seattle was denounced by activist groups for making a joke about illegal immigration, which protestors branded an "ethnic slur." Before a rally of 250 students, Gerberding apologized and agreed to enroll *himself* in a "multiracial awareness" course aimed at curing bigoted tendencies. See Michael Park, "Gerberding Issues Public Apology," *Daily Campus Newspaper,* University of Washington at Seattle, May 16, 1990, p. 1.

17. All signs point to the multicultural revolution on campus expanding its reach.

• Recently the Middle States Association of Colleges postponed accreditation for Baruch College in New York City, citing insufficient progress in preferential recruitment of faculty and students. Both the Middle States Association and the Western Association of Schools and Colleges have announced that institutional commitment to diversity will now constitute an essential criterion for accreditation.

• Proportional representation has extended to some cases of campus discipline, for example, when a firebomb exploded on the Wesleyan campus in May

1990, minority activists insisted, and university investigators agreed, that regardless of where circumstantial evidence pointed, white and black students should be interrogated in roughly the same proportion as their group representation in the student body, to avoid the appearance of prejudicial inquiry.

• As censorship codes have grown more expansive, previously innocuous conduct is now prosecuted—thus at Southern Methodist University, the judicial committee recently punished one student for referring to Martin Luther King, Jr., as a communist and singing "We Shall Overcome" in a "sarcastic manner," and another student for calling a classmate a Mexican "in a derogatory manner" even though the student immediately apologized for the perceived slight.

• Finally, group classification based on ethnicity has become increasingly nuanced at the University of California at Davis, where Latino activists have organized hunger strikes to protest the Spanish department's alleged bias toward the Castilian language, spoken in Spain, over colloquial Spanish, spoken in Mexico.

See Ed Wiley, "Agencies Likely to Incorporate Diversity Standards," *Black Issues in Higher Education,* May 24, 1990, p. 4; Kirk Johnson, "Racial Graffiti Found on Walls at Wesleyan," *New York Times,* May 5, 1990; "Three Bias Incidents Provide Lessons for Class on Race," *New York Times,* May 6, 1990, Campus Life, pp. 53–54; Eric Brazil, "Irked Latino Students Castigate Castilians at California College," *Washington Times,* May 17, 1990.

18. I believe that the moral power of the idea of victimhood derives from Christianity. The Greeks elevated the heroic virtues, while Christianity elevated the sacrificial virtues. It was Christianity which invented the doctrine of the sanctified victim. Previously victims were, for the most part, despised and degraded. Christ, however, was the victim who, even in defeat, emerged triumphant. Modern racial and gender politics seems to be a new version of this *tableau,* without Christian themes of penance and regeneration.

19. Thomas Sowell argues that deep-seated cultural grievance often manifests itself in repressive ways. White Afrikaners in South Africa nurtured a profound isolation and "seige mentality" that they used to justify their policies of apartheid. Similarly, Hitler exploited a German sense of grievance and humiliation, engendered by the defeat in World War I and the Treaty of Versailles, to justify the irridentism and mass brutality of World War II.

Shelby Steele finds that some blacks on campus "badger white people about race almost on principle. It's a kind of power move for them."

This perception is shared by writers entirely sympathetic to the causes of minority victims. Frantz Fanon writes that the historical victim "is overpowered but not tamed . . . he is patiently waiting until the settler is off his guard to fly at him. The native is an oppressed person whose permanent dream is to become the persecutor."

Albert Memmi observes, "The oppressed want to forge ahead by themselves, to find their own particular and individual path, entirely cut off from their former overlords, and at first in direct opposition to them—from now on, they will acquiesce in the ugliness of their own reactions, which they will no longer attempt to disguise; indeed they will make use of them, inducing in themselves hideous paroxysms of hate."

Thomas Sowell, "Affirmative Action: A Worldwide Disaster," *Commentary* (December 1989); Shelby Steele, "I'm Black, You're White, Who's Innocent?" *Harper's* (June 1988): pp. 45–52; Frantz Fanon, *The Wretched of the Earth* (Grove Press, New York, 1963), p. 53; Albert Memmi, *Dominated Man* (Beacon Press, Boston, 1969), p. 9.

20. "I have learned that success is to be measured not so much by the position that one has reached in life, as by the obstacles which [one] has overcome while trying to succeed." Booker T. Washington, *Up from Slavery,* reprinted in John Hope Franklin, ed., *Three Negro Classics* (New York: Avon Books), p. 50.

21. See John Leo, "The Class that Deserves Cutting," *U.S. News & World Report,* May 29, 1989, p. 58.

22. Cited in Glenn Ricketts, "Multiculturalism Mobilizes," *Academic Questions,* Summer 1990, p. 57.

23. Harvard Law School professor Randall Kennedy says that it is possible to find cases where tests and standards are biased, but "the proper response is not to scrap the meritocratic ideal" but rather "to abjure all practices that exploit the trappings of meritocracy to advance interests that have nothing to do with the intellectual characteristics of the subject being judged." See Randall Kennedy, "Racial Critiques of Legal Academia," *Harvard Law Review* 102 (1989): 1745–1807.

24. Comment of President James Freedman of Dartmouth College, cited by Edward Fiske, "Redefining Dartmouth New President's Quest for Private Selves,' " *New York Times,* August 23, 1988, p. E–24.

25. Manfred Stanley, "The American University as a Civic Institution," *Civic Arts Review* (Spring 1989): 6.

26. See, e.g., Edward Said, *Orientalism* (New York: Pantheon Books, 1978).

Delusions about other cultures are not simply an ancient phenomenon but are evident in this century. Disgruntled with race relations in America, Paul Robeson visited the Soviet Union in the early 1930s, and returned with high praise for Stalin's ethnic policies. "The Soviet Union is the only place where ethnology is seriously considered and applied." See Paul Robeson, "I Breathe Freely," *New Theater* (July 1935): 5.

More recently, in 1979, Richard Falk of Princeton University found in the Ayatollah Khomeini a progressive alternative to the Shah of Iran. Embittered by U.S. support for the Shah, Falk was certain that Khomeini would champion the progressive cause:

> The depiction of Khomeini as a fanatical reactionary and the bearer of crude prejudices seems certainly and happily false. What is also encouraging is that his entourage of close advisers is uniformly composed of moderate, progressive individuals [who] share a notable record of concern for human rights. In Iran, the Shiite tradition is flexible in its ap-

proach to the Koran. . . . Khomeini's Islamic republic can be expected
to have a doctrine of social justice at its core. Iran may yet provide
us with a desperately needed model of humane governance for a Third
World country.

See Richard Falk, "Trusting Khomeini," *New York Times,* February 6, 1979;
Richard Falk, "Khomeini's Promise," *Foreign Policy* (Spring 1979): 28–34.

Paul Hollander of the University of Massachusetts at Amherst argues that
Western intellectuals have since the 1930s searched for a peasant paradise abroad.
The quest began with Stalin's Russia, then Mao's China, Castro's Cuba, and
most recently Ortega's Nicaragua. Every time irrefutable evidence surfaced showing how bloodthirsty were the regimes that Westerners revered, the Western fantasy moved on to the next destination. Hollander argues that foreign countries
are often experienced by Western intellectuals as a projection of their own domestic alienation and self-hatred. See Paul Hollander, *Political Pilgrims* (New York:
Oxford University Press, 1981).

27. Even a careful reading of the Vedas or Analects will not transplant young
Americans into the culture of which those important works are a part. It would
take years, perhaps a lifetime, of experience and study for an outsider to penetrate
the inner reaches of another culture—as difficult as it would be for a Chinese
to become an expert on Mark Twain or Henry James. This is not only beyond
the capacity of most students, but also of most faculty. There are only a handful
of teachers who could even approach such comprehension, and probably none
of them teaches general undergraduate courses. Consequently, non-Western study
is better aimed at the narrower but more practical goals of widening the Western
scope of familiarity, preparing the Westerner for travel and cultural exchange,
and learning how to empathize with others who are very different from oneself.

28. Michael Novak at the American Enterprise Institute points out that most
Western classics aim at the production of universal knowledge. Adam Smith did
not write "The Wealth of Scotland" but rather *An Inquiry into the Nature and
Causes of the Wealth of Nations.* The Declaration of Independence does not
state that "all Americans" but rather that "all men are created equal and endowed
by their creator with certain inalienable rights." Again, the founders intended to
make a universal statement, even if they neglected to use gender-inclusive language. The Western tradition, at its best, teaches self-criticism toward itself and
openness to other cultures.

29. See Allan Bloom with Harry Jaffa, *Shakespeare's Politics* (New York:
Basic Books, 1964).

30. W. E. B. Du Bois, "The Spirit of Modern Europe," cited by Herbert
Aptheker, ed., *Against Racism* (Amherst, Mass.: Amherst College Press, 1985),
pp. 52–54.

31. Paul Robeson, *Here I Stand* (Boston: Beacon Press, 1957), p. 26.

32. Paul Robeson, "Reflections on Othello and the Nature of Our Times,"
The American Scholar (Autumn 1945): 390.

33. For example, while the number of humanities majors plummets, the American Council of Learned Societies boasts, "Precisely those things now identified as failings in the humanities indicate enlivening transformation." See "Speaking for the Humanities," American Council of Learned Societies, Paper No. 7, New York, 1989 p. 3.

Contributors

MOLEFI KETE ASANTE is professor and chairman of the Department of Afro-American Studies at Temple University and editor of the *Journal of Black Studies*.

MICHAEL E. BAUMAN is professor of theology and culture at Hillsdale College in Hillsdale, Michigan. Among his many works are *Milton's Arianism* and *Man and Marxism*.

FRANCIS J. BECKWITH, lecturer of philosophy at the University of Nevada, Las Vegas, and senior research fellow, Nevada Policy Research Institute, is the author of several books, including *Politically Correct Death: Answering the Arguments for Abortion Rights* and *David Hume's Argument Against Miracles: A Critical Analysis*.

WILLIAM R. BEER is professor of sociology at Brooklyn College, City Unviersity of New York.

ALLAN BLOOM was, until his death in the fall of 1992, co-director of the John M. Olin Center for Inquiry and Practice of Democracy at the University of Chicago, where he was also a professor in the Committee on Social Thought. He authored the bestselling *The Closing of the American Mind* on university education.

DINESH D'SOUZA is a research fellow at the American Enterprise Institute, Washington, D.C. He is the author of *Illiberal Education: The Politics of Race and Gender on Campus.*

ROSA EHRENREICH, a graduate of Harvard University, is now a Marshall Scholar at Oxford University.

CHESTER E. FINN, JR., professor of education and public policy at Vanderbilt University and director of the Educational Excellence Network, served as assistant secretary of education from 1985 to 1988.

STANLEY FISH is professor of English and law at Duke University. A Milton scholar and literary theorist, he is the author of several works, including *Doing What Comes Naturally: Change, Rhetoric, and the Practice of Theory in Literary and Legal Studies.*

IRVING HOWE, co-editor of the journal *Dissent,* is a distinguished social and literary critic. He is the author of many works, including the recent *Selected Writings: 1950–1990.*

DIANE RAVITCH is adjunct professor of history and education at the Teacher's College of Columbia University.

GEORGE REISMAN, professor of economics at Pepperdine University's School of Business and Management, is the author of *The Government Against the Economy.*

THOMAS SHORT is associate professor of philosophy at Kenyon College in Gambier, Ohio.

CATHARINE R. STIMPSON is university professor and dean of the Graduate School at Rutgers University. In 1990 she served as president of the Modern Language Association (MLA).

JOHN TAYLOR is a writer for *New York* magazine.

STEPHEN S. WEINER is executive director of the Western Association of Schools and Colleges.